THE COMPLETE BORZOI

The Complete BORZOI

by LORRAINE GROSHANS

FIRST EDITION
Third Printing 1989

HOWELL BOOK HOUSE Inc.
230 Park Avenue
New York, N.Y. 10169

Library of Congress Cataloging in Publication Data

Groshans, Lorraine.
    The complete borzoi.

    Includes bibliographical references.
    1. Russian wolf-hounds.   I. Title.
SF429.R8G76   636.7'53   81-4377
ISBN 0-87605-057-7   AACR2

Contents

About the Author

LORRAINE GROSHANS typifies the ideal choice for the author of a dog breed book. For 25 years she has bred, shown, studied and researched Borzoi. She is a member of six dog clubs, having served three of them in official capacities. She has been importantly involved in four publications devoted to Borzoi prior to this book.

Under the *Loral* prefix—a contraction of the first letters of her and her husband Albert's first names—48 Borzoi and Whippet champions have been bred. Loral Borzoi rated among the "Top Ten" in the breed in 1979 and 1980 with many specialty, group and best in show wins.

The American Kennel Club approved Mrs. Groshans as a Borzoi judge in 1969 and later approved her also for Whippets, Greyhounds and Salukis.

She served the Borzoi Club of America as secretary in 1962-1970 and 1973 and as president in 1975-1977. She is an honorary life member of the Lehigh Valley Kennel Club, having served it in various offices including as president in 1968-1969, the first woman to hold that office in the club's 72-year history. President in 1976-1977 of the Pennsylvania Federation of Dog Clubs, she has been its delegate from the Lehigh Valley Kennel Club since the state Federation was founded in 1970.

Her work on behalf of Borzoi publications includes the chairmanship of the committee for the BCOA booklet *The Borzoi* published in 1963; committee member for the BCOA book *The Borzoi* for which she wrote several chapters in 1973; and editor of the BCOA Yearbooks in 1975 and 1976.

Though Borzoi are her favorite breed, she has owned one or more dogs in the following breeds: Miniature Pinscher, English Foxhound, Afghan Hound, Silky Terrier, Italian Greyhound, Dachshund (Smooth and Wire), and German Wirehaired Pointer.

Her club memberships include the Borzoi Club of Delaware Valley, Pennsylvania Dachshund Club and Dog Judges Association of America.

The Borzoi fancy is fortunate to have such an experienced and well-informed authority to record the lore of this noble breed.

From the Author

THE FIRST BORZOI I owned was the first Borzoi I ever remember seeing. Even though I had owned and shown Dachshunds for a few years before that first Borzoi, there had never been any Borzoi entered at the shows where I had exhibited. In fact, after acquiring my first Borzoi and entering her at a few shows, there was still no competition in the breed. It wasn't until the 1955 Borzoi Club of America Specialty at the Westchester show in Rye, New York that I first saw other Borzoi and met other Borzoi owners. Ch. Rachmaninoff was best of breed that day and soon-to-be-champion Lisa Denton was best of opposite sex. Being benched next to Lisa, I had the good fortune to meet her owners Lawrence and Erma Denton. Erma became a good friend and a great source of help and encouragement over the years. If I were to dedicate this book to anyone it would most certainly be to her memory with my deepest gratitude.

In 1950 Erma Denton spent many hours researching the early history of the Borzoi. Help on early foreign history was extended to her by Mary Taviner who later incorporated much of that information in her Borzoi magazine *Riders of the Wind*. When Erma passed on, her husband Lawrence sent me all the files and records of her research. To a great extent I have relied on these in the belief that all her time and efforts should not be wasted.

A list of all those who have offered generous help and assistance in securing information and pictures would be lengthy. My deepest gratitude is extended to all of them. Special thanks must go to talented artist Sandra Cody for the sketches in the chapter on the interpretation of the Standard. Without the help from all these friends, this book would not have been possible.

—*Lorraine Groshans*

1

The Origin of the Borzoi

"ONCE UPON A TIME..." So many fables, myths, children's stories begin with this phrase. Almost every attempt to write of the origins of the Borzoi should also start out in this same manner. Breeds that have evolved since the beginning of the 20th century have written records of great accuracy to which one can refer. The beginnings of more ancient breeds are cloaked in mystery, clouded by assumptions and confused in and by fables and fantasies.

The most common "once upon a time" claim for the origin of the Borzoi is the crossing of a Persian greyhound or Saluki-type dog with the heavier coated, hardier Russian boarhounds or sheepdogs. The Tatars in their travels could well have acquired the Saluki-type coursing hounds and through selective breeding tried to make them more adaptable to the more rugged northern climates. The changes undergone by these hounds could also have come about through natural adaptation and through natural variation within the hounds themselves, although judicious outcrossing could have speeded up the process. Supposedly this was during the 13th and 14th centuries. A reference to hare-coursing dogs of a Borzoi type at the Court of the Grand Duke of Novgorad was made in Russian documents in 1260. However, it was many years, even centuries, before more descriptive information became available.

In *The Modern Dog Encyclopedia*, Henry P. Davis claimed that the Borzoi descended from the type of greyhound dog shown in early Persian and Egyptian art, there being two schools of thought regarding the development of the longer coat. One maintains that centuries of existence in the bitter cold of Russian winters produced it; the other contends that it was developed by crossbreeding with the wolf. Hutchinson, in his 1930 *Popular Dog Encyclopedia*, also claimed that the Borzoi stems from the early Egyptian greyhound type of dog.

In *The March of Muscovy* by Harold Lamb published in 1948 by Doubleday, we learn that Sigismund von Herberstein, an Austrian nobleman, traveled to Moscow in 1516 to try to arrange a state of peace between Vaily the Great Prince, son of Ivan III, and Poland and Lithuania. His mission was a failure, but he must have been quite a success personally for when he left for home he was presented with many costly gifts including several wolfhounds.

Perhaps one reason for so many theories and so little knowledge of the origin of the Borzoi may be that what recorded information we do have comes to us from Russia, and that country was backward in the development of her literature. It was not until the 18th century that we find the prose and verse of Lomontov, the drama of Sumarokov and the poetry of Derzhawin. Therefore, it may be considered rather remarkable that in the 17th century, around 1650 to be more exact, a book of rules for Borzoi hunting, dedicated to Czar Alexis, was published. The book contained a detailed description of Borzoi type but no mention of color was made. The Borzoi was considered a working dog then and color was of little importance compared to the prime requisites of speed and strength. The Borzoi was cross-bred whenever his owner thought such a breeding would produce a better working dog. This could have destroyed the breed had not the great distances and difficulties of transportation forced breeders to inbreed their own stock to such an extent that the crossbreeding done later did little harm. Because the Borzoi was so highly prized as a hunting and coursing dog, the crossbreeding was very carefully done, usually with a greyhound type.

There were two distinct types of early Russian Borzoi—the Siberian and the Circassian. The Siberian had a close thick undercoat and the coloring was usually white with lemon, tan or brindle markings. The Circassian type had a flat coat of about two inches but with profuse feathering of the front legs and thighs and thick curls about the neck. The legs of the latter were longer and the head shorter than in the Siberian. The Circassian type also included black and tan coloration.

After Borzoi were exhibited at a show in Moscow in 1824, a change was noted in the general attitude toward the breed. Crosses were no longer deemed advisable as the owners were anxious to produce show-winning specimens as well as good hunting dogs. Later in that same century, Artem Boldaroff stated that he would not hunt with any dogs that were not pleas-

The first known portrait of a Borzoi in England. By courtesy of Gerald Massey in London, England, we have this photograph of the watercolor by F. Heicehl of a Russian Borzoi bred in the kennels of the Czar and given to Sir J. Saville Lumley, K.C.B. by Count Fersen, Imperial Grand Verein, October 31, 1864.

Gold medal Woronzova Hunt wolf-team with huntsman.

ing in appearance. Obviously he was trying to strike a balance between type and soundness, or beauty and ability, in his breeding program at his Woronzova Hunt. At one time self-colors and black and tan Borzoi were barred from official expositions in Russia although many dogs of these colorations were found among the best known kennels in Russia. Extremely curly haired Borzoi were also looked upon with disapproval as this was thought to come from an infusion of blood from the Courland Greyhound (now extinct) from the Courland province in the Baltic area.

At this period in its history, the Borzoi was not only the aristocratic dog, he was the dog of the aristocrat. Color became an item of supreme importance. Various colors were favored by different Hunts often as their hallmark.

The Czar's Imperial Kennel is legend. He, and others of the nobility, maintained fabulous establishments for Borzoi complete with extensive staffs whose sole duty was the care of the dogs. It was considered unthinkable for any nobleman to sell one of these hounds although they were sometimes presented as gifts to honored guests. In that manner, they finally made their way beyond the borders of Mother Russia.

It is small wonder that the Borzoi was valued so highly. One has only to recall historians' accounts of how all of Europe (and no doubt Asia as well) had been overrun by wolves for centuries. King Ethelred campaigned against the wolf and had him exterminated in England and Wales in the 10th century by publishing an edict that tribute might be paid in wolves' pelts instead of the coin of the realm. It is surprising that the Borzoi type of hound was not imported and used in this campaign in England at that time, but such was not the case. Accounts of Borzoi in England did not appear until several centuries later. Where the Borzoi-type hound was used he did indeed prove his worth. Here was a breed that could be taught to chase, overtake and hold the vicious wolf until the hunter could destroy it. A team of Borzoi would run along either side of a wolf, grasp his neck firmly close behind an ear and throw him over on his back where he would be pinned to the ground by the dogs until the hunter killed him or captured him to use for training of young stock back at the kennel.

But while wolf hunting with Borzoi served some useful purpose in depleting the wolf population and protecting livestock from their depradations, it was also a colorful sport. There was keen competition among the various kennels or hunts with great sums of money and favors won and lost on wagers. Wolf hunting with Borzoi evolved into a sporting event with as much color, pomp and pagentry as sports favored by the aristocracy in other lands such as horse racing and fox hunting.

Hunting was the national sport in Russia, and the most elaborate preparations were made for the hunting parties. If Hollywood could have

Martynow portrait of the white and grey Nagrajdai, grand gold
medal winner owned by G. Tchebyshow.

Martynow portrait of the white and grey Pobedim, grand silver
medal winner owned by S.S. Kariew.

Martynow portrait of the white and grey Opromet, grand gold medal
winner owned by H.I.H. Nikolai Nikolaievitch.

Martynow portrait of the white and sable Tcharodei, grand gold medal
winner owned by the Grand Duke Nicholas.

imported one of these events, the movie moguls would have had a spectacle worthy of their overlooked term "colossal." The cast would have consisted of faultlessly dressed huntsmen, Borzoi equipped with collars and leads in colors matching the hunters' costumes, the finest of horses, and men and other animals numbering in the hundreds at least. Wealthy estate owners kept hundreds of Borzoi for this purpose; less affluent estate owners and farmers kept as many as they could, sometimes going to unbelievable lengths to acquire them since they were not generally for sale. For instance, Mrs. Winifred Chadwick in her book *The Borzoi*, first published in England in 1952, says, "Legend related that a rich landowner of the Province of Tarnoff gave his daughter, as wife, to an ignorant country squire in exchange for a single Borzoi. The descendants of the pair, however, regarded this story as a slight to them and maintained that the deal was not over a Borzoi but a *Svora*, i.e. three Borzois."

Many Russian writers recount tales of the wolf hunts. Leo Tolstoy in his novel *War and Peace* gives an account of a hunt consisting of 130 dogs and 20 horsemen. Tolstoy's friend and countryman Ivan Nazhivin, in his book *The Dogs*, writes a story of Russian life on the great estates before, during and after the Revolution. There is a vivid account of a wolfhunt with two noblemen pitting their Borzoi against each other for high honors in the field. As the years pass in Nazhivin's story and the Revolution nears its end, there is a graphic accounting of the confusion and horror as roving bands of peasants and soldiers killed and destroyed everything associated with the aristocracy including, of course, the Borzoi. Perhaps the most vivid, true account of wolf hunting in Russia is to be found in the story of "The Perchino Hunt" by His Excellency Dimitri Walzoff. A translation of this work is included in Mrs. Chadwick's book, and it is probably the most accurate and most detailed accounting of wolf hunting to be found anywhere.

In 1887 the Grand Duke Nikolai Nikolaivitch gave added impetus to the effort to restore Borzoi breeding to its former high level by purchasing the Perchino* estate in Tula and producing Borzoi whose reputation for quality was and is world-wide. The Grand Duke had previously owned foxhounds on his father's estate Peterhof. His first Borzoi was Udar followed by Osornoi purchased from the Tumanoffski Hunt in Novgorad

---

* It should be noted by students of history and pedigrees that the price of fame is such that there have been at least three well known kennels since the Grand Duke's Perchino Hunt became synonymous with quality in Borzoi: the Perchina Kennels of Lois Kellogg in the United States, one in Australia and one in South Africa. The "o" and "a" at the end of the name are found interchangeably in various accounts on all four kennels.

To the American Amateur of the Borzoi Hound

The famous "Pershino" Borzoi Kennels, belonging to H.I.H. the Grand Duke Nicolas Nicolasovitch, beg to announce that they have always ready for immediate delivery, first class Borzois, of the purest ancient Russian type, good for show, coursing, breeding and hunting purposes.

The Pershino Kennels have always won all championship prizes, and first class medals at exhibitions and coursings, where they were represented. The Breeding Kennels of H.I.H. consist of three hundred borzois; and borzoi-hounds trained on wolves are a feature.

Photographs of representative specimens will be illustrated in future issues.

Communications may be addressed to and further information obtained from Worthington Whitehouse, 573 5th Ave., New York.

N. Kosheleff, Supt.
Pershino, Government of Tula, Russia

American Champion Bistri of Pershino, Bred By H. I. H. the Grand Duke Nicolas
The Best Borzoi outside of Russia

and Chitschny and Atlan from the W.P. Wojekoff's Hunt. In 1884 the Grand Duke disbanded his Hunt at Peterhof when he left to take command of the Imperial Hussar Regiment. When he re-established his Hunt, it was on the estate owned by the personal secretary to the Czar in the District of Sepuchoff. Within three years after the purchase of Perchino he had bought Borzoi from many Hunts, always striving to perfect his breeding program according to his conception of the ideal Borzoi with a balance of type and soundness. Later, the Grand Duke created the "Society for the Development of the Qualities of Hunting Hounds" in St. Petersburg and became its first president.

An interesting advertisment appeared in the March, 1908 issue of the magazine *Country Life in America*. This was over the name: N. Kosheleff, Supt., Pershino, Government of Tula, Russia. The ad displayed a photo of American Champion Bistri of Pershino, "the best Borzoi outside of Russia," The copy in the ad included the following statements. "The famous 'Pershino' Borzoi Kennels, belonging to H.I.H. The Grand Duke Nicolas Nicolasovitch, beg to announce that they have always ready for immediate delivery, first class Borzois, of the purest ancient Russian type, good for show, coursing, breeding and hunting purposes. The Pershino Kennels have *always* won all championship prizes, and first class medals at exhibitions and coursings, where they were represented. The Breeding Kennels of H.I.H. consist of 300 Borzois; and borzoi-hounds trained on wolves are a feature." Obviously, the Borzoi in Russia at the turn of the century had exchanged his status of royal gift for one of commercial commodity.

A leading Russian artist during the latter half of the 19th century, N.A. Martynow, son of the celebrated artist Andrei Efymovich Martynow (1768-1826), was commissioned to do a series of paintings of winning Borzoi exhibited by the Imperial Society of Russia from 1874 to 1879. While these paintings are interesting, they must be studied allowing for artistic license as they lack the accuracy of actual photographs.

The Imperial Kennels of the Czars—known as Gatchina—were started in 1613. In the late 19th century Prince Galitzin was Master of the Imperial Hunt. At one time during his stewardship Gatchina housed in the neighborhood of 60 couples of Borzoi, 20 couples of English foxhounds, 8 couples of Bearhounds and 100 horses. Hunting of various sorts was indeed a royal sport.

The inventory of dogs, horses and staff at Perchino was even greater according to Walzoff. There were at the time of his count 365 dogs (100 foxhounds, 130 hunting Borzoi, 20 retired Borzoi, 15 greyhounds, 100 Borzoi puppies), 87 horses, and 78 persons on the staff for the kennels and stables. Perchino was said to be the only Borzoi hunt in all of Russia existing on such a scale.

Another Russian hunt, active in Borzoi breeding at the end of the 19th century whose name is familiar to all who search for knowledge of the best of the breed was Woronzova located in the Province of Tamboff and owned by Artem Bolderoff. In 1896 he became the owner of this hunt which had been first established by his uncle Nikolai Arkadievitch Bolderoff.

These hunts and others survived and prospered until the Revolution in 1971 when there was an end to the nobility and a permanent abolition of all large estates.

Although Borzoi were not well known in England or in Western Europe at the time, two Borzoi-type dogs were pictured in Le Compte Buffon's revised *Historie Naturelle* published in 1798. Buffon described two dogs brought by his son from St. Petersburg in 1773 as white with a few markings of color, greyhound in form but larger with long silky coats, fine-boned with overall refinement. The first mention of the breed in English literature was in the book *A Picturesque Representation of the Manners, Customs, and Amusements of the Russians* by J.A. Atkinson and James Walker published in 1812 in which the authors described the hunting of wolves by the "fan-tailed greyhound" after a visit to Russia. However, these two descriptive items and others following did not create an immediate demand for Borzoi outside of Russia.

There were many published treatises on dogs and their classifications which are of historical if not specific interest. The earliest printed attempt at canine classification in English was the *Book of St. Alban's* written by the Prioress of St. Alban's, Dame Juliana Berners, in the mid-15th century. The next classification came about a century later written by Dr. John Caius, physician to Queen Elizabeth, published in 1576 dividing all known dogs into six groups: those hunting beasts, those used for fowling, spaniels and others of the toy types (the "comforters"), and two groups of various shepherd and working types. Dr. John Henry Walsh (who used the pseudonym Stonehenge) was Editor-in-Chief in the mid-19th century of *The Field*, and English sports publications. It was Dr. Walsh who encouraged and promoted the establishment of a stud book and the written description, or standard, for all recognized breeds in England. In 1874 Frank Pierce compiled the first all breed stud book.

In 1890 *The Illustrated Book of the Dog* by Vero Shaw was published in England. This is a most comprehensive book on all the recognized English breeds of that day giving the history and detailed descriptions of them and including many lovely color plates. In content and format this book closely resembles *The Complete Dog Book*, an official publication of American recognized breeds of the American Kennel Club today. The Borzoi in the Shaw book is referred to in the section on foreign dogs under

In this picture, taken about 1913, the hounds of the
Imperial Hunt of the Czar are being taken to the field.

Persian.   English Greyhound.   Deerhound.
Italian.   Siberian Wolfhound.

THE GREYHOUND FAMILY.

The Greyhound family from Vero Shaw's book *The Illustrated Book of the Dog* published in
England in 1890. Note that the Borzoi is called the Siberian Wolfhound.

19

the heading of the Siberian Wolfhound. The author states that the breed was scarce at that time in England although appearing occasionally at dog shows where they always generated great interest and admiration. He compares the Siberian Wolfhound to the Scotch Deerhound with differences in coat length, texture and color. The best specimens known to the author were those owned by the Rev. J.C. Macdona and Lady Emily Peel. A general illustration of the "Greyhound Family" appeared in the chapter on the Greyhound and included the Siberian Wolfhound.

In 1897 Hugh Dalziel writing under the pen name "Corsincon" in his book *British Dogs: Their Varieties, History, Characteristics, Breeeding, Management, and Exhibition* had the following to say about the Siberian Wolfhound.

"This is a dog of the Scotch deerhound type, and much the same in size. The most striking difference is in the colour. The grizzle, almost universal in the deerhound, gives place here to a mixture of colours. The majority of those exhibited at our shows are white, with fawn or yellow markings; but a gentleman who reported a dog show at Moscow for 'The Country,' when there were about 50 exhibited, describes the prevailing colour of the *Barsee*, as these hounds are called, to have been white and dark grey; and Minski, shown at Burton-on-Trent, is a mixture of light and dark grey and white; but certainly the majority we see here are white and fawn or yellow.

"They are scarce in this country, which is to be regretted, as they are strikingly handsome and majestic. The best specimens I have seen are Lady Emily Peel's Czar, by the Duke of Hamilton's Moscow out of the Rev. J.C. Cumming Macdona's Sandringham; and the latter bitch is also a grand one. Czar is a splendid fellow, white and lemon coloured, in build corresponding with our best deerhounds; he has a good deep chest, well sloped shoulders, airy neck, and noble head with rather full, almost amber-coloured eyes, which show bead-like, surrounded as they are with white. He is altogether a dog of fine proportions and noble appearance, and a first-rate specimen of the breed.

"The texture of the coat is finer than in our deerhounds, and, from their colour partly, they have a milder look than their name and work would lead us to expect.

"As an ornament and companion they are to be commended, and I hope to see them become more plentiful."

It may be strange that the English people had not embraced the Borzoi long before they did because of their devotion to the sport of hunting, but we should remember the wolf had not menaced the British Isles since the 10th century so the incentive to use these hounds for their original purpose did not exist. When the Borzoi finally made his appearance in

20

Ch. Velsk and White Czar. Maude Earle's painting of two of the Duchess of Newcastle's Borzoi at the turn of the century. They are full brothers by the imported Russian dog Korotai (by Atman ex Soodarka) out of Ch. Vikhra (by the Russian import Golub ex Vedma).

A son of Ch. Velsk out of Gatchina bred and owned by Queen Alexandra whelped in 1907 named Vassilka. — Vandyke

Ch. Tsareta, the last Russian-bred Borzoi that was purchased by the Duchess of Newcastle. The bitch was sent to England as a present from Count Stroganoff of Russia to his English Greyhound trainer. Tsareta won several show honors and, when bred to Ch. Velsk, produced Ch. Tatiana, Ch. Velsk Votrin, Ch. Theodora, Master Velsk and Atloffs Boris.

England, due to the Russian custom of presenting him as a gift, he was adopted and prized mainly for his regal beauty.

It is believed the Czar presented the first pair of Borzoi to Queen Victoria. The Prince of Wales, later King Edward VII, received Molodetz and Owdalzka. The Princess of Wales, later Queen Alexandra, received Alex, and the Duchess of Manchester was given Katae. Katae was the first Borzoi exhibited in England and this was in 1863. This was the public's first opportunity to see these hounds and may be considered the beginning of their popularity in England.

In 1865 Lady Innes-Ker started her Borzoi kennel, and Lady Emily Peel exhibited Borzoi occasionally. There is a Landseer painting of the latter with her Russian Borzoi. At the Crystal Palace show three Borzoi were shown in 1872. Lady Emily had shown a brace at an earlier show at the same location. These and others at that time were entered as Siberian Wolfhounds.

In retrospect, these events seem mere preliminaries to the debut of the dog Krilutt in 1888 at the Alexandra Palace show as Krilutt became the first English champion Borzoi. As a consequence, Krilutt was considered by many to be the pillar of the breed in that country. He was sired by Dorogai from General Toharoff's line out of Nagla from Mr. Yermoff's line bred by Mr. Korotneff of Oriel, Russia, whelped April 27, 1886. He was a white dog with silver markings, stood 30¼ inches at the shoulder, had a 33 inch girth, and 11½ inch long head and a 21 inch tail. As he had won the silver medal at the 1888 Moscow exhibition, he was a good specimen but evidently not the best. He was owned by Mrs. Wellesley of Merton Abbey in Surrey, whose husband Colonel Wellesley had served as British Military Attache in Russia.

In 1890, Her Grace Kathleen Duchess of Newcastle entered the Borzoi fancy by establishing her kennels at Clumber in Nottinghamshire using the suffix "Notts" although her kennel name was Clumber. This was one of the great milestones in the history of the breed. Often the interest of a well-known personality stimulates an increase in popularity for a particular breed because of the human habit of following a fashionable leader. This was not mere fly-by-night venture on the part of the Duchess, however, as she was a practical expert who understood dogs. She was a highly respected judge of the breed and served in that capacity from 1897 to 1948, and her devotion to the breed continued until her death in 1955.

The Duchess of Newcastle first exhibited Borzoi in 1890 and won a breeder's medal with her six young entries; home-bred ones by Ivan II, a French dog, out of Spain, a gift to her mother by a Spanish nobleman. Constantly seeking perfection in the breed, she sent agents to Russia several times to procure better Borzoi than were available in England and

22

Sandringham Kolpitza and Sandringham Moscow owned by Queen Alexandra. — *Russell*

Alex, owned by Queen Alexandra. Alex was gift to her when she was Princess of Wales from her brother-in-law, Czar Alexander II of Russia.

Borzoi were often associated with royalty in many countries at the turn of the century. The children of the German Crown Prince are shown here with their Borzoi in 1910.

even made one trip there herself to gain information through talks with prominent Russian breeders. One of the first Borzoi she owned was a self-fawn Ch. Ooslad (Artem Bolderoff's Ataman ex Podrooga II from Dmitri Walzoff's kennels) bred by General Sokoloff. Through this dog's son Windle Earl he is found in the pedigrees of Champions Sunbeam, Statesman, Showman, Ivan Turgenoff and Miss Piostri, all important Borzoi winners at the turn of the century.

The Borzoi Club was organized in England in 1892 with the Duke and Duchess of Newcastle serving as the first presidents jointly for several years. In 1912 there were over 50 members—just twenty years after the club's beginnings. The Duchess was Patroness of the Club at the time of her death 63 years after she first became president.

Also in 1892, 50 Borzoi were exhibited at a show at the Agricultural Hall in Islington. Twenty of these were owned and entered by the Russian Imperial Kennels, and the announcement that the dogs were to be sold at auction after the show created much excitement. The Duchess of Newcastle purchased Oudar, considered the best one, for the sum of 200 pounds.

William Wade of Hulton, Pennsylvania, is credited with having introduced the Borzoi to America in 1889 when he purchased a bitch named Elsie from Freeman Lloyd in England. In the stud book of the American Kennel Club, Volume 8, in 1892, the only Borzoi registered were Vladimir (Ch. Krilutt ex Elsie) and his litter sister Princess Irma, both strong show winners owned and bred by Harmony-Hornell Kennels in Covert, New York.

The first American to visit Russia and import Borzoi directly from that country was Charles Stedman Hanks of Boston, Massachusetts. He and his wife traveled to Russia in 1889 to visit a cousin Major General Henry T. Allen who was the Military Attache at the American Embassy in St. Petersburg. During their stay they met several officials in the Czar's household and staff. One of these gentlemen, Colonel Dietz, was very much interested in Borzoi and was instrumental in assisting Mr. Hanks in acquiring some for export. Mr. Hanks had expressed his desire to bring Borzoi to the United States so that the people of this country might learn to know and appreciate these most beautiful of hounds.

In the report of the Class of 1879 of Harvard College, Mr. Hanks wrote in his profile in 1890 that he had established a kennel in Manchester-By-The-Sea, Massachusetts, by the name of "Seacroft." This record also states that Mr. Hanks was a member of the New England Kennel Club. Seacroft housed many imported Borzoi including two who attained their American championships: Ch. Vinga bred by Prince Boris Galitzin and Ch. Svodka bred by A. Schermetieff.

There must have been quite a number of Borzoi imported about the same time, for Paul H. Hacke of Pittsburgh, Pennsylvania purchased several dogs from Russia through correspondence with A.J. Rousseau in St. Petersburg. Many of these died in transit, and the best remembered survivor was Zloeem. Mr. Hacke also owned Ivan that he entered in a show in Chicago in 1890. Mr. H.W. Huntington, secretary of the National Greyhound Club, imported several from England. The best known was Argoss bred by General Sokoloff in 1887 and imported when several years old, attaining his American championship shortly thereafter. Mr. Huntington's interest in the breed lasted but a very short time before he returned to the greyhound fancy. A Mr. King showed Ivan Romanoff in New York City in 1890, and a Mr. Tefft registered a Borzoi with the AKC in 1893.

When Mr. Hanks turned his attention to Greyhounds, his desire that Americans would adopt the Borzoi breed was an accomplished fact. No one was more devoted to the breed that the Seacroft Kennel manager Thomas Turner who took over the Seacroft Borzoi, exhibiting them for several years. By the time Mr. Turner's interest waned, there were many others who knew and admired the breed, and its popularity rapidly increased after the turn of the century.

Several of the Borzoi at the Seacroft Kennels in Massachusetts around 1890.

Ch. Sorva of Woronzova, imported from Artem Balderoff's kennel in Russia, was owned by Joseph Thomas. She was best opposite sex at Westminster in 1904 through 1907 and again in 1909.

Yarki of Perchino, bred in the Perchino Kennels of HIH Grand Duke Nicholas, was imported by Joseph Thomas for the Valley Farm Kennels. Enroute to the United States, he was bred in England to Queen of Olives who was also sent to the U.S.

Ch. Kopchic O'Valley Farm was bred by Valley Farm. He was used extensively at stud and may be found in extended pedigrees here and abroad, especially in Holland and Belgium.

27

2

Early History of
The Borzoi in America

WHEN A NEW BREED is introduced to a country, it usually takes a few years for the novelty and curiosity concerning the breed to settle into true understanding and appreciation. This is brought about by a few devoted breeders and soon taken up by others who become interested in the breed.

In a previous chapter, the beginnings of Borzoi in the United States were traced through the importations from England and Russia by a few people. While Mr. Hanks of the Seacroft Kennels did extend his interest from his original importations to a limited number of breedings, the interest of most of the other importers began and ended with their first few Borzoi.

The dawn of the twentieth century saw the beginning of serious interest and breeding of the Borzoi. The story has been told more than once about Joseph Thomas' interest in the breed and his search for quality foundation stock in Russia.

The most famous kennel name in American Borzoi history is Valley Farm. The kennel became the cornerstone of the best Borzoi stock in America. To this day, it is recognized in other countries of the world as the premier American Borzoi kennel which in itself speaks volumes for the quality it produced.

The Valley Farm kennel name was registered with the American Kennel Club in December of 1901 with Joseph B. Thomas as owner. However, Valley Farm was actually owned by a syndicate made up of Joseph

Ch. Khotni O'Valley Farm (by Zyclon of Perchino ex Olga O'Valley Farm) represents some of the best and most successful breeding done at Valley Farm.

Ch. Nega O'Valley Farm, a cross of Valley Farm and imported Dutch lines, was a beautiful sable bitch owned and exhibited by the Vladimir Kennels. Later she was sold to Louis Murr's Romanoff Kennels.

Ch. Ivor O'Valley Farm was part of the great hunting team bred and owned for a while by C.E. Miller of Wisdom, Montana. He was shown at Westminster in 1925 and won best American-bred in show.

Thomas Jr., Ralph H. Thomas, A. Douglass Dodge, Howard H. Mossman and Chauncey J. Hanlin. Mr. Mowbray M. Palmer acted as secretary until 1915 when Mr. Thomas transferred the kennel and registered name to him. Miss Lois Kellog became a partner in 1921. It was a stormy partnership which lasted until 1929 when Valley Farm was again transferred solely to Mr. Palmer while Miss Kellogg went on to establish her own kennel of Perchina. Mr. Palmer was the sole owner until his death in 1932 at which time the ownership of the Valley Farm affix went to Mrs. E.T. Biesel, mother of Miss E.C. Biesel of Vladimir Kennels. Miss Biesel used the Valley Farm affix on a few Borzoi of her Vladimir breeding based on Valley Farm stock for a few years after that.

Joseph Thomas bought his first several Borzoi from the kennels of Tom Turner, the former manager of the Seacroft Kennels. Then he purchased some from Mrs. J.G. Kent's Terra Cotta Kennels in Toronto, Canada. His most noteworthy purchases came as a result of three trips he made to Russia on behalf of the syndicate in search of Borzoi that would consistently reproduce according to type. He visited Artem Baldaroff's Woronzova Kennels and the Perchino Kennels of the Grand Duke Nicholas where he acquired the white and gray Bistri of Perchino (by Almaz of Perchino ex Ptachka of Perchino), the white and tan Nayada of Perchino (by Armavir of Perchino ex Podrousky of Perchino), the white and tan Schaloste of Perchino (by Vakhlak of Perchino ex Zarka of Perchino), the white and tan Nenagladni of Perchino (littermate of Nayada), the white Sorva of Woronzova (by Kousnetzoff's Lioubezny ex Boldaroff's Rasskida), the white Atamanka of Woronzova (by Boldaroff's Kolpchik ex Prelest of Perchino), and the white Rasskida of Woronzova (by Pochvall ex Zmieka). These were all purchased in 1903 and 1904. In 1911 he imported the brown brindle Zyclon of Perchino (by Groznyj ex Zaplia II), the grey Yarki of Perchino (by Yestreb ex Grosa), and the tan and white Postrel of Woronzova (by Pobildim ex Alaska).

One of the hounds that descended from these imports was one of the finest studs in America, Ch. Kopchic O'Valley Farm, a white and tan dog whelped in 1905 (by Bistri of Perchino ex Schaloste of Perchino). When he was bred to Sorva of Woronzova, he sired Sorvina who in turn produced Sorvina II whelped in 1911 and owned by the Sippican Kennels. The Vladeska Kennels used him with Variadne (by Ch. Podar of Toula ex Ch. Lasca) to get Ch. Varatai of Vladeska. Miss M.K. Bird of Westbury, New York bred him to her Tousky (by Sverkay '95 ex Stonefield Ziska) imported by Miss Bird from the Duchess of Newcastle to get Ch. Westbury Rattler sold to the Tatiana Kennels. Dr. John E. DeMund had imported Princess Vedma (by Velasquez ex Vedma) from the Duchess of Newcastle and subsequently bred her to Nenagladni of Perchino to get the two excel-

puppy days, but only when the two were alone together. In public, the wolf remained aloof although he never openly resented any attention from strangers.

"He was not so tolerant of dogs, however, and woe to any dog that ventured to cross his path. As a joke, I once entered him as a 'buffalo hound' at one of the big bench shows. He was accepted, benched and behaved himself perfectly, though I did take the precaution to put a wire screen between him and the public.

"Only once did he even threaten trouble. That was when I was leading him past a bench of the Russian Wolfhounds, who instantly leaped to the ends of their chains, eyes blazing, teeth bared, while their savage barking brought every dog in the show to its feet.

"The great wolf whirled about facing the foremost dog, Champion Bistri O'Valley Farm. The calmness of the wild brute was in marked contrast to the excitement of the dogs. As he stood there firmly on his four legs, the hair on his back and neck rising in a tall mane, menacing fangs unsheathed, and those cold, merciless eyes gazing straight into his sworn enemy, I wondered what was going on in the back of that big gray head. Perhaps he was wondering how many dogs of that caliber he could account for in a fair open fight taking one at a time. Then I dragged him off, mane tossing, and with many a backward glance at the splendid dogs who were just as eager as he to come to grips."

Dr. John E. DeMund's Lorraine Kennels in Brooklyn, New York, were active during the early years of Valley Farm's existence. He owned the two champions Lasca and Zoraida and their offspring already mentioned. He bred Lasca to Ch. Pojar of Toula (by Abrek ex Outechka), a tan and white male bred by N.T. Kochaleff in Russia and owned by Dr. J.P. Hoguet of Byoak Kennels in New York. The ensuing litter of Novosti, Lasky, Belkis and Variadne all carried the Lorraine prefix and all finished their championships. Dr. DeMund retained ownership of Novosti and Belkis. Later, he gave Novosti to Alva Rosenberg, only 14 or 15 at the time but even then quite a "dog man", to compensate for his disappointment in a Borzoi he had received from one of Lasca's earlier litters. Mr. Rosenberg later wrote that Novosti "was a big white dog with light tan markings—somewhat straight behind and light in eye, otherwise quite typical, but now that he is dead I might day that I considered him the worst of the four despite that on one occasion or so he beat his brother Lasky, who was white marked with black—an unpopular color those days—and was a very handsome upstanding hound. However, I think Dr. DeMund considered Ch. Belkis, a white with some brindle markings, the pick of the lot. She never grew much of a coat but her quality and conformation left little to be desired." Mr. Rosenberg's comments about early Borzoi are extremely valuable to any student of the breed as he maintained an absorbing interest in Borzoi from the early years of his love for Ch. Lasca until his death in 1973. He was a well-known and highly respected all-breed judge for many years and had the reputation of being one of the most competent and impartial judges of the Borzoi.

Dr. DeMund was elected to various offices in the Russian Wolfhound Club of America and served that organization faithfully for many years. As president of the American Kennel Club, a position he held for several years, his knowledge and abilities so generously given to the cause of pure-bred dogs benefited not only Borzoi but all breeds.

The Bailiff Kennels of Dr. Wilson C. Bailey in Camden, New Jersey began breeding Borzoi about 1906. Dr. Bailey furnished one of the foundation bitches for the Vladeska Kennels when he sold Valeska Bailiff at the age of nine weeks to Mr. J. Bailey Wilson. Dr. Bailey owned Ch. Obilska (by Ch. Sorvan O'Valley Farm ex Valley Farm Hilka), a white dog with lemon and brindle markings bred by Copperburg and Merriman of Fairview Kennels in Simsbury, Connecticut. When Obilska was bred to the white and lemon bitch Aube O'Valley Farm (by Ch. Bistri of Perchino ex Atamanka of Woronzova), he sired Teddy Bailiff. He also sired Vladimir Bailiff and Valeska Bailiff, all three becoming champions and going to other kennels to continue their contributions to the breed in various breeding programs.

The Holmes Kennel, owned by Forrester H. Scott of Merion, Pennsylvania, was most active in the breed from about 1908 to 1918. Ch. Holmes Boris and Ch. Holmes Thor are still to be seen in extended pedigrees. Ch. Holmes Sonia (by Ch. Obilska ex Zulika) when bred to Ch. Laska produced Ch. Ronia, a white and black bitch. After discontinuing his kennel operations, Mr. Scott was without Borzoi for many years. True to form, however, Borzoi-lover Scott could not give up the breed forever. In the early 1960's he attended the December show in Philadelphia to watch the Borzoi judging and could not resist arranging to purchase a puppy companion from Priscilla Sanner of the Petrikov Kennels.

Mr. R.W.K. Anderson of Plainfield, New Jersey introduced his kennel name Boreas to the Borzoi fancy in 1908. Two of the best known Borzoi purchased by him were Ch. Teddy Bailiff and Ch. Novo O'Valley Farm (by Rasboi O'Valley Farm ex Siberia O'Valley Farm). Ch. Teddy Bailiff sired Boreas Avenger and Boreas Ursula, the sire and dam of Ch. Lada of Delmac bred by Delmac Kennels but owned by J.L. Jones' Agnedelldoll Kennels.

It was during the same decade as the previously mentioned kennels began that Mr. J. Bailey Wilson of Media, Pennsylvania brought Valeska Bailiff to his Vladeska Kennels. The bitch established quite a record for herself winning hundreds of first and special awards during her show career. She also proved herself as an exceptional brood bitch. When bred to Lasky she produced Vera and when bred to Varatai of Vladeska she produced Valan and Valectra, all of Vladeska and all champions. Vera, when bred to Nogais O'Spring Valley produced Ch. Vanestra of Vladeska.

The best of breed award at the Kennel Club of Philadelphia annual show is a gold medallion carrying the bas-relief of a Borzoi head and a Bulldog head. According to William Kendrick, long time president of the kennel club, the Borzoi head was modeled by Mr. Wilson's Ch. Valeska Bailiff which he co-owned with his sister Mrs. R.G. Stewart.

Other early American Borzoi stemmed from the Tatiana Kennels of Mrs. James C. Hadley of Erie, Pennsylvania who chose this kennel name in honor of the first Borzoi she owned, Princess Tatiana (by Kuroki ex Tama) bred by Otto F. Behrend. Mrs. Hadley was an ardent exhibitor in the eastern, midwestern and central southern states. She showed Ch. Kopchik O'Valley Farm's son Westbury Rattler and Nenagladni of Perchino's son Vionga O'Valley Farm to their championships. Vionga's daughter out of Vishera of Tatiana, Ch. Viatka of Tatiana, when mated to Ch. Lasky produced Ch. Valievo of Tatiana. Mrs. Hadley purchased Valisan of Vladeska and added yet another championship title to her kennel's record.

Mrs. Carama Chantler of Shreveport, Louisiana began breeding Borzoi in her Iskra Kennels with the purchase of Major B (by Ch. Kopchic O'Valley Farm ex Petersburg O'Valley Farm) bred in 1912 by Harvey Brown in Nebraska. Both his sire and dam may be traced back to Bistri of Perchino. Her next purchase was Ch. Princess Troubetskoy (by Blistai F.R. ex Austin's Kasa) in 1918 bred by V.T. Pisarra in New Jersey. Princess was another descendent of Bistri so the mating of these two dogs brought a maximum of his fine qualities to Iskra.

Some years later Mrs. Chantler bought the strikingly handsome Ivanovitch of Glenwild (by Ch. Duke Boris of Cliffview Manor ex Divinia of Glenwild) a champion that won the Sporting Group nine times out of the ten shown and took best in show twice. (It should be remembered that in those days sporting dogs and hounds as we know them today were all in a single sporting group.)

Mrs. Chantler owned Ch. Miss Piostri of Vladimir (by Ch. Boi O'Valley Farm ex Dawn of Vladimir) bred by Miss Biesel. In Miss Piostri's pedigree can be found Yarki of Perchino and Queen of Oltves, the English bitch that was bred to Yarki in England when he was en route to America from Russia. Also owned was Ch. Grozny O'Valley Farm (by Ch. Boi O'Valley Farm ex Ch. Nastia O'Valley Farm), another of Miss Biesel's breeding and winner of three best in show awards with two of them at his first two shows when he was only 13 and 14 months of age. Another outstanding winner for Mrs. Chantler was the bitch Ch. Zohra of Vladimir (by Graybar of Vladimir ex Vladimir's Mojave Girl) also bred by Miss Biesel. This bitch finished her title of champion by winning three consecutive groups. In 1933 Mrs. Chantler imported Brynzga of Bransgore (by Gordey of Addlestone ex Ch. Sandra of Addlestone) from Mrs. Gingold in England.

Iskra Borzoi were exhibited extensively from the 1930's through 1948 after which Mrs. Chantler discontinued breeding Borzoi and turned her attention to the breeding of Salukis. In 1956 Mrs. Chantler acquired a Borzoi bitch of English and Scottish breeding from the Malora Kennels with the idea of returning to the Borzoi fancy. However, before plans for a revival of Iskra Borzoi activity could materialize, Mrs. Chantler died in 1958.

About 1914 the Arkansas Valley Kennels came into being. It was owned by Mr. D.C. Davis of Cimarron, Kansas who began breeding Borzoi with some Valley Farm hounds sired by Ch. Khotni O'Valley Farm out of Nazimova O'Valley Farm. A white male of this breeding, Kohotna of Arkansas Valley, was reputed to be an outstanding Borzoi due to his beautiful outline, fine ears and exceptional coat.

A contemporary of the Arkansas Valley Kennels was the Anoakia Kennels of Mrs. Anita Baldwin of Santa Anita, California, a daughter of one of California's early settlers. The late well-known judge Chris Shuttleworth was associated with this kennel when he first came to America from England. Mrs. Baldwin imported the English Ch. Ramsden Radium (by Ramsden Ranger ex Miss Piostri) from Major Borman's kennels. From Mrs. Vlasto's English kennels she acquired the 1915 Cruft's winner Rolf of Addlestone (by Trumps of Addlestone ex Sylvia of Addlestone) and the bitch Lotka of Addlestone (by Michael of Addlestone ex Yenia). From Valley Farm Mrs. Baldwin obtained Ch. Konzka O'Valley Farm (by Bistri of Perchino ex Siberia O'Valley Farm) and Grom O'Valley Farm (by Lasky ex Kacke O'Valley Farm).

Among the many excellent Borzoi bred by Mrs. Baldwin we find Radium, Ramsden and Khoza—all of Anoakia (by Ch. Ramsden Radium ex Ch. Konzka O'Valley Farm). When Rolf of Anoakia was bred to Princess Ski, he sired Princess Natacha bred by Miss Janet Miller of Los Angeles. Natacha, under the ownership of Miss Marietta Gregory, set a world record for high hurdle racing. Miss Gregory was in partnership with Miss Edith Green in the Natacha Racing Kennels in the San Fernando Valley until about 1945.

Princess Natacha came by her racing ability naturally. Her grandfather was Rolf of Addlestone and the Addlestone hounds were great racers. In 1928 when the Tia Juana, Mexico dog track first opened, there was one race a day for Borzoi only. Natacha loved to course jackrabbits and often accompanied Miss Gregory on her rides through the open fields so she was in good racing condition both mentally and physically. She was taken to Tia Juana winning her first four races and setting a new track record in the fourth.

The Orloff Kennels of William S. Johnston of Esterville, Iowa also appeared in 1916. His stock was based on the Russian-bred Yarki of Perchino, and he bred Borzoi of superior quality that were often purchased by topflight breeders all over the country. His Ch. Johnston's Krilenko went to Mrs. Cluxton and sired many champions for her Glenwild Kennels. His Yona of Orloff (by Johnston's Balderoff ex Grozny of Orloff) went to the Vladimir Kennels in New York owned by Miss Biesel.

In the 1920's a new roster of kennel names arose to add their share to the perpetuation of the breed. A lion's share it proved to be for the Glenwild Kennels of Mrs. W. Harold Cluxton of Chicago. In the comparatively few years this kennel was active, it consistently produced Borzoi of the highest quality that were in demand by breeders and fanciers throughout the United States. The Glenwild name is a very important one far back in Borzoi pedigrees. The foundation of the Glenwild stock may be credited to Ch. Johnston's Krilenko and Ch. Duke Boris of Cliffview Manor (by Blistai FR ex Ruszka of Romanov) bred by Dr. S. DeSayda at this Cliffview Manor Kennels in Red Bank, New Jersey. Both of these studs were frequently bred to bitches Mrs. Cluxton had obtained from Mrs. Janet Patterson's Romanoff Kennels in Canada.

Some of the famous Glenwild Borzoi were: Ch. Kuropatkin of Glenwild (by Johnston's Krilenko ex Neva of Romanoff); litter brother Ch. Boris of Glenwild; Ch. Almaz of Glenwild (by Duke Boris of Cliffview Manor ex Zaplin of Ralova); littermates Ch.Kronstadt of Glenwild, Ch. Olga of Glenwild, Ch. Sascha of Glenwild, Ch. Petrofski of Glenwild and Ch. Peterhof of Glenwild (by Duke Boris of Cliffview Manor ex Neva of Romanoff). Ch. Borgia of Glenwild (by Duke Boris of Cliffview Manor ex Zahftra of Romanoff) won her title undefeated and became a group as well as best in show winner in 1925 and 1926. In addition, Borgia produced daughter Ch. Pobieda of Glenwild (by Ch. Kuropatkin of Glenwild) who also finished undefeated and won sporting groups in 1929 and 1930. Miss Harriet S. Crane of Montclair, New Jersey owned Ch. Sascha of Glenwild and Ch. Ivan Truvor of Glenwild (by Ch. Kossack of Glenwild ex Marya of Glenwild). Ivan was bred to Tamas of Recall (by Ch. Casimir O'Valley Farm ex Zanoza of Recall) to sire Ch. Lady Sara Loundes H.S.C and Ch. Navosti H.C.S.

Mrs. Cluxton had a huge trailer equipped wtth stalls for twelve Borzoi and a cot for the kennel man. She trained some of her dogs in obedience work and transported them in the trailer to various fashion shows and to children's homes where their performances delighted many an under-privileged child. Her Ch. Czar III of Glenwild was the first Borzoi to earn an obedience title of companion dog in this country.

Mrs. Cluxton loved the richly colored Borzoi and was a great pro-moter of the self-blacks and self-mahoganys even though she often had to overcome deep-rooted prejudice against the dark colors so prevalent in those days. It is a shame that Mrs. Cluxton did not live to see the turnabout in acceptance of these favorite colors thirty and forty years later as Ch. Black Falcon of Twin Elms and Ch. Bronze Falcon of Woodhill garnered their many group and best in show honors in the same midwest area where she exhibited for so many years.

The Zenovia Kennels owned by Frank and Nellie Martin of Hatfield, Pennsylvania were registered early in the 1920's. They produced Ch. Zan of Zenovia and his litter sister Ch. Zanoza of Zenovia (by Ch. Romanoff Peterhoff ex Valeska of Vladeska). The basis of their breeding stock came from the Vladeska Kennels and was combined with selected specimens from the Canadian Romanoff Kennels. Nellie Martin is probably remem-bered most today for her book *The Russian Wolfhound* published by the Judy Publishing Company in 1931.

Another active breeder of this period was Kenneth L. Douglass of Akron, Ohio with his Ladoga Kennels. His foundation stock was largely Valley Farm and included the bitch Salta O'Valley Farm (by Dagonay O'Valley Farm ex Annia O'Valley Farm). When Salta was bred to Pojar of Ladoga (by Nasskok O'Valley Farm ex Agnedelldoll Zanoza) she pro-duced the dark mahogany Yarki of Ladoga and Yona of Ladoga and Ch. Yetive of Ladoga. Pojar was sold in 1935 at the age of eight to Louis Murr and his Romanoff Kennels. This Ladoga kennel is not to be confused with the Ladoga Kennel in England nor with the Ladoga Kennel that appeared in the United States about 15 years later owned by Wilda Woehr.

Althea Farms, owned by Col. Howard Stout Nielson and Sam Walley of Darien, Connecticut, bred Borzoi for a few years during this period but sold their last hounds to Miss Lois Kellogg in 1930. It was from Althea, founded mostly on Valley Farm stock, that Louis Murr purchased the great Ch. Vigow O'Valley Farm, a Borzoi that brought a wealth of honors to his kennel.

To Vlad O'Valley Farm (by Ch. Ostrand O'Valley Farm ex Cresta Bielaja O'Valley Farm), a puppy purchased by Miss Emma Biesel about 1920, goes the honor of naming her Vladimir Kennels at Niverville, New York although the name was not registered until 1925.

Some of the better known Borzoi bred by Miss Biesel were: the lovely gray Graybar of Vladimir (by Vlad O'Valley Farm ex Yona of Orloff); Ch.

Ch. Duke of Fergovia was one of the several champions bred and owned by Villa Smith at her Fergovia Kennels in Manchester, Missouri. *Brown*

Miss Piostri of Vladimir (by Boi O'Valley Farm ex Dawn of Vladimir) and her litter brother Ch. Nadkin Ousland of Vladimir; Ch. Nastia Alliaska O'Valley Farm (by Ch. Boi O'Valley Farm ex Ch. Nastia O'Valley Farm) and her littermate Ch. Grozny O'Valley Farm who was sold to Valley Farm and later to Mrs. Chantler's Iskra Kennels. Miss Biesel also owned the beautiful sable Ch. Nega O'Valley Farm (by Nasskok O'Valley Farm ex Bessberk's Cresta O'Valley Farm) and the well known Ch. Boi O'Valley Farm (by Ch. Appraxin O'Valley Farm ex Zohra du Zwaenhoek).

The Woronzova Kennels of Mrs. Marie Roach of Zionsville, Indiana had its real inception when Mrs. Roach saw her first Borzoi at a show in Florida in 1925. Her first purchase was the noted bitch Russian Beauty, winner of many awards throughout the country defeated only once in her show career and then by her kennelmate Ch. Romanoff Lasky (by Pertzoff O'Valley Farm ex Lady of Romanoff) bred by Janet Patterson and owned as an intermediate owner by the Glenwild Kennels. Mrs. Roach owned the great producing stud Kasoss of Madiera (by Romanoff Lasky ex Zorka II of Glenwild). When Kasoss was bred to Russian Beauty II, he sired Zorina of Woronzova who in turn became the dam of Ch. Duke of Woronzova when he bred to Ch. Boi Woronzova OVF. The Duke sired Ch. Balvan O'Baron's Wood out of Laska O'Baron's Wood.

Mrs. Roach owned the lovely bitch Ch. Nega of Woronzova, a red sable with cream markings. Nega was bred by Mrs. F. Stuart Foote (by Kervan O'Valley Farm ex Nayada Kavkaz O'Valley Farm). She earned not only several group placings but also a best in show at Indianapolis in 1933. When Mrs. Roach bred Nayada to Ch. Boi O'Valley Farm she was granted permission to use the Valley Farm suffix by Miss Biesel in naming her Ch. Boi Woronzova OVF.

Mrs. Villa L. Smith of Manchester, Missouri purchased her first Borzoi Lady Alova (by Kazan of Mississippi Valley ex Countess of Crozon) from Mrs. J.D. Roberts in 1925. At that time Mrs. Smith's kennels were located in the small town of Ferguson near St. Louis so her kennel was named Fergovia.

Lady Alova (bred to Ch. Nicholas Romanoff II from the Canadian Romanoff Kennels) gave Mrs. Smith her first champion Ch. Nicholas of Fergovia. This was in 1927. Her second champion was Ch. Spotnazi of Fergovia (by Romanoff Allin ex Patsonya of Fertovia) followed by Ch. Duke of Fergovia from the same sire and dam a year later. Mrs. Smith also bred Ch. Ivan of Fergovia (by Joreck of Fergovia ex Lady Russonya) and Ch. Komarovski of Fergovia (by Tzar of Fergovia ex Allah of Fergovia). She owned Ch. Fergovia's Sonya of Millvale (by Ch. Kuzjani of Millvale ex Ch. Natalie of Romanoff) bred by Mabel Millichip.

After several years away from active breeding and showing of Borzoi,

Boris of Romanoff and Ch. Sarvoi of Romanoff bred and owned by LeRoy Pelletier in the early days of his American Romanoff Kennels. This kennel was owned later by Louis Murr.

Ch. Vigow O'Valley Farm, bred by Valley Farm, first owned by Col. Neilson, later sold to Louis Murr.

The three most important Borzoi studs at the Romanoff Kennels of Louis Murr: Ch. Vigow of Romanoff, Ch. Vigow O'Valley Farm and Ch. Otrava of Romanoff. *Hopton*

The winning team of Louis Murr and Ch. Vigow of Romanoff.

Mrs. Smith made a brief reappearance on the scene when she shared her home with Martha Taylor in the early 1960's, Mrs. Taylor returning to Missouri after an absence of some 30 years. While living there at Fergovia, Mrs. Taylor bred her Zcerlov's Zoltka (by Ch. Suntan's Malchik of Alpine ex Tanya of Malora II) to Ch. Dark Star of Sleeping Bear (by Abernant ex Ch. Natascha of Sleeping Bear). From this breeding Mrs. Taylor kept two puppies both of which finished after she moved back to California: Ch. Zcerlov's Morning Star and Ch. Zcerlov's Red Star.

The American Romanoff affix has been owned by four individuals: Mrs. F.C. McAllister was the first, then Leroy Pelletier, then the brewer scion Norman A. Pabst and finally Louis J. Murr. Mr. Murr—through all of his efforts to promote and improve the breed, his contributions through the national breed club, and later his application of knowledge and experience to the judging of all breeds—established his name and coincidentally that of his Romanoff Borzoi Kennel as a fixture in the canine hall of fame. He was the son of Basque parents born in northern Italy. At the age of fourteen he made his way to the United States to become a permanent resident. Afterwards, whenever asked about his ethnic background, Mr. Murr would reply only "I am an American." This was in no way a reflection on his ancestry but more a statement of his love for and belief in his adopted country.

Far back in the pedigrees of many of the present day American Borzoi, the predominant name seems to be that of the cream colored Ch. Vigow O'Valley Farm (by Appraxin O'Valley Farm ex Zohra du Zwaenhoek) whelped by the Valley Farm Kennels in 1926. He was first owned by Col. Neilson of Althea Farms but in 1929 was sold to Mr. Murr. He sired many a champion whose bloodlines appear in countless other champion's pedigrees. Among his offspring bred by the Romanoff Kennels we find: Ch. Tiranka of Romanoff (ex Ch. Tamara of Romanoff); Ch. Lasky of Romanoff (ex Tiranka III of Romanoff) and Lasky's little sister Yura of Romanoff eventually owned by John L. Hensey; Ch. Bransgore Akuratai of Romanoff exported to Mrs. Lucy Gingold in England; Ch. Otrava of Romanoff (ex Zanoza of Recall) owned by Mrs. Rosanelle W. Peabody; Otrava's litter brothers Ch. Tibor of Romanoff and Ch. Vigow of Romanoff. There have been many Borzoi with the name of Vigow from the Romanoff line, but this last one mentioned is the one always brought immediately to mind when the name Vigow is mentioned. Because he established such a great record in the show ring and because he was the major part of the winning team with his breeder-owner, Ch. Vigow of Romanoff was then and remained always the favorite of Louis Murr. The first time shown Vigow went from classes to best of breed to first in group to coveted best in show under the expert judge Mrs. H.

Ch. Khan of Romanoff, another multi-best in show winner bred at Romanoff, was owned by Richard Herbhold of Brooklyn, New York.

Ch. Prince Igor of Romanoff, shown with owner Beverly Traglio of Portland, Oregon and Judge Lewis Spence, dominated the shows in the Northwest during the early 1950's with his many group and best in show wins. *Roberts*

Hartley Dodge at Capital City Kennel Club show in April of 1934. He was shown 77 times and was never defeated in the breed. With 67 group wins and 21 best in show wins it was indeed a proud record. At that time the American Kennel Club offered an annual award for the best American-bred dog based on wins at shows held by AKC member clubs. Vigow not only won the award in 1935 but also in 1936 becoming the only dog ever to win the award more than once.

Ch. Vigow of Romanoff sired many notable Borzoi, some of which were: Ch. Adam's Bolshoi (ex Czarina Anna Semenovna) bred by Annie Adams and sold to John Hensey; Ch. Count Leban (ex Randa Rosyka) bred by Mrs. Peabody and then sold to Mr. Murr and later to Mrs. Adams; Ch. Viouga of Romanoff (ex Lizetta); Ch. Nikita O'Baron's Wood (ex Tanya of Romanoff) in Mrs. Oldmixon's kennels; and two good producing bitches Juna and Adana both of Romanoff.

Down through Ch. Vigow O'Valley Farm, throughj Ch. Otrava of Romanoff out of Magna of Romanoff, through Ch. Ajax of Romanoff out of Juna of Romanoff came another renowned stud Ch. Tyddo of Romanoff bred by Mrs. Stewart Jr. Tyddo sired Ch. Vigow OVF of Romanoff (ex Adana of Romanoff) sold by Mr. Murr to Mrs. Arnold J. Brock. This Vigow won five best in show awards in the States and Canada; shown in group 78 times, he was left out of the ribbons only four times. His victories during the war years of the 1940's did much to counteract the lull in popularity of the breed at that time. Before he died at the age of 14 in 1953, he had sired many famous Borzoi among which were Ch. Dostoievsky of Fleetstone (ex Ch. Snigouriska) bred by Fairfield Pope Day and owned by Mrs. Brock; Ch. Bolshoi of Romanoff and Ch. Ninotchka of Romanoff (both ex Adana of Romanoff) with the latter owned by Mrs. Brock; the best in show Ch. Khan of Romanoff (ex Czarina Zhe) bred by Alfred Albert and owned by Mr. R.A.E. Herbhold; and Ch. Prince Igor of Romanoff (ex Czarina Zhe) owned by Miss Beverly Traglio of Portland, Oregon.

When Ch. Vigow O'Valley Farm died at the age of 16, his skeleton was donated to the Smithsonian Institute in Washington D.C. It is not mounted but is kept with numerous other dog skeletons in the research collection of the Division of Mammals. A few years later a second Borzoi skeleton was donated by Harold Gross to the collection—his Ch. Haljeans Nazan. Ch. Vigow of Romanoff died of injuries inflicted by an unwilling bitch when she was taken to him for breeding. (Mr. Murr always believed in natural, unassisted breedings in his kennel.) This Vigow's skeleton was donated to the Peabody Museum of Natural History in Massachusetts to be used as part of a project to demonstrate the structural differences within a family brought about by evolution under human selection. The project, unfortunately, was never completed and the unmounted skeleton remains in storage.

One of the last Borzoi owned by Louis Murr, when his kennel doors closed after he turned his attentions to professional judging, was Vigow of Romanoff II (by Ch. Khan of Romanoff ex Adana of Romanoff II) who was never shown but remained as Mr. Murr's companion. Vigow II was used by several breeders and appears in the early pedigrees of Tam-Boer, Majenkir, Conamor and Loral lines. In the early 1960's Mr. Murr bought Ch. Tatiana of Alpine (by Yermak's Tuman ex Ch. Uda Adams) for his daughter. Tatiana was bred to the Tam-Boer-owned Ch. Vigow of Romanoff III to produce Ch. Chudak of Romanoff owned by Mrs. Irmgard Thompson, probably the last Borzoi to carry the Romanoff name. Mr. Murr remained an active all-breed judge until his death early in 1978.

In 1929 Miss Lois Kellogg II founded the Perchina Kennels in Peekskill, New York when she dissolved her partnership in the Valley Farm kennel with Mowbray Palmer. In the 1929 Stud Book in the AKC library it can be noted that 84 Borzoi were transferred to Perchina from the Valley Farm and five from the Althea Farm signifying that this new kennel opened on a grand scale. Miss Kellogg exhibited on a grand scale too with at least a dozen entries at each show. Later, she moved to California driving the entire distance with 102 Borzoi in a trailer. The Perchina Kennels were finally located in Arlemont, Nevada where Miss Kellogg continued to breed Borzoi until her demise. Although the kennel housed many hounds and Miss Kellogg exhibited extensively, very few of her Borzoi were sold to others. One she let go was Ch. Rubles Perchina (by Rinaldi Perchina ex Omega Perchina) whelped in 1944 and sold to Helen and Charles Colstad as a foundation for the Perchinoff Kennels in California.

In the 1930's Mrs. Frances Oldmixon's Baron's Wood Kennels, named after her father's estate in England, were located in New York. Most of her foundation stock came from the Romanoff kennels. Two of her outstanding Borzoi both in the show ring and as studs were Ch. Volk O'Baron's Wood and Ch. Prince Igor O'Baron's Wood (by Ch. Lasky of Romanoff IV ex Yona of Ladoga). Prince Igor was sold to Mr. Murr in 1939 and then to Alfred Papile in 1942. A white and silver bitch bred by Mrs. Oldmixon and seen often in extended pedigrees was Nikita O'Baron's Wood (by Ch. Vigow of Romanoff ex Tanya of Romanoff). After Mrs. Oldmixon's death, Miss Katherine Shvetzoff acquired the Baron's Wood affix and bred Borzoi until she moved west in 1953. Her Ch. Duke O'Woronzova, bred to Laska O'Baron's Wood, sired her excellent stud Ch. Balvan O'Baron's Wood.

A contemporary of Baron's Wood was the Mogedo Kennels owned by Mr. and Mrs. George Mendel of Steubenville, Ohio. The Mogedo

The famous "Brown Boy," Ch. Korichnevi Malchik of Mogedo, owned and bred by Mr. and Mrs. George Mendel.

Ch. Lady of Romanoff, bred by Louis Murr and owned by Beverley Traglio, was a hound group winner and the dam of several champions.

bloodlines were based on Valley Farm, English and Canadian Agatestone lines. One of the most distinquished Borzoi owned by the Mendels was "Brown Boy" registered as Ch. Korichnevi Malchik of Mogedo (by Ch. Dagmar-Markada of Mogedo ex Sniegurka) bred by S, Kapitanoff. His sire (by Harosi-Malchik ex Laurelzamar) was bred by the Mendels. When Brown Boy was bred to Pletska of Bransgore, he sired their beautiful Ch. King of Mogedo.

Mrs. Rosanelle Peabody of Maplewood, New Jersey bred Borzoi for a short time during the late 1930's. The one most often remembered is Ch. Count Leban (by Ch. Vigow of Romanoff ex Randa Rosyka) purchased by Louis Murr in 1939 and later by Annie Adams.

Mrs. Annie Adams of Lincoln Park, New Jersey opened a Borzoi kennel in 1938 with one bitch, expanded rapidly until at one time she had 46 brood matrons. In 1946 she won the Borzoi Club of America Breeder of the Year trophy donated by Mr. R.A.E. Herbhold for having bred the greatest number of Borzoi during that year. (How times and emphasis have changed since then!) Her stock was mainly Valley Farm and Romanoff. Many champions have borne the Adams' name among the better known being the foundation stock of Alpine Ch. Marvola Adams and Ch. Uda Adams. The kennel was disbanded in 1951.

3

Recent History of
The Borzoi in America

THE HISTORY of the Borzoi in America from the first important imports at the turn of the century to about the time of World War II in the 1940's was covered in the previous chapter. Because breeding and traveling was severely curtailed by war-imposed restrictions on travel, food and other necessities for activating sound and progressive breeding programs, that particular decade forms a natural dividing line between the past and the present as far as the history of Borzoi in the United States is concerned. Some kennels successfully survived the war years continuing their influence on the Borzoi world over a long period of time. Because their influence extends to the present time, they are included in this chapter on recent history. Twenty or thirty years from now some of the kennels included herewith might be excluded while others will be added as their successful operations come to the fore. Time is the only master of perpective.

William and Marion Woodcock first owned Whippets in the early 1920's in their California Suntan Kennels. Marion and Marietta Gregory worked together training and conditioning dogs. They both put great emphasis on conditioning prior to coursing or racing by steady, controlled walking for miles each day. Marion fell in love with Borzoi by association with those owned by Miss Gregory and soon added them to her kennel.

Astor von Nordseestrand was imported about 1925 by Harold F. Wilson. Bred to Lebideska Milka in 1930 by Mr. Wilson, Astor sired the Woodcocks' first Borzoi Maska Marcoff of Suntan. When Maska Mar-

Ch. Taras Bulba of Suntan owned and handled here by James Forry and Ch. Malinki Kukla of Suntan owned and handled here by Marion Woodcock with Judge Leo Meeker.

Ch. Bellona of Rydens, bred in England by Mrs. Stanley Young, was imported by Mrs. Ashton and eventually owned and finished by Marion Woodcock. *Ludwig*

Ch. Suntan's Mythe Maxim of Alpine, bred by Bobbye Potter and owned by Bill and Marion Woodcock, is shown here with Marion and Judge Donia Cline.

Ch. Oakshade's Dona Ysabel with Betty Forry and multi-specialty winner Ch. Oakshade's Don Paco of Marbob with June Forry and Judge Betsy Prior. *Ludwig*

coff was bred to Vanja of Agatestone, imported by Miss Gregory, a litter was produced which included Petrusky, Kiprensky, Katusha, Alisha—all of Suntan and all champions. Kiprensky and Katusha were often shown as a brace. In 1941 at the Golden Gate show they captured both the winners dog and winners bitch spots and then went on to best hound brace in show. They were shown together not only at dog shows but also appeared together in many movies.

After World War II, Afghan Hounds became quite popular and the Woodcocks added this breed to their expanding sighthound kennel. They showed and finished several Afghans in the 1940's and 1950's.

Also at about that time three new Borzoi were purchased and finished: Ch. Haljean's Illyann of Suntan (by Ch. Haljean's Nazan ex Amber of Kerch) and the litter brothers from the Alpine Kennels Ch. Mythe Mazeppa of Alpine and Ch. Mythe Maxim of Alpine (by Ch. Ataman of Alpine ex Markina of Mantavani). Marion Woodcock had always loved the beautiful white and lemon English bitch Ch. Bellona of Rydens (by Rimski of Rydens ex Olga of Lenoken), so when she was offered for sale Bill bought her as a gift for his wife. Bellona was bred to Mazeppa and produced an excellent litter in 1954. Ch. Hasi Murat of Suntan, Ch. Malinki Kukla of Suntan and Ch. Mariska of Suntan were kept at the Suntan Kennels. Ch. Taras Bulba of Suntan was sold to the Forry's Oakshade Kennels. Mazeppa was bred to Suntan's Maryanya of Alpine owned by Burton and Maria Norbury and produced Ch. Bur-Mar's Larina of Suntan.

Due to ill health Bill and Marion moved to Pearblossom at the edge of the Mojave desert. After Bill died, Marion could not physically handle the kennel of large dogs so she concentrated on her whippets during the 1960's. In 1968 Marion had a series of strokes and spent the remaining three years of her life in nursing homes.

In 1953 James and Elizabeth Forry purchased a puppy later to become Ch. Zonazo Perchinoff C.D. owned and trained by their Oakshade Kennels in California's Topanga Canyon. This kennel already housed older full brother Karloff Perchinoff C.D. (by Ch. Rubles Perchino ex Ch. Lady of Bolshoi). Zonazo was best of breed at the Borzoi Club of California specialty in 1957. His son out of Marbob's Toniscott of Malora (by Barinoff Ambassador ex Lucky Lady of Barnaigh) Ch. Oakshade's Don Paco of Marbob was best of breed at the same specialty in 1962 and 1964. Also in that same litter were Ch. Oakshade's Dona Blanca, Oakshade's Don Diego and Ch. Oakshade's Dona Ysabel. In 1954 the Forrys obtained Ch. Taras Bulba of Suntan mentioned earlier.

While living in California, the Oakshade hounds were most active in public appearances at fashion shows, movies and such. The fact that the

Ch. Oakshade's Don Diego with June Forry and Judge Marion Woodcock. *Ludwig*

Ch. Boris Worthing, bred by Eileen Worthing, was the winner of eight hound groups and two bests in show.

Shere Khan of Malora, owned and bred by Eileen Worthing, represents the Canadian lines imported by Malora.

53

Forrys' daughter June was so active in training and showing the hounds in breed, obedience and junior showmanship also led to much interest and acclaim.

In the early 1960's as Jim retired, Oakshade moved to Oregon. Breeding and exhibiting were given up for a while as the new house and kennel demanded most of the time available. However, daughter June also moved to Oregon with her husband Marvin Clark and their two sons in the 1970's. With their help Oakshade resumed breeding and showing with litters sired by Ch. Inca Jo Ao of Vala Rama and Ch. Comanche of Phantom Lake.

Mrs. Eileen Worthing probably did more Borzoi breeding in her Malora Kennels (first located in St. Paul, then Phoenix and finally in California) than any other American breeder during the first fifteen years after World War II. However, the history of Malora goes back many years prior to that.

Eileen started with Lovely Lady Ozette (by Clown ex Princess Anna) producing the first Malora litter in 1934. A few years later she imported Rubinoff Babe (by Ch. Rubinoff Boy ex Ch. Betty of Hortoff), an auburn colored bitch with white trim bred in 1934 by Florence Kibbin in Canada. This Borzoi soon became a champion with many best of breed wins proclaiming her excellence in the show ring and famous offspring to prove her worth as a brood matron. When bred to Ch. Adams Bolshoi she produced Ch. Kosloff Vigow Kanduit, a two time best in show winner, and his litter brother Ch. Boris Worthing whelped in 1941. Another bitch that produced well for Malora in the early days was Princess Volga sired by Silveroff of Canadian Romanoff lines out of Duchessy sired by the imported Dutch Borzoi Bessberk's Ejoff in turn sired by the French Ch. Volga du Nord.

After the war in 1949, Eileen imported Barinoff Ambassador (by Mazeppa Brazhnikoff ex Zula of Whitelilies), a white dog with black markings and tan points bred by J. Barratt in England. He was not exhibited in this country because of a defect left by distemper but proved to be a most valuable stud. In 1950 Eileen imported the litter sisters Lucky Lady of Barnaigh and Lovely Lady of Barnaigh (by Menthe's Yerres von Bergland ex Domino of Barnaigh) bred by Mrs. McNeil in Scotland. When Ambassador was bred to Lucky Lady for three litters, they produced many champions including Splendour of Malora, Zelda Shaun of Malora C.D., Jaguar Jehan of Malora and Firebird of Malora.

Other imports of note owned by Malora were from France, England and Scotland. The black masked white and red bitch Weschika (by Esky v Marcolid ex Tolka de L'Ar-Vro-Goz) bred by Madame Jouan in France was imported by Dr. Bralove and sold to Mrs. Worthing in 1954. Another of Madame Jouan's breeding was Ch. Warona de L'Ar-Vro-Goz (by Fr. Ch. Esky von Marcolid ex Sleza de Kezan) imported also by Dr. Bralove, sold to Jeannette Whisler and then resold to Mrs. Worthing in 1955. Also in 1955, Malora imported the white and orange bitch Dionne des Mariettes (by Fr. Ch. Asmodey de Morton Hall ex Yrina de Morton Hall) and her litter brother Dikar des Mariettes bred in France by Mme. Raulin. Late in the same year Winjones Paskoss (by Ch. Winjones Ermolai ex Winjones Dunyashka) bred by Winifred Chadwick in England was imported. The following year more Borzoi crossed the Atlantic to take up residence at Malora: Mara of Barinoff (by Mazeppa Brazhnikoff ex Fencewood Griselda) bred by A.G. Warnes in England, Black Watch of Barnaigh (by Ch. Reyas Romancer ex Red Cloud of Barnaigh) bred by Mrs. McNeil of Scotland and Bright of Barnaigh (by Ch. Reyas Romancer ex Olga of Barnaigh) also from Mrs. McNeil. All of these imports appear frequently in pedigrees of most leading kennels of today.

Eileen Worthing and James Barr of Sunbarr worked closely on many breedings often exchanging stud services and dogs so that many of the same Borzoi appear in pedigrees of stock produced by both kennels. When Eileen moved to California, she took with her several Sunbarr bitches that were subsequently leased out on breeding terms with all puppies produced carrying the Malora name. At the present time no breeding or exhibiting is being done at Malora, but the influence of Malora is still extensive with Malora-bred dogs figuring prominently in the pedigrees of the majority of the top Borzoi of today.

The Borzoi kennel with the longest history of active breeding and exhibiting still in existence today is the Trezor Kennels of Russell and Cleoh Everhart in Ann Arbor, Michigan. Their first two Borzoi were whelped in 1929 out of Montana hunting stock: Prince Volga and Lady Diana (by Borese of Envilla ex Sourja of Envilla). While these two carried magnificent coats, they had little else to offer in a breeding program that the Everharts were determined to start. Unlike others who might have tried to upgrade from pet stock, Russ and Cleoh decided to secure quality stock to start their Arborzoi Kennels, the name originally used.

At the Detroit show in 1930 they met Mrs. H.A. Dengler who had her Ch. Krassai of Kameneff entered that day for exhibition only. Mrs. Dengler was so impressed with the Everharts' sincere desire to obtain good breeding stock that she leased Krassai's dam and a litter sister to them and then assisted them in securing the services of Valley Farm studs that were owned by Mrs. F. Stuart Foote as well as studs from the Woronzova and Ladoga kennels. Mrs. Foote was the breeder of Ch. Nega of Woronzova, a lovely bitch the Everharts felt was their ideal Borzoi.

One of the first of their home-bred greats was the red-sable and white

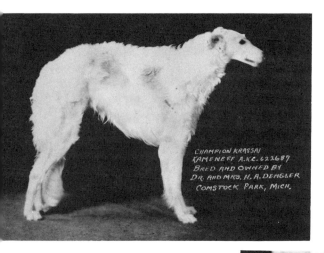

Ch. Krassai Kameneff, bred and owned by Dr. and Mrs. H.A. Dengler in Michigan.

Arborzoi Zvezda, bred by Russ and Cleoh Everhart, was owned by Mary Taviner in Nebraska.

Ch. Trezor Boris, bred and owned by Russ and Cleoh Everhart, is shown winning best of breed under Judge Louis Murr. *Norton of Kent*

Ch. Trezor (by Yarki of Ladoga ex Serna Kameneff), a spectacular winner in the 1930's. Later when the breed name was changed from Russian Wolfhound to Borzoi, the AKC would no longer allow the Everharts to use the kennel affix of Arborzoi as part of the registered name of their Borzoi. It was at this time that the kennel name was changed to Trezor in honor of their first big winner Ch. Trezor.

During the first years Russ and Cleoh proudly exhibited their Borzoi, their dogs were entered at the same shows as the Glenwild Borzoi of Mrs. Cluxton. Often, as in 1941 at Detroit, the Glenwild and Trezor entries were benched together with no bench separations displaying a long line of up to a dozen Borzoi, all beautiful, all peaceful. Mrs. Cluxton once wrote, "The Arborzoi dogs have the finest expression and disposition of any Borzoi in America."

After World War II, the Everharts found it almost impossible to procure stock of unmixed Valley Farm bloodlines so they became hosts to a few good English imports which became the basis for further breeding.

In 1944 a Ch. Trezor daughter (ex Rega of Wieckert Farm) Arborzoi Zvezda was sold to Mary Taviner's Ramadan Kennels in Nebraska. In the early 1950's after they had attained their American championships, Ch. Winjones Janda and Ch. Winjones Balvoniza were sent by Mrs. Taviner to live with the Everharts. Janda was bred to Ramadan Koraleva Chevry (by Gay Cavalier of Yadasar ex Ivanda of Yadasar) to produce the black and white brothers Ch. Trezor Boris and Ch. Trezor Briansk. Littermates of Koraleva Chevry, Ramadan Righ and Ramadan Nur Jehan were also sent to the Everharts. In 1954 littermates Ch. Firebird of Malora and Ch. Jaguar Jehan of Malora (by Barinoff Ambassador ex Lucky Lady of Barnaigh) were purchased from Mrs. Worthing's Malora Kennels. Both Firebird and Jaguar produced very well for Trezor. Jaguar was used also quite successfully by other kennels as well. Firebird was bred to Ramadan Righ to produce Ch. Trezor Alupka who was sold to Dr. Charles Conally. For Alupka's second litter, she was leased back by the Everharts and bred to Ch. Ramadi of Sunbarr Ranch (by Ch. Tobolzkoi Krasnoje Selo ex Solo of Barnaigh) to produce their fabulous "I" litter in 1962 which included Ch. Trezor Ivan, Ch. Trezor Ramadi of Vala Rama, Ch. Trezor Ivanda and Ch. Trezor Iskra. Ivan was a top producer and it will be so noted in the profiles of many of the kennels to follow in this chapter. In a breeding very similar to that which produced Alupka, Jaguar was bred to Ramadan Koraleva Chevry to produce Ch. Trezor Dzhalinda.

In 1966 at the Midwest specialty at Detroit three unique "trophies" were offered by the Midwest Borzoi Club through the generosity of James Barr. While the premium list stated only "special certificates," those certificates turned out to be the registration certificates for three puppies

Ch. Jaguar Jehan of Malora, owned by Russ and Cleoh Everhart, was a great producing stud for Trezor and other kennels. *Norton of Kent*

Cleoh Everhart with Ch. Trezor Iskra and Russ Everhart with Ch. Trezor Ivan, two from the great Trezor "I" litter.

Ch. Trezor Alupka, bred by Trezor, was owned by Dr. Charles Conally pictured here. Alupka was leased back by the Everharts to produce the "I" litter.

Brown

59

given to the owners of the winners bitch, winners dog and best of breed Borzoi that day. Cleoh's Trezor Kervan (by Ch. Trezor Ivan ex Ch. Trezor Dzhalinda) was winners dog thereby making the Everharts the new owners of the Borzoi who became Ch. Trezor Valdai of Sunbarr (by Malora's Blaise of Sunbarr ex Dezdra of Sunbarr Ranch). Littermates of Kervan were Ch. Trezor Kara, Ch. Trezor Kolpitza owned by Dorothy Baranowsky, and Trezor Krosotka. Krasotka was bred to Valdai to produce Ch. Trezor Molodetz owned by Mrs. Baranowsky and the spectacular bitch brace Ch. Trezor Meta and Ch. Trezor Modjeska. After Mrs. Baranowsky's untimely death both Molodetz and Kolpitza went to William Cunningham who established his Borzoi breeding program based mainly on those two at his Dacun Kennels.

Ivan was bred to Trezor Eudoxia (by Ch. Jaguar Jehan of Malora ex Ramadan Koraleva Chevry) to produce Ch. Trezor Lubyanka C.D. owned by Janet Shelton and Ch. Trezor Lancer of Buk's owned by Chester and Irene Bukwaz. Lubyanka was used by the Everharts to sire a litter out of Meta which contained Ch. Trezor Tamara going to Timothy and Ginger Pruss as a foundation bitch for their Tremara Kennels and Ch. Trezor Trasanya C.D.X., T.D. owned by Ernestine and Janet Shelton. Trasanya has the great distinction of being the first Borzoi to earn a tracking degree. Also from that "T" litter Gail McRae Roberts bought Trezor Taneyev of Markova. Bred to Gail's Ch. Markova's Kazhaan of Volga she produced the lovely red and white, group placing Ch. Mirioschka of Markova.

During the late 1970's the breeding and exhibiting of Trezor hounds was left mostly up to others as Russ and Cleoh gradually cut down the size of their kennel. However, they are still active in their various club affiliations with all-breed clubs as well as specialty clubs.

Ch. Bolshoi of Romanoff (by Ch. Tyddo of Romanoff ex Adana of Romanoff) bred by Louis Murr was the "Commander-in-Chief" of all the dog forces at the Millvale Kennels of Mrs. Mabel Millichip in Parkville, Missouri until his death in 1953. Ch. Molotov of Millvale earned a best in show in 1946 to put Borzoi back in the limelight following World War II. Probably the best remembered stud at Millvale was Ch. Kuzjani of Millvale (by Ch. Bolshoi of Romanoff ex Orel of Romanoff) as he appears in the pedigrees of many of the important kennels of today. After her husband's death, Mabel closed the doors of Millvale. Later after remarrying and moving to Florida, Mabel Millichip Lehman is again appearing on the Borzoi scene but this time in the role of judge at many of the shows across the country.

Lewis Godfrey of Hastings, Michigan was active for about ten years in breeding Borzoi noted for their obedience and hunting abilities at his

Ch. Trezor Ramadi of Vala Rama and litter brother Trezor Keeper of the Flame VRF, bred by the Everharts in their "I" litter were owned by Dr. and Mrs. Charles Conally.

Am. and Can. Ch. Brandegor Kachevnik, sired by Ch. Vala Rama's Phoenix of Sunbarr, is owned by his breeders Peter and Heather Higson. He is shown here with Peter being awarded the winners ribbon at the BCGNY specialty by Judge Alfred Curnow from England. *Ashbey*

61

Whiskey Run Hill Kennels. Later were added English lines through the use of Sleeping Bear and Ramadan studs. Black Knight of Whiskey Run (by Ch. Winjones Janda ex Ninotchka of Whiskey Run Hill C.D.) went to the Everharts' kennel. When Mr. Godfrey retired from active breeding, the dogs he owned at that time were transferred to the Wisconsin Sunbarr Kennels of James Barr.

John L. Hensey of Hensey Hobby Farm in Washington, Illinois specialized in Animal Husbandry and Genetics at the University of Illinois, rather an advantage in breeding his Borzoi. He owned Ch. Adam's Bolshoi (by Ch. Vigow of Romanoff ex Czarina Anna Semenovna) a white and tan dog bought from Annie Adams in 1941. Bolshoi was the sire of numerous Borzoi champions and appears in many extended pedigrees. A few of his offspring were: Ch. Adam's Alexis (ex Orel of Romanoff), Ch. Boi (ex Honey Baby of Neva Jeskra) owned by Mrs. J.C. Lindsey, Ch. Boris Worthing (ex Rubinoff Babe) bred by Malora and owned by William Schmidt, Ch. Kosloff Vigow Kanduit (ex Rubinoff Babe) owned by LeRoy Burkette, Ch. Nicholas of Sleeping Bear (ex Zorina of Ashwell) bred and owned by Major and Mrs. Chester Clark, Ch. Rubinoff of Hensey Hobby Farm (ex Black Belle of Romanoff) owned by Mrs. Clark. Mr. Hensey also owned Nickola of Glenwild and Orlick (by Can. Ch. Krasna Peterhof ex Czarina of Ladoga).

Mr. and Mrs. Arnold J. Brock of Scarsdale, New York, once quite active in the national breed club, used the affix Happy Ridge. They owned the three champions previously mentioned: Ninotchka of Romanoff, Vigow OVF of Romanoff and Dostoievsky of Fleetstone. Ninotchka was bred in 1946 to Ch. Kosloff Vigow Kanduit to produce their home-bred champion Nadya of Happy Ridge.

In 1946 Mrs. Ethel Bromley purchased one of Ch. Tyddo of Romanoff's grandsons Czarowitz (by Lemurr Adams ex Irina Adams) from Annie Adams for her Yelmore Kennels in Hudson Falls, New York. In 1947 she acquired Ver-Sam's Patrusha (by Bolkov ex Krasny Volga), and in 1959 she sold Yelmorb Natasha of Sirhan (by Yelmorb Kolchak ex Ch. Walhof Fraun) to Audrey Benbow in Canada.

Dr. Charles R. Conally of Detroit, Michigan owned the Vala Rama Kennels, and his stock possessed the Mogedo, Arborzoi, Glenwild and Romanoff lines found principally in the pedigree of his excellent home-bred stud Ch. Jascha (by Miya Ten ex Nusia of Mogedo). Charles added English and Scotch lines when he acquired Trezor Alupka (by Ramadan Righ ex Firebird of Malora) from breeder Russell Everhart. Alupka was leased to the Everharts later after her first litter for Vala Rama to be bred to Ch. Ramadi of Sunbarr Ranch which produced a litter of great quality. Charles took two males from that litter, Ch. Trezor Ramadi of Vala Rama

The two Borzoi representing the Haljean's foundation: Peter the Great of Key's Farm (by Count Chris of Key's Farm ex Lady Wanda of Metropolis View) and Ballerina (by Ch. Vigow of Romanoff ex Czarina Anna Semenovna).

Ch. Winjones Janda, bred in England by Winifred Chadwick and imported by Mary Taviner, was kept and shown by Russ Everhart pictured here. "Hippo" was the first English Borzoi to take the breed at Westminster and the first English Borzoi to be awarded the best of breed annual award by the BCOA. *Frasie*

Ch. Vala Rama's Funny Girl is shown here with her breeder-owner Grace Conally. *Booth*

and Trezor Keeper of the Flame VRF. Flame died in an unfortunate kennel accident while still quite young. Many considered him even better than his brother Ramadi.

Shortly before the acquisition of these red and white brothers, Charles had married Grace Heller who had owned a few Borzoi prior to that time. Grace had always wanted a self-black Borzoi, and her search for one led her to purchase the puppy that became Ch. Vala Rama's Phoenix of Sunbarr in 1966 (by Wilolea Casanova ex Moja of Sunbarr Ranch). As he grew older, Phoenix developed brindle trim as well as the white trim. Phoenix was one of Grace's favorites and she bred him to a number of fine bitches. One outstanding Phoenix son is Am. and Can. Ch. Brandegor Kachevnik (ex Xanadu's Lara) bred and owned by Peter and Heather Higson of Ottawa, Ontario. Kachevnik was one of those dogs that never bothered with small wins, only big ones such as majors at specialties.

Vala Rama's Lure of the Fflame (by Ch. Nightsong Thor of Sunbarr ex Ch. Nightsong Alix of Sunbarr) was obtained from Joyce and Henry Brandin's Nightsong Kennels. This bitch was leased by Anna Ungerleider and bred to her English import Int. Ch. Zomahli Evolgo (by Zomahli Dyasha ex Ch. Zavist of Carradale). The Conallys obtained Ch. Vala Rama's Janda of Windy Hill and Ch. Vala Rama's Jewel of Windy Hill from that litter. From Sunbarr again, came Ch. Vala Rama's Pandora of Sunbarr (by Beau Geste of Sunbarr ex Sophia of Sunbarr Ranch) who was bred to Ramadi to produce Ch. Vala Rama's Funny Girl, the specialty winning Ch. Vala Rama's Man for All Seasons and Ch. Phaedra of Vala Rama sold to Phyllis Brettell. Pandora was bred to Phoenix to produce Ch. Soyara's Foxy Lady of Vala Rama sold to Prudence and Gregory Key and Ch. Inca Jo Ao of Vala Rama sold to Phyllis Brettell.

After the death of Dr. Conally in 1972, the breeding activities at Vala Rama were carried on for a while by Grace and then gradually curtailed.

Mrs. Jeannette Whisler's Haljeans Kennels in Manassas, Virginia housed the Mogedo dogs when that kennel was dispersed including the famous "Brown Boy" Ch. Korichnevi Malchik of Mogedo. Jeannette owned the English import Amber of Kerch (by Ivan of Lenoken ex Doborah of Tangmere) bred in 1943 by the Chichesters but brought to Canada by Pat Tripp. While in Canada, Amber was bred to Dagmar of Mogedo to produce Tra-Varish of Pat-Mer the sire of Ch. Pat-Mer's Czar of Wyndhaven owned by Mrs. Clyde Ritchie and Can. Ch. Rasputin owned by Mrs. Bobbye Potter. Jeannette Whisler bred Amber to Haljean's Nazan and two of the ensuing litter were sold to other breeders: Ch. Haljean's Ilyann of Suntan went to Marion Woodcock and Haljean's Mazurka went to Eileen Worthing.

Another import at Haljeans was Ch. Warona de L'Ar-Vro-Goz (by

Eng. and Am. Ch. Winjones Balvoniza, bred in England by Winifred Chadwick and imported by Mary Taviner, is shown here with her handler Wilda Woehr winning one of many hound groups. *Frasie*

Like his owner Jeanne Sundt, Ch. Midtfyn's Boja had an active career as a model. He appeared on the cover of *Collier's* with Kathleen Norris. *Willinger*

Ch. Esky von Marcolid ex Sleza de Kazan) bred by Madame Jouan and brought to the States from France by Dr. Bralove. Toni, as she was called, had eleven of her championship points including three majors by the time she was a year old placing in the group at ten months. She produced an outstanding litter in 1954 when bred to Barinoff Ambassador.

Jeannette added German bloodlines to her American, French and English stock by breeding two of her bitches to Ch. Amurat v Merdody owned by Clarence DeCraene. She seldom exhibited her own dogs but many were purchased and shown by others. Several went to various other kennels to be used as breeding stock: Kostenov, Sunbarr, Suntan, Malora, DeCreane, Bachelor Forest, Petrikov to name a few.

As noted above Dr. Richard Bralove imported a few Borzoi bitches from France which were then sold to the Haljeans and Malora kennels. After several years away from the Borzoi world, Drs. Richard and Olga Bralove returned to the fancy in the 1960's first finishing Ch. Wilolea's Prince Igor (by Trezor Krassai ex Chelan of Rancho Gabriel). They imported the self-red Quelle Belle des Mariettes from France and Springett Sheer Vanity from England. Belle bred to Igor produced Ch. Bralova's Gaucho Lindo. Vanity bred to Ch. Adage Duncan C.D. produced Ch. Bralova's Chara of Wilolea. After finishing Chara and specialing her for a while, the Braloves once again closed the doors of Bralova in 1975.

The Ramadan affix was used by Mary M. Traviner of Omaha, Nebraska starting in the years just after World War II. In 1944 she purchased Arborzoi Zvezda (by Ch. Trezor ex Rega of Wieckert Farm). In 1950 she imported two Borzoi from the Winjones Kennels in England. The first was the English champion and later American Ch. Winjones Balvoniza known as Julie (by Balalaika of Rydens ex Winjones Bistri). At the time she left England Julie held the post-war record for challenge certificates for bitches. She continued her winning ways in the States by winning hound groups under the hand of Wilda Woehr. The other import was the self-black male Winjones Janda (by Mazeppa Brazhnikoff ex Astrakan of Barnaigh) with an American championship and some hound group wins to his credit as he matured. After he finished, Janda (affectionately known as Hippo) and Julie were permanent guests at the Everharts' kennel in Michigan where Hippo was shown occasionally by Russell Everhart. From a litter out of Ramadan Koraleva Chevry, Hippo was the sire of the black and white brothers Ch. Trezor Briansk and Ch. Trezor Boris. In 1955 Mary imported Ivanda of Yadasar in whelp to Gay Cavalier of Yadasar. The litter was uniform and excellent in type. A male Ramadan Righ and a bitch Ramadan Nur Jehan went to Russell Everhart. Two males Ramadan Kanetz Raduga and Ramadan Cynge went to Carla Alioshin of Yermak Kennels in California. A son of Ramadan Cynge and

66

Ch. Ataman of Alpine, bred and owned by Bobbye Potter, figures prominently in the pedigrees of many fine Borzoi.

Ch. Saturn Petrovitch of Alpine, bred and owned by Bobbye Potter, was donated to the 27th Wolfhound Regiment after which he was known as Kolchak III.

67

Ch. Zelda Shaun of Malora was the sire of Ivanda's next litter. His name was Ch. Millrock's Bronze of Malora C.D. Also in this litter was Ramadan Rio Rita U.D. owned and trained by Ed and Joanne Weaver in California.

As can be seen by this partial listing, Ramadan Kennels had a policy of using English stock exclusively after the first Borzoi Zvezda. Mary carried on an extensive correspondence with Borzoi breeders in all countries of Europe and had a vast knowledge of foreign Borzoi lines. In the mid-1950's she edited the bulletin of the Midwest Borzoi Club but in 1956 started the publication of an international magazine devoted to Borzoi "Riders of the Wind" which continued until 1963 when ill health forced Mary to discontinue.

Jeanne and Harald Sundt, Jr. of San Marino, California, owners of the Sundra affix, spent a year touring Europe and visiting Harald's former home in Oslo, Norway immediately after World War II. While staying at an old inn in Ireland, they saw a Borzoi which so impressed them they started a search for one of their own. Some months later Jeanne saw one at a dog show in Denmark and knew she had to have him for her own. After much negotiating with the breeder, Mrs. Marie Barlebo, they were able to purchase Midtfyn's Boja (by Finis Pjotr ex Hollywood's Lola). They also bought a bitch Gandil (by Helmarhoja Wladimir ex Finis Katja) bred by Mr. P.J. Peterson. They returned to the States with both dogs in 1947 where both Borzoi earned their American championships and Boja won a hound group.

Boja's most outstanding son was Ch. Ataman of Alpine. Ataman, as one of Mrs. Potter's extensively used studs, carried Boja's name into a great many pedigrees of California-bred Borzoi.

Boja and Gandil brought the breed to the attention of the general public on many an occasion as they appeared in many fashion shows, magazines and movies. Boja was pictured in color with Ilona Massey in the *American Magazine* and he was on the cover of *Colliers* in 1950. Boja was in two Bob Hope movies: *The Great Lover* starring Bob Hope and Rhonda Fleming and *Fancy Pants* with Bob Hope and Lucille Ball.

Mrs. G. Clifton Potter had her Alpine Kennels at Stockton, California. In 1927 she attended a dog show and saw a red Borzoi bitch that she thought to be the most beautiful dog in the world. She bought her and showed her several times before breeding her. This was Lady Balteach (by Kalman of Balteach ex Countess Avella II) bred by the Cowell brothers. She was bred to Ch. Sovereign of Rual (by Tersia of Corwindell ex Duchess of Ribstone). The resulting litter had twelve puppies and Bobbye Potter learned early the joys and worries of raising and selling such a large number of puppies. For the next several years Bobbye's time and energies turned to marriage and the establishment of a new home. In the 1940's she bought two young bitches from Annie Adams both of which were to finish their championships: Ch. Marvola Adams (by Ch. Kuzjani of Millvale ex Ver-Sam's Patrusha) and Ch. Uda Adams (by Lumurr Adams ex Irena Adams). Although Uda Adams was a great producer being the dame of twelve champions, many considered Marvola a Borzoi of better type. Marvola was bred to Ch. Midtfyn's Boja. In her first litter was Ch. Ataman of Alpine, Ardagan of Alpine C.D. and Ch. Holka of Alpine. Ataman was the sire of twelve champions and Ardagan was the first Borzoi on the West Coast to earn an obedience degree. Ardagan was such an enthusiastic, willing worker that he was known to one and all as Happy Harry. In 1951 the English import Markina of Mantavani produced an Alpine litter sired by Ataman. In that litter were Ch. Mythe Maxim of Alpine and Ch. Mythe Mazeppa of Alpine, both going to the Suntan Kennels of the Woodcocks, and Ch. Mythe Marova of Alpine kept by Bobbye.

Ataman was bred to Krassina of Hensey Hobby Farm to produce Ch. Gotchina of Grador and Ch. Gradina of Grador for Dorothy Sweet. He was bred to his daughter Nebeca Petrova of Alpine to produce Ch. Corps de Ballet Fouette for Randi L'Ete. His litter out of Donna Marie of Malora gave breeder Dixie Bilodeau Ch. Zina Petrovna O'River Ranch. Ataman was bred to Uda Adams to produce Ch. Saturn Petrovitch of Alpine who was donated to the Wolfhound Regiment based in Hawaii and was thereafter known as Kolchak III.

A brief history of the Wolfhound Regiment is in order at this point. The 27th U.S. Infantry Regiment, known as the Wolfhound Regiment, has been stationed in Hawaii. The regiment earned its Wolfhound name when it was sent to Siberia in August of 1918 as part of the Allied Expeditionary Forces used in the pursuit of hostile forces. In almost two years of action in that cold, bleak land they fought several major battles and many minor skirmishes often substituting brilliant military tactics for lack of sufficient fire-power. The basic purpose of their action was to assist the White Russian armies in protecting the Trans-Siberian Railroad from the Bolsheviks. The outcome was glory and commendations for the 27th, but the finest tribute came from their adversaries, the Bolsheviks, who compared their advances to the fleetness and tenacity of the Borzoi's wolf-coursing exploits and called the regiment "The Wolfhounds," a name they bear proudly to this day. In October, 1952 the Department of the Army officially recognized this name and authorized its use as a parenthetical designation to follow the numerical one, and it is so used on all orders, records, letters and other official papers.

The head of the Borzoi does not conform to the rules of heraldry so their insignia is a wolf's head set in a rectangular sable field bordered in

Ch. Zonazo Perchinoff C.D., bred by Charles and Helen Colstad, was owned by June Forry. He is pictured here with Judge Leo Murphy winning best of breed at the BCOC 1957 specialty.

Loral's Chaan Kazah, bred by Lorraine Groshans, was renamed Kolchak V when he became the mascot of the Wolfhound Regiment. He is shown here in Hawaii with his handler Sgt. Harold Moore and Major General Fred C. Weyand, commanding general 25th Infantry Division.

Ch. Rubles Perchino and puppy Prince Miboi O'Kolstad owned by Charles and Helen Colstad.

The Llebasi team of black and white Borzoi shown winning Best Team in Show, handled by June Forry under Judge Halpern at the 1958 BCOC Specialty.

gold. Underneath is their motto *Nec Aspera Terrent* liberally translated to mean "Undaunted."

The Borzoi mascots of the 27th have all been named after Aleksandr Kolchak, the able Russian Admiral who led the White Russians during the regiment's tour of Siberian duty. The first one, Kolchak I, was given to the 27th in September of 1929. Kolchak II arrived in April, 1940. Shirley Temple was made an honorary colonel of the 27th when she was a little girl and posed frequently for photographs with Kolchak II. Kolchak III was donated by Bobbye Potter in March of 1956. Two years later Lorraine and Bernard D'Essen of Animal Talent Scouts in New York sent Kolchak IV. In July of 1962 Al and Lorraine Groshans sent Loral's Chaan Kahzar (by Ch. Mikhail of Woodhill ex Loral's Alpha Yurochka) to become Kolchak V. All donors were made Honorary Wolfhounds by the regiment.

Charles and Helen Colstad of Portuguese Bend, California owned the Perchino Kennels, a name deriving from the origins of their first Borzoi Ch. Rubles Perchino (by Rinaldi Perchino ex Omega Perchino), one of the last of the Perchina line as bred by Lois Kellogg. Rube was purchased in 1945 and the following year the Colstads added Ch. Lady of Bolshoi (by Ch. Bolshoi of Romanoff ex Adam's Zanoza Millichip), a lovely white and cream bitch bred by Mildred Millichip. These two were bred in 1950 to produce Ch. Walzoff Perchinoff, owned by Mrs. Martha Taylor, a consistent winner at an early age as well as a veteran winning a specialty best of breed under Alva Rosenberg at the age of nine years. Martha also owned Ch. Zcerlov's Zanoza O'Perchinoff from the repeat breeding in 1953.

Two other noteworthy Borzoi from the Perchinoff second litter were Ch. Zonazo Perchinoff C.D., the first West Coast champion to also earn an obedience degree owned and handled by June Forry and Ch. Zinaldi Perchinoff owned by Mrs. Forrest Griffeth. Zinaldi earned his American title in three shows and his Canadian title in three shows with two hound groups for good measure.

In 1958 Helen and Martha were co-breeders of a litter out of Zcerlov's Zoltka sired by Ch. Walzoff Perchinoff. This litter produced Ch. Perchinoff Ciadona O'Zcerlov and Ch. Perchinoff Gorki O'Zcerlov both owned by Andre Legere, Ch. Perchinoff Rubles O'Zcerlov kept by Helen, and Ch. Campaigner's Alix owned by Toxey and Renee Smith. Alix was indeed a true campaigner as she racked up an impressive record as a special. Later she was bred to Ch. Bronze Falcon of Woodhill to produce Ch. Mojave's White Falcon and Ch. Mojave's Kia.

Breeding and showing at Perchinoff gradually tapered off during the late 1950's. Even the land on which the lovely Perchinoff home stood in those earlier years may disappear from view as in true California manner it is currently slip-sliding into the ocean.

72

Ch. Tamazar of Twin Elms, a major stud at the Twin Elms Kennels of Gordon and Sylvia Sohr in Wisconsin.

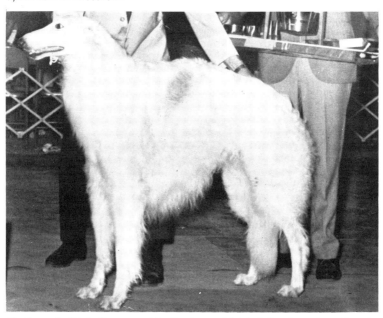

Ch. Gregori of Twin Elms owned by Gordon and Sylvia Sohr. Gregori was the winner of two specialties and a best in show before his tragic death enroute to a California specialty.

Gordon and Sylvia Sohr established their Twin Elms Kennels in Racine, Wisconsin and came into the spotlight right after World War II with their obedience work. In 1946 Gordon started lessons with the lovely golden bitch Bourtai of Malora (by Prince Sergei Ivanovitch ex Honey Babe of Neva Iskra). She earned her C.D. after only two months of training. Then it was time out to raise a family. Bourtai became the first U.D. Borzoi in 1950.

The Twin Elms history was interrupted on several occasions by tragic accidents that would have deterred less devoted breeders and fanciers. A bout with distemper nearly wiped out the kennel during its early years. After restocking the kennel and breeding several outstanding litters, many of the dogs were killed from inhalation of a poisonous spray carried to the kennel from the neighboring parkland which was being sprayed for insects. Undaunted, the Sohrs started again to build up the kennel. In 1969 their top winning Ch. Gregori of Twin Elms died during a flight to a California show. Having made him a central part of an extended breeding program, it was almost like starting over a third time after that, as all breeding plans had to be revamped. It has always been my opinion that it is only after facing tragedy and misfortune of one kind or another, coping with it, and going on successfully and courageously that a breeder can be truly called a breeder. Certainly Sylvia and Gordon qualify as true, devoted breeders of Borzoi.

In 1953 Twin Elms produced Ch. Black Falcon of Twin Elms from a breeding of their Nadja of Twin Elms C.D. to Boris Batyi of Wieckert Farms. Black Falcon was purchased by Nellie Hilsmier and went on to a fabulous show career under her Woodhill banner handled during his years in the ring by Wilda Woehr, then Ed Bracy and finally Dick Cooper. While Twin Elms did indeed produce a variety of colors, the majority of those kept by the kennel were white or nearly white which became their hallmark. When Nadja was bred to Zork of Twin Elms, she produced Ch. Zabu of Twin Elms C.D.

The Sohrs acquired Ch. Tzarina Borgia of Frontier from Andrew Cunningham. When she was bred to Ch. Tobolzkoi Krasnoje Selo she whelped the "T" litter that had so much influence on many pedigrees from coast to coast. Ch. Tamazar of Twin Elms was kept by the Sohrs as was the white bitch Ch. Taia of Twin Elms.

Ch. Talix of Twin Elms from the same litter was the main character of a cinderella story passing from one owner to another several times until finally discovered accidentally by Jayne Stepnoski who took him to her home in California after establishing his registered identity. At her Olympus Kennels he was bred to her foundation bitch Ch. Sonoma of Rancho Gabriel (by Ch. Solentse Ternovnek of Alpine C.D. ex Ch. Milka of Ran-

The Twin Elms twins Ch. Garush of Twin Elms and Ch. Gregorovitch of Twin Elms at eleven months. Greg died at a young age but Garush went on to some impressive group wins. *Heinz*

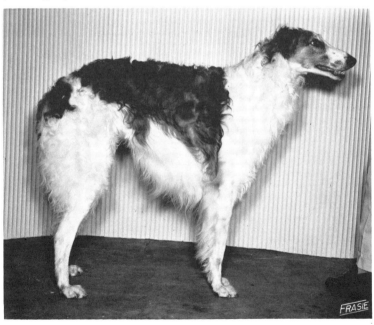

Ch. Dark Star of Sleeping Bear, bred by Major and Mrs. Chester Clark and owned by Mr. and Mrs. Henry Mackh. *Frasie*

cho Gabriel) producing among others Ch. Artemis of Olympus and Ch. Aphrodite of Olympus. The breeding program at the kennel then involved mainly close line-breeding and in-breeding. Talix was bred to both of these white bitches producing Ch. Pegasus of Olympus (ex Artemis) and Ch. Aphrodite's Eros of Olympus (ex Aphrodite). Aphrodite was owned by Diane and Delbert Weaver. Ch. She-Za-Ne of Rancho Gabriel was bred to Talix and Jayne bred the bitch from that litter, Ch. Shasta of Rancho Gabriel, back to Talix. Shasta's litter brother Ch. Rogue of Rancho Gabriel was kept by the breeder Phydelma Gillette. Jack Boyd, of Los Prados Kennels bred his Ch. Milka of Rancho Gabriel to Talix to produce his Ch. Galina of Los Prados. Ch. Juno of Olympus (by Talix ex Artemis) was bred to Ch. Rysiu's Igor of Heathcliff (by Kura Kamar of Malora ex Locksley Hall's Easter Star) to produce Ch. Apollo of Olympus and Boreas of Olympus who were sent East to Cecilia Dougherty. Shown as a brace, these two white brothers won five groups (including Westminster in 1971) and two best brace in show.

To get back to the Twin Elms history, Malora's Talisman of Twin Elms was bred to Ch. Zabu of Twin Elms C.D. to produce Ch. Czaru of Twin Elms. When Czaru was bred to Sunbarr's Yasna of Twin Elms (by Haljean's Tarquin of Malora ex Noelle of Malora) Ziada of Twin Elms was the result. Ziada was bred to Ch. Barin Borisky (by Count Boris Patri ex Artemis the Huntress DelVos) to produce the winning Ch. Gregori of Twin Elms whose record included two specialty wins and a best in show. After his death in 1969, in an effort to produce another Gregori, a Ch. Barin Borisky son, Ch. Borin Leo Tolstoy, was bred to a Borisky and Tamazar granddaughter Ch. Serebro Zvezdah of Twin Elms (by Ch. Duke Alexander of Twin Elms ex Ch. Ballerina of Twin Elms) to produce the white brace Ch. Garush of Twin Elms and Ch. Gregorovich of Twin Elms. After successfully campaigning Garush for several years, the breeding and exhibiting by Twin Elms gradually diminished during the 1970's.

Mr. and Mrs. Henry Mackh owned Borzoi on their Friendship Acres estate in Wayne, Illinois during the early 1950's. Mr. Mackh had owned Borzoi since childhood but did not exhibit them until he and his wife acquired Katherine and Czarina of Ladoga (by Boi ex Pola of Ladoga), litter sisters bred by Grace King. These two bitches became the first Friendship Acres champions. The Mackhs added English bloodlines to their kennel by means of Sleeping Bear stock. One of those additions was Ch. Dark Star of Sleeping Bear (by Abernant ex Ch. Natascha of Sleeping Bear) bred by the Clarks. When they retired to Tryon, North Carolina they gave up all their Borzoi. However, as could be expected, they again bought another as a companion in the late 1960's—Trezor Tigran (by Ch. Trezor Lubyanka C.D. ex Ch. Trezor Meta).

Ch. Rachmaninoff, owned by Weldon and Kay McCluskey, is shown winning best of breed at the 1957 BCOA Specialty under Judge Arnold Brock. *Shafer*

Ch. Nicholas of Sleeping Bear, owned by Major and Mrs. Chester J. Clark, is shown with his owner winning a best in show in Canada. *Kilbreath*

The Woronsova Kennels furnished the basic stock for Mrs. Walter Wieckert's Wieckert Farm Kennels in Appleton, Wisconsin with Nayada Woronzova and Ch. Boris Batyi of Wieckert Farm appearing often in pedigrees of Borzoi bred there. Nayada was bred by Marie Roach while Boris was a home-bred whose sire Batyi was purchased from Dr. Richard Bralove.

Dorothy Harris had the Grador Kennels in California. As mentioned previously, she bred Krassina of Hensey Hobby Farm (by Ch. Krasna Peterhoff ex Nichola of Glenwild) to Ch. Ataman of Alpine to produce a litter containing Ch.Gotchina of Grador which she kept, Ch. Gradina of Grador which she bred once and then sold and Saiga of Grador sold to Andrew Cunningham's Frontier Kennels in Buffalo. Saiga was bred at Frontier to Miss Mythe of Sleeping Bear (by Ch. Nicholas of Sleeping Bear ex Ch. Musidora) to produce Arlekeen of Frontier, the foundation bitch of Loral Kennels. When bred to Barishyna of Frontier, Saiga produced Ristovia's Brizhi of Frontier, an important brood bitch at the Ristovia Kennels. Bred to Savona of Frontier, he sired Ch. Tzarina Borgia of Frontier, an important bitch in the history of Twin Elms as we have seen.

Dorothy was taken by a picture in Nellie Martin's book *The Russian Wolfhound* of a black and white Borzoi closely resembling her Gotchina. She also owned Ch. Golupka (by Ch. Saturn Petrovitch of Alpine ex Ch. Uda Adams), a happy white bitch. Mrs. Harris bred Golupka to Gotchina in hopes of getting puppies resembling Gotchina but she was disappointed as not one puppy in the litter had black markings. Isabell Walton obtained Golupka on a co-ownership and repeated the breeding. In this second litter eleven of the twelve puppies were black and whites!

In 1958 Dorothy married Arthur Sweet. In that manner Ch. Marbob's Don Kazan of Malora (by Barinoff Ambassador ex Lucky Lady of Barnaigh) went to live at Grador although Dorothy never used him at stud. Shortly after her marriage, interest in Borzoi gave way to interest in Shetland Sheepdogs. After the death of Arthur in 1970 Dorothy continued to judge for a few years and then turned in her judging license so that she could become a show superintendent with Isabell Walton and others in California.

Isabell V. Walton started her Llebasi Kennels in El Monte, California in 1948 with a litter brother and sister Llebasi's Nicholette Murr and Llebasi's Rachmaninoff (by Lumurr Adams ex Tanny Adams) purchased from the Malora Kennels. The next addition was Volk O'Baron's Wood and some puppies sired by him out of Ch. Bellona of Rydens and a bitch Rona of Ashtonia from a previous litter of the same breeding. Two of the puppies that Isabell kept became Llebasi's Verra Zorenna and Ch. Llebasi's Rushan Vodka. Isabell moved to Arizona in 1952 where she lost

Catherine Dean with Baron and Lady Wolfschmidt who traveled widely as promoters of Wolfschmidt Vodka.

all her Borzoi, except Vodka, from the extreme heat, so she returned to California in 1955 to obtain two bitches, Gratina and Grasina of Grador (by Gotchina of Grador ex Ch. Golupka of Alpine), from Dorothy Harris. Grasina was a promising puppy but died at the age of ten months of a brain tumor.

Still undaunted by misfortune, Isabell purchased Melisande of Rancho Gabriel (by Mythe Ivanoff of Alpine ex Ch. Obvorozevat Laska of Alpine) bred by the Gillettes. In 1959 Ch. Melisande and her companion Llebasi's Anna Pavlova received as much, if not more, attention than the slot machines in Las Vegas when they appeared in two shows nightly with Mae West in the Congo Room of the Sahara Hotel.

When Isabell acquired co-ownership of Ch. Golupka of Alpine and bred her to Ch. Gotchina of Grador, she was back in the puppy business with a litter of eleven. As mentioned above, she and Dorothy were co-owners of the litter. She showed four of these puppies as a team at the 1958 Borzoi Club of California specialty where they went all the way to the top for best team in show handled by June Forry. They were Llebasi's Prelude, Sonata, Concerto and Nocturne. Of these Sonata finished her championship.

In the early 1960's Isabell moved to Houston, Texas where she was associated for a while with Joanne Jelke's Jobi Kennels. Isabell purchased Ch. Lisa of Rancho Gabriel (by Ch. Solentse Termovek of Alpine ex Aldo of Rancho Gabriel). Lisa was bred to Granaldee of Grador to produce Ch. Llebasi's Czarina O'The Oaks and Ch. Llebasi's Czar O'The Oaks and Ch. Jobi Rowena. The breeding of Gradonn of Grador to the bitch Llebasi's Shalimar produced Ch. Llebasi's Little Stinker and the Baeton's Ch. Springhurst Tanya of Llebasi.

In 1967 Isabell obtained Llebasi's Prince O'Lutolf (by Ch. Akin Saba of Wolfschmitzoff ex the French import Sasha Duchesse Narishkin) from breeder Joseph Lutolf. Prince was specialed for a few years placing often in groups and winning one best in show in Texas. Bred to Cossack's Aphrodesia he produced Ch. Kristull Image. Used by Nadine Johnson on two of her French bitches he produced Ch. Rising Star Ghost Dancer C.D., Ch. Blythe Spirit of Rising Star, Ch. Blue Diamond of Rising Star (ex Q'Ariana d'Ymonville); and Ch. Balzax of Rising Star (ex Int. Ch. Q'Blietzka des Balileika).

Major and Mrs. Chester J. Clark of Glen Arbor, Michigan started out with Romanoff and Valley Farm bloodlines in their Sleeping Bear Kennels adding some English lines with a number of imports in the 1950's. Ch. Nicholas of Sleeping Bear was a consistent show winner with a Canadian best in show to his credit. The Clarks imported a number of Borzoi from Mr. E.H. Guy in England, chief among them Ch. Fearless Lass and

Ch. Blue Train (by Challenge ex Godiva). They imported the three littermates Musidora, Abernant and Nimbus (by Ch. Blue Train ex Ladoga Varya). Musidora earned her American title in 1953. Abernant was bred to Ch. Natascha of Sleeping Bear, a litter sister to Nicholas, to produce Ch. Dark Star of Sleeping Bear.

The Baronoff Kennels of Weldon and Katherine McCluskey started on Long Island, moved to Wenonah, New Jersey and then on down to Sewell, New Jersey. One of their best known early Borzoi was Ch. Rachmaninoff (by Nayan of Romanoff ex Neuhoff's Roxanna of Millvale) in 1951. For a while Rocky was owned by George E. Mosley in New York City but soon returned to Baronoff. The McCluskeys also bred Baron and Lady Wolfschmidt (by Ch. Mazar Lustik of Pavlov Crest ex Neuhoff's Roxanna of Millvale) in 1954 whose chief claim to fame is that they travelled over 100,000 miles by air in less than one year earning their beef and kibble by advertising vodka.

Robert Beck bred his Ch. Major Zorka of Pavlov Crest to Rachmaninoff and in lieu of a stud fee, the McCluskeys took Sascha of Baronoff. After finishing her championship, Sascha was bred back to her sire to produce Ch. Bolshoi of Baronoff and Ch. Anna Pavlova of Baronoff and Tiranka of Baronoff. Tiranka was bred to Ch. Prometheus of Rancho Gabriel (by Ch. Hollister of Rancho Gabriel ex Ch. Garsova Ivanova of Alpine C.D.) when he was in the East for a few years with his owner Bill Thompson. Tiranka produced the huge self-gold Gogol of Baronoff who was bred to his granddam Sascha to produce Ch. Kislov of Baronoff and look-alike son Ch. Kalmyk of Baronoff and Nicole of Baronoff. Tiranka also produced Ch. Aleksandra of Baronoff who became the foundation bitch of the Pheasant Hill Kennel of Polly Clement. The McCluskys bred their Anna Pavlova to Prometheus and had even better luck as she produced Ch. Prince Rurick of Baronoff sold to Mary Horton, Ch. Prince Igor of Baronoff, Ch. Tartar's Diana of Baronoff and Ch. Tartar's Adonis of Baronoff, the latter two taken to California by Bill Thompson with Diana later going to Jack Boyd. Nicole also went to California where she was bred to Ch. Vastri of Rancho Gabriel, a Prometheus son. Falconhurst Vaz of Baronoff from that litter was sent back to Baronoff. Cordova Borcia of Baronoff (by Kalmyk ex Leafwood's Cara of Cordova) bred to Vaz produced Ch. Tonia of Baronoff C.D.X., the BCOA obedience award winner in 1975 owned by Kathryn Kirby in New Hampshire.

Sascha was bred to Ch. Mikhail of Woodhill. As a stud puppy from that litter Louise Heaton chose a red and white bitch who later became the outstanding Ch. Cordova Mishka of Baronoff. In addition, Louise bought the black and white litter brother Ch. Cordova Batyi of Baronoff, winner of a BCOA specialty a few years later. Several years later the Mc-Cluskeys bought two of Mishka's puppies sired by Ch. Galand's Alexander who were to become Ch. Milov and Ch. Misha of Cordova. Ch. Sabrina of Baronoff C.D. had been sold to Jim and Jacqueline Lynch who bred her to Ch. Adage Duncan C.D. to produce Ch. Aries Allegra who returned to Baronoff.

The McCluskeys were very active in various Borzoi clubs with Mac serving as president and AKC delegate of the BCOA. After Kay's death in 1976, most of the breeding activities at Baronoff were curtailed and Mac turned his attention to judging the breed at shows from coast to coast.

The foundation bitch of the Pheasant Hill Kennels of Polly Clement in Media, Pennsylvania was Ch. Aleksandra of Baronoff (by Ch. Prometheus of Rancho Gabriel ex Tiranka of Baronoff). For her first litter she was bred to Ch. Kalmyk of Baronoff to produce Ch. Dashenka of Pheasant Hill owned by Marcia Melamed and Ch. Sverkai Troika of Pheasant Hill owned by Terry Fulmer. Marcia and Polly will never forget the time they entered Dashenka as a class bitch at Westminster the year of the Big Snow, the year cars and trains headed for New York were stranded for hours, even days. Their normally two-hour trip took close to ten hours. Dashenka took it all in stride and, showing more animation than ever before in the ring, not only won the points but also walked away with best of breed. For her second litter, Aleksandra was sent to California to be bred to Ch. Vastri of Rancho Gabriel (by Prometheus ex Ch. She-Za-Ne of Rancho Gabriel) to produce Ch. Chara Troika of Pheasant Hill, co-owned with Terry Fulmer, and Ch. Lubim of Pheasant Hill. Chara bred to Ch. Loral's Iossif Ivanevitch produced the lovely bitch Ch. Czarina of Pheasant Hill owned by Mary Shoaf, Ch. Perun of Pheasant Hill owned and shown by Polly's son and Ch. Rugay Aspor of Pheasant Hill owned by Ed and Ann Filetti of West Chester, Pennsylvania. Rugay was a versatile Borzoi earning not only his bench championship but also a C.D.X. degree and a field championship.

In the 1960's Dog Land, a park at which dogs of all recognized breeds were on permanent display, was established in Florida. Joseph and Mary Horton fell in love with the Borzoi and had to have him. After much negotiation a replacement was sent down from Baronoff and the Hortons took Ch. Prince Rurick of Baronoff (by Prometheus ex Anna Pavlova of Baronoff) home to their Wolfschmidtzoff Kennels in Jacksonville, Florida, which later moved to Atlanta, Georgia. Three bitches were quickly added: Baba Yaga of TamBoer, Ch. Whitchie of TamBoer and Katrina Czarina of TamBoer (all of Ch. Allah of TamBoer ex Ch. Natasha of TamBoer). In due time Rurick was bred to Whitchie producing Ch. Elena of Wolfschmidtzoff, Ch. Our Mary of Wolfschmidtzoff, Ch. Akim Saba

Ch. Nicky of Baronoff shown with his breeder-owner Kay McCluskey, winning a match show group first under Jane Jantos. *M&R Creative Images*

Ch. Prometheus of Rancho Gabriel with his co-owner Bill Thompson and Prometheus' daughter Tartar's Eos of Rancho Gabriel.

Ch. Hollister of Rancho Gabriel is shown winning one of his many specialty bests of breed in 1960 with his grandmother Ch. Obvorozevat Laska of Alpine, a specialty winner herself. Both were owned by Lyle and Phydelma Gillette. *Ludwig*

83

Ch. Perchotin's Byankaj Gabriel, a son of Troyka van Borjoschka, was imported by Phyl and Lyle Gillette in 1973. *Bennett*

Otto Newmar of Rancho Gabriel (owned by Jean Lau), Asa Newmar of Rancho Gabriel (co-owned by Stanton and Gillettes) and Hoit Newmar of Rancho Gabriel (owned by Gillettes) — the first champion offspring of the Dutch Int. Ch. Troyka van Borjoschka at Rancho Gabriel.

84

of Wolfschmidtzoff and Laylya of Wolfschmidtzoff. Laylya bred to Ch. Ristovia's Count Karajan produced Ch. Karahanz of Wolfschmidtzoff and Jowag's Count de la Tuque. Count de la Tuque bred to Elena produced Ch. Zoloshka of Wolfschmidtzoff while Karahanz bred to Our Mary produced Ch. Chayka of Wolfschmidtzoff, sold to the LaMac Kennels, and Ch. Zongore of Wolfschmidtzoff. Elena bred to Ch. Elain-Ward's Katawba v Sunbarr (by Malora's Bede of Sunbarr ex Hoheit v Bergland) yielded Ch. Wolfschmidtzoff Beaujolais. The Hortons purchased Ch. Saul of Rancho Gabriel (by Ch. Deucalion of Rancho Gabriel ex Ch. Moselle of Rancho Gabriel) from the Gillettes in California. Cbet of Wolfschmidtzoff (by Rurik ex Whitchie) bred to Saul produced Ch. Tanya of Wolfschmidtzoff. The list of the Hortons' breedings and the champions they produced could go on and on. After about ten years of very active breeding, the Hortons moved their kennel to Alabama where Borzoi breeding gave way to the breeding of racing greyhounds.

Also in Georgia are the LaMac Kennels of Nate McCannon and Joe Lashley. Most of their foundation stock was from Wolfschmidtzoff with Ch. Wayside Dawn (by Ch. Prince Rurik of Baronoff ex Katrina Czarina of TamBoer) and Ch. Katrinka of Wolfschmidtzoff (by Pascha of Wolfschmidtzoff ex Ch. Katrina of Wolfschmidtzoff) and Ch. Truelov of Wolfschmidtzoff (by Ch. Don Pedro of Wolfschmidtzoff ex Ch. Kislov of Baronoff). Truelov was taken to Ch. Makhayl of TamBoer to produce the bitch Ch. Makhaylia of LaMac while Katrinka was taken to Ch. Sorvan of TamBoer to produce the dog Ch. Dagan of LaMac. In 1973 Nate saw Loral's Talaironda (by Ch. Loral's Nika Timofe ex Loral's Charisma of Sunbarr) at a show and fell in love with the silver brindle marked bitch. He and Joe put a championship title on her and then sent her to Majenkir for breeding to Ch. Majenkir Apollonian Tsar. From the litter they retained Ch. Prince Basil of LeMac, a champion, a group winner and best of breed at the national specialty in Philadelphia in 1977.

Lyle and Phydelma Gillette both grew up with a deep love for animals of all sorts so it was only natural that when they married and had the space for dogs, they should establish their Rancho Gabriel Kennels first located in Saratoga, California, and later moved to other locations in northern California and in Oregon. They have been involved in several breeds of dogs such as Beagles, Silky Terriers, Salukis as well as Borzoi, but the Borzoi has always placed first in their hearts. In 1952, they owned Georgia of Alpine. When she died within a year, they acquired three littermates sired by Ardagan of Alpine C.D. out of Ch. Uda Adams. These were Ch. Solentse Ternovnek of Alpine C.D., Sontse Onyat of Alpine C.D. and Ch. Obvorozevat Laska of Alpine. The following year they purchased the bitch Ch. Garsova Ivanova of Alpine C.D. (by Mythe Ivanoff of Alpine ex

Ch. Uda Adams). Ternovnek and Laska constituted their foundation stock.

There have been many successful breedings at Rancho Gabriel producing many champions (64 to date) many of which have contributed significantly to the breeding programs of other kennels. In 1957 they whelped Ch. Hollister of Rancho Gabriel (by Ch. Solentse Ternovnek of Alpine C.D. ex Aida of Rancho Gabriel). Jarvis, as he was known, made the Rancho Gabriel name a household word in the Borzoi world. His show record included group wins as well as specialty wins. In addition, he sired twelve champions for his own kennel; he was never offered at public stud. In 1959 Laska was bred to Jarvis to produce the champions Ney-Che, Chin-Dee and She-Za-Ne. This last named bitch was the dam of eleven champions placing her as one of the outstanding brood bitches at Rancho Gabriel. During the next several years Jarvis sired several champions out of Ch. Garsova Ivanova of Alpine C.D. including the Rancho Gabriel champions Hera, Prometheus, Niobe, Champagne, Moselle, Timon, Oberon and Lancelot.

Ch. Prometheus of Rancho Gabriel, who contributed so much to the Baronoff breeding program as we have seen, was bred to She-Za-Ne in 1964 and 1965 to produce champions Vastri, Mazeppa, Adana, Markina, Aeneas, Deucalion—all of Rancho Gabriel—and Ch. Tartar's Eos. Deucalion was bred to Ch. Moselle of Rancho Gabriel to sire champions Gideon, Saul, Rachel and Serenade.

Up to this point in time the Rancho Gabriel line was highly linebred and most of the Borzoi produced were white or self-cream or self-gold. In the years that followed several outcrosses were tried, most quite successfully, to add certain improvements to the "center line" as Lyle and Phyl refer to their originally established type.

In the 1960's the Gillettes imported Elfield's Flightmaster C.D. from Australia. Flightmaster (by Ch. Elfield's Golden Fleece ex Ch. Elfield's Glad Tidings C.D.) was a brilliant self-red and added a variety of colors to the Rancho Gabriel produced Borzoi during the next few years. Sauvignon of Rancho Gabriel bred to Flightmaster produced Cacciatore of Rancho Gabriel. Cacciatore and Markina produced Ch. El Cazador of Rancho Gabriel U.D. owned, shown and trained by Del and Donnelle Richards.

In 1969 a leased bitch, Ch. Whirling Celeste of Malora (by Sunbarr Hercules of Malora ex Sunbarr Atlanta of Malora), was sent to Holland to be bred to the outstanding winner Int. Ch. Troyka von Borjoschka. From this litter came the Rancho Gabriel champions Hans Newmar, Otto Newmar, and Hoit Newmar. This was the beginning of the Dutch blend at Rancho Gabriel, a blending of the Borjoschka line with their center line. In 1973 Lyle and Phyl imported a Troyka son (ex Tanjuscha von Bergland, a Troyka daughter) soon to become Ch. Perchotin's Byankaj Gabriel. Bred recently to Ch. Hoit Newmar of Rancho Gabriel, he sired Ch. Rancho Gabriel Masterpiece and Ch. Rancho Gabriel Classic.

Both Lyle and Phyl have always taken a most active part in various Borzoi clubs and have been most instrumental in the promotion of both open field and lure coursing. Their Borzoi have often been trained in obedience as the titles on several of the above listed dogs indicate. They were very active in the formation of the Borzoi Brigada by the Mission Trail Borzoi Club, an obedience drill team that put on many demonstrations for various groups bringing to public attention the abilities of the Borzoi in obedience.

The Yermak Kennels were started by a turn of the wheel of fortune. Carla and Dmitri Alioshin of Sacramento, California went to a dog show in 1950 with the express purpose of watching Dachshunds. At the show they saw twelve Borzoi on the benches. Dmitri, a White Russian refugee formerly an official on the Manchurian Railway, recalled Laska the Borzoi his family had owned when he lived in Russia before the Revolutionists drove his parents from their home and killed the dog. The show featured a raffle the prizes for which were puppies. Carla held a winning ticket and as her prize picked out the only Borzoi in the group of puppy prizes, an eight week old silver and white male soon named Yermak of Marbob, bred by Marie Whitney. And so a puppy and a kennel were named after the Cossack Yermak, the Conqueror of Siberia. This puppy was by Ch. Damon of Ashtonia out of Anninka of Twin Elms. Soon after this a bitch was purchased from the Alpine kennels who became Ch. Zvezda Petrovna of Alpine (by Ch. Ataman of Alpine ex Ch. Uda Adams). She was bred back to Ataman for a litter of eight puppies. Her second litter was by Mythe Ivanoff of Alpine to produce three champions: Ch. Yermak's Rurik, Ch. Yermak's Ekaterina and Ch. Yermak's Platon.

In 1955 Mary Taviner sent Ramadan Kanetz Raduga to live at Yermak. He was by Ch. Gay Cavalier of Yadasar ex Ch. Ivanda of Yadasar and was a promising show dog winning at the tender age of seven months. Unfortunately, he did not survive his first year, so his litter brother Ramadan Cygne was purchased. When Cygne was bred to Ch. Zelda Shaun of Malora C.D. he sired Ch. Millrock Bronze of Malora C.D. After going to California, Cygne was bred to Ch. Uda Adams to produce the gold male Chuda of Alpine who in turn sired the black and tan Vrozyat Alpine Tartar Prince and Vrozyat Alpine Chuda out of Ch. Nadja of Alpine. Tartar Prince, known as Petey, made his home at Yermak.

In 1958 Mary Taviner sent the black and white bitch Barinoff Promise True to Yermak. Trudi had been imported from England where she had been bred by G. Sarson by Dewarne's Zagavor ex Ledvedka Perchina.

Carla is a most talented artist and has contributed much of her talent to various club publications. She was associate editor of "Riders of the Wind" with Mary Taviner.

Mrs. Nellie Wood Hilsmier bred Norwegian Elkhounds in her Woodhill Kennels in Ft. Wayne, Indiana for many years before becoming captivated by the Borzoi. She purchased the self-black Ch. Black Falcon of Twin Elms (by Boris Batyi of Wieckert Farms ex Nadja of Twin Elms C.D.) and campaigned him successfully with two bests in show to his credit in the midwest in the mid-1950's. Black Falcon did more than any other Borzoi to put to rest the prejudice against black Borzoi. Also purchased at about the same time from Mrs. J.S. Lindsey were the littermates Ch. Prince Mykye of Woodhill and Ch. Princess Anya of Woodhill (by Ch. Kuzjani of Millvale ex Ch. Sari). Nellie also purchased Ch. Tania of Ladoga (by Boi ex Pola of Ladoga) from her breeder Wilda Woehr. Wilda handled Black Falcon to some of his wins at the beginning of his show career. She was the owner of the Ladoga Kennels, not to be confused with the earlier kennel by the same name.

Black Falcon was bred to Ch. Tania producing a new list of champions bearing the Woodhill affix: Falconette, Bronze Falcon and Riuske. Bronze Falcon was the image of his sire except in color as he was a self-red. He continued his father's record in the show ring with several best in shows. He was bred to several bitches and was responsible for champion foundation stock in the Ungerleiders' Windy Hill Kennel, the Cordova Kennel, the Mojave Kennel as well as adding additional champion stock to the Woodhill and DeCraene kennels.

The White Swan Kennels of Mr. and Mrs. C.R. DeCraene, Jr. in Keyport, New Jersey specialized in German imports. Two of the more important ones bred by Frau Hanne Muller were Djumber von Bergland (by Ch. Asmaley v Merdody ex Ch. Banjani v Bergland) and Fandanga von Bergland (by Ch. Yukon von Bergland ex Adina Hel-Jagers-Meute) both imported in the mid-1950's. American bloodlines were introduced to White Swan by the mating of Fandanga to Ch. Black Falcon of Twin Elms. Ch. Toski of Woodhill was produced from that breeding and went to Woodhill.

Mr. and Mrs. Clarence DeCraene Sr. of Hazlet, New Jersey imported Ch. Amurat v Merdody (by Anselmi v Smoorenburg ex Antje v Urbanshof) in 1955 from Frau Charlotte Merdody in Germany. Admiral, as he was called, was a handsome dog, though quite small, with a very profuse deep gold and white coat. He finished his American championship by going best of breed at the 1956 BCOA specialty show. He was bred to Lydia Suchoff's Laska of Romanoff (by Vigow of Romanoff II ex Baba Yaga of Romanoff) to produce Ch. Shura of Don and Ch. Hussar of Don

Ch. Tersai of Gwejon, a top producing stud for Gwen and John Pinette in New Hampshire.

The self-black Ch. Black Falcon of Twin Elms, owned by Nellie Hilsmier, winner of 17 groups and two bests in show. He is handled here by the first of his several handlers-Wilda Woehr. *Frasie*

Ch. Amurat von Merdody, imported from Germany by Clarence DeCraene, is shown here winning best of breed at the 1956 BCOA Specialty.

Ch. De-Ray's Red Magic, a son of Ch. Bronze Falcon of Woodhill, owned by C.R. DeCraene.

89

The well-matched Gwejon hounds Ch. Vosmoi of Gwejon C.D. and Ch. Vershok of Gwejon, owned by John and Gwen Pinette, shown being awarded their tenth Best Brace in Show by Judge Elsworth Howell in 1969.

Ch. Galand's Alexander, bred and owned by Chester and Kathy Galek in New York. Alexander was leased for a short time by Mrs. Cheever Porter, but it was under the hand of his owner Kathy that he earned his specialty and best in show wins. *Gilbert*

for Lydia's Don Kennels. Another male from that litter, Kazak of Don, was bred to Admiral's daughter Ch. DeCraene's Liebchen (ex Haljean's Moonlight of Malora) to produce Ch. Kazak of DeRay who went also to Lydia's kennel. Another in that litter was Ch. Taroh of DeRay owned by Yoichi Hiraoka.

Liebchen was bred to Nellie Hilsmier's Bronze Falcon and the litter was split between the two kennels. Nellie picked Ch. Mikhail of Woodhill later sold to Dean and Louise Heaton and Ch. Czarina of Woodhill which she kept. Clarence took the red male Ch. DeRay's Red Magic and the bitch Ch. Amber Morn's Copper Lady.

Gwen and John Pinette in Claremont, New Hampshire combined their talents and names to form the Gwejon Kennels in the 1950's. Their first serious venture in Borzoi was the purchase of littermates Barasha HHF of Gwejon and Ch. Czarina HHF of Gwejon C.D.X. (by Ch. Kuzjani of Millvale ex Seiga of Hensey Hobby Farm) from the breeder John L. Hensey. Czarina earned her obedience titles both in the States and Canada. In fact, she was the first Borzoi to win the Dog World Award of Distinction for her outstanding scores earned in Canadian obedience trials. With scores for all three novice legs well over 195, she was highest scoring hound at all three shows and highest scoring dog in the latter two shows. Czarina was bred to her brother to produce Ch. Tersai of Gwejon who figures prominently in the foundation stock of such kennels as Galand, Marshann, Ridgeside and others.

When Czarina was taken to the Woodhill kennels to be bred to Black Falcon, the trip was unsuccessful in that regard but most successful in another. On a side trip to the Trezor Kennels in Michigan, they discoverd Ch. Jaguar Jehan of Malora to whom Czarina was later bred to produce Ch. Belka of Gewjon. Belka, bred to Tersai, produced the twin brothers Ch. Vosmoi of Gwejon C.D. and Vershok of Gwejon who established quite a show record both as a brace and as individuals. At the Midwest specialty at Detroit in 1966 Vosmoi was best of breed and third in group. Later with his brother he was part of the best brace in show.

The Belka-Tersai breeding also produced Ch. Gwejon Zagreus of Kostenov owned by Byron and Louenna Avery, Ch. Gwejon Ziaka of Marvita owned by Anita and Marvin Davis and Rusalka of Gwejon. Rusalka bred back to her sire produced Ch. Gwejon Kosoi. The success of the limited Gwejon breeding program was a tribute to the intelligent use of inbreeding planned and executed by the Pinettes.

Ch. Tersai of Gwejon was chosen by Chester and Kathy Galek as a stud for their Ch. Galand's Nina Peshkov (by Baron Alex Rachmaninoff ex Baroness Alexandria). The resulting litter had five champion males: Ch. Czar owned by Alfred Edlin, Ch. Galand's Alexander, Ch. Galand's

Baronoff, Ch. Galand's Michailoff and Ch. Galand's Andrejenko. Alexander was leased for about two years by Mrs. Cheever Porter but achieved his most notable wins while at the Galand Kennels handled by Kathy, wins including a specialty and a best in show. Baronoff, after Kathy's untimely death, was sold to the Tserevna Kennels of Art and Mary Neal on Long Island, New York. There, he was bred to their Ch. Ristovia's Tserevna Sheeba to sire Ch. Tserevna's Brandy Alexander, finished by the Neals and then sold to Pat Wahlig's Beowolf Kennels in Missouri.

The Tam-Boer Kennels of Mr. and Mrs. Leonard Tamboer and daughter Lena are located in Mahwah, New Jersey. In the early 1950's they bought several Borzoi from Louis Murr's Romanoff Kennels. All of their dogs since then have stemmed from those during the last 25 years. In fact, while the kennel has taken in a few puppies from litters sired by their various stud dogs, none of them has been incorporated into any serious breeding programs, so the lines of Tam-Boer remain direct and unadulterated back to the original Romanoff purchases.

The breeding of their Lady Gretchen of Tam-Boer to Vigow of Romanoff II in 1955 and the exhibiting of the litter that ensued produced Valia, Elena, Natasha and Elizavetta—all of Tam-Boer and all champions. When Lady Gretchen was again bred to Vigow II, she produced among others Ch. Dutchie of Tam-Boer and Ch. Sunday of Tam-Boer, the latter a bitch sold to Joyce Larsen in Virginia.

Ch. Vigow of Romanoff III was purchased from Louis Murr later and put in Lena's name. After earning his American championship, he was taken to Bermuda to become the first American Borzoi to earn a title in that country. Louis Murr bred his Ch. Tatiana of Alpine to this dog to produce Ch. Chudak of Romanoff owned by Irmgard Thompson and used so successfully by several kennels as we shall see later.

Dutchie was bred to Ch. Little Joker of Tam-Boer (by Vigow of Romanoff II ex Snow Witch of Romanoff) to produce Ch. Ducies Wild of Tam-Boer, the kennel's big winner in the early 1960's. Vigow III bred to Elena sired Ch. Vigow of Tam-Boer who, when bred to Valia, sired Ch. Allah of Tam-Boer. Allah bred to Natasha produced the best in show winner Ch. Nicolai of Tam-Boer owned by Mrs. Herbert C. Klipfel of western New York and ably handled by Bud Moser.

In 1963 Little Sweetheart of Tam-Boer (by Vigow of Romanoff II ex Lady Gretchen of Tam-Boer) was bred to Ducies to produce what many consider to be the best of the Tam-Boer Borzoi, Ch. Makhayl of Tam-Boer, a white and gold-brindle dog. He may well be the only Borzoi to have finished by obtaining his majors by defeating breeds other than Borzoi. While he won winners several times for points, he earned his required two majors by taking two bests in show. After finishing his championship he continued his winning ways by winning two more bests in show.

The pictures of Tam-Boer dogs on this page and the following page were kindly sent to the publisher by Lena S. Tamboer who credits Louis Murr's Romanoff line and her parents' use of it for the excellence of the Tam-Boer dogs.

Right, Harmony's Bistri of Tam-Boer, with Len Tamboer.

Ch. Nickolai of Tam-Boer, owned by Eva Klipfel, bred by Tam-Boer Kennels, winner of Best of Breed at the 1964 Borzoi Specialty. Later, his handler Bud Moser piloted him to a Best in Show.

Am. Can. Ch. Ducies Wild of Tam-Boer, sire of Am. Can. Ch. Makhayl of Tam-Boer.

Am. Can. Ch. Makhayl of Tam-Boer, multiple group and Best in Show winner.

Jessie Hamersma of Midland Park, New Jersey, has always been closely associated with the Tamboers. Indeed, many have thought her to be Lena's sister as they always traveled to shows together and in the beginning they often dressed alike. From the 1956 litter of Vigow II and Snow Witch, Jessie owned Ch. Nicky the Great of Tam-Boer. Her brother William owned the specialty winner Ch. Flying Dutchman of Tam-Boer (by Ch. Allah of Tam-Boer ex Ch. Lady Gretchen II). Jessie also owned Ch. Sorvan of Tam-Boer (by Makhayl ex Lady Gretchen II).

Mrs. Elizabeth Allison in Delaware, New Jersey bred her first Borzoi Alcyone Delvos (by Atlas ex Princess Sylvia of Millvale) to Vigow of Romanoff II in 1956 at her Kalevala Kennels. Ch. Nicholas Siberius and Ch. Andrea Alexis from that litter were sold to Mrs. Grace Dusenbury and Miss Harriet Crane respectively. Elizabeth retained a white bitch from that litter, Snow Princess, and subsequently bred her to her litter brother Nicholas to produce Ch. Tanya Majenkir of Kalevala C.D. sold to Karen and Jim Staudt. Tanya became the foundation bitch of Karen's Majenkir Kennels. Another bitch from that first litter, Sylvia Carrara, was bred to Erma Denton's Prince Nicholas (by Ivan's Georgi Zhukov ex Platina Adams) to produce Kalevala Victoria. When Victoria was bred to Ch. Loral's Alpha Sverkai (by Ch. Nicholas Siberius ex Arlekeen of Frontier) she produced the lovely black and white Ch. Tarnoff's Suzee Samovna owned by Carol DiGioacchino of Warminster, Pennsylvania who used the affix Tarnoff for the few litters she bred subsequently. A male from that litter was sold to Ronnie Ingenito of Brooklyn, New York later to become Ch. Frederick Peter La Paurie. When Victoria's litter sister Kalevala Melissa was also bred to Sverkai, she produced the black and white bitch who became Ch. Shadow Flight of Rannock Moor owned by Mrs. Pierpont Schreiber of New Jersey.

In 1960 Alcyone was bred to Sasha's Sensation. The only dark marked male in the litter was sold to Canada. There he was discoverd by Audrey Benbow, rescued and rehabilitated to become Ch. Topaze as we shall see in the next chapter.

In their River Ranch Kennels in Madera, California, Bill and Dixie Bilodeau bred Donna Marie of Malora to Mrs. Potter's Ch. Ataman of Alpine to produce Can. Ch. Zina O'River Ranch and their own gold Ch. Zlato O'River Ranch. Dixie also owned two other well known champions: Ch. Holka of Alpine (by Ch. Midtfyn's Boja ex Ch. Marvola Adams) and Ch. Solntse Petrovitch of Alpine (by Ch. Ataman of Alpine ex Ch. Uda Adams), winners dog at the first Borzoi Club of California specialty in 1954. After Bill died in an auto accident in 1965, Dixie remained in their lovely home built at their vineyard near Madera but discontinued breeding and exhibiting.

Swedish, Norwegian and American Ch. Leicro's Zandor was imported by Joe and Charlotte Wheeler from Sweden. *Callea*

Ch. Tarnoff's Suzee Samovna, bred by Elizabeth Allison, owned by Carol DiGioacchino, is shown here finishing her championship with a best of breed from Judge Heywood Hartley. *Shafer*

Int. and Nordic Ch. V'Indra's Vanity, bred by Charlotte Wheeler and exported to Lillemor Leifors and Cony Croneryd in Sweden. *Boöbe*

Mex. and Am. Ch. Yermak's Rurick was the first Borzoi owned by Sid and Marge Cox of Hethivar in California.

In the 1950's in his Corps de Ballet Kennels, Randi L'Ete of California bred Ch. Corps de Ballet Fouette (by a father-daughter mating of Ch. Ataman of Alpine to Nebeca Petrovna of Alpine). Nebeca bred to Tzar Bolvi of d'Lisitsa produced Ch. Corps de Ballet Fokine. Fouette's litter sister Corps de Ballet Sissone bred to the Tzar produced Ch. Corps de Ballet Maestro.

The V'Indra Kennels of Joe and Charlotte Wheeler have been breeding Borzoi for many years. However, the most interesting breeding program seems to be the current one involving as it does the combination of lines from many foreign countries with those of the American lines with which the Wheelers have been involved. The kennel located in San Juan Bautista, California combined English lines with Alpine to produce Ch. V'Indra's Roxanne of Alpine (by Can. Ch. Keepers Gabriel ex V'Indra's Alpine Phantom Flight). V'Indra's Elizaveta is truly cosmopolitan in her lines as she was sired by the English import Ice Snow of Index out of the bitch Samovaroff Top Lady imported from France although of Swiss and German lines. Charlotte and Swedish breeder Lillemor Leifors have exchanged Borzoi both of which have earned multiple championships. Charlotte imported Ch. Leicro's Zandor, a white and brindle dog with championships in Sweden and Norway as well as in this country. V'Indra Vanity (by V'Indra's Saint George ex V'Indra's Alpine Phantom Flight) was sent to Sweden soon to earn an international and Nordic championship.

Sidney and Marge Cox of California bred Borzoi under the kennel name of Hethivar. Their first champion was Ch. Yermak's Rurik (by Mythe Ivanoff of Alpine ex Ch. Zvezda Petrovna of Alpine) bred by Carla Alioshin from a half-brother half-sister mating. They also owned Ch. Alta of Alpine (by Yermak's Tuman ex Ch. Mythe Marova of Alpine). When Rurick and Alta were bred they produced the best in show winning brace Ch. Sascha Kochab of Hethivar C.D.X. and Ch. Shahzana Kochab of Hethivar C.D. owned by daughter and son-in-law Gail and Charles McRae. After losing their dogs to a series of tragedies at their home, a new self-red bitch was acquired from Sunbarr, Ch. Sunbarr Ruby of Hethivar (by Beau Geste of Sunbarr ex Nedra of Sunbarr Ranch). Ruby was bred to Ch. Trezor's Ramadi of Vala Rama to produce the Hethivar jewel litter which included Ch. Hethivar Diamond Baymiller. In 1966 Gail McRae Roberts separated herself from Hethivar and started using her own kennel name of Markova.

The Loral Kennels of Al and Lorraine Groshans in Center Valley, Pennsylvania were devoted mainly to Dachshunds until a black and white Borzoi bitch was purchased in 1955 by the name of Arlekeen of Frontier (by Saiga of Grador ex Miss Mythe of Sleeping Bear). In 1960 Arlekeen

Ch. Loral's Alpha Nicholai, the first Borzoi champion at the Loral Kennels of Lorraine Groshans.

Ch. Loral's Iossif Ivanevitch, a much sought-after stud, bred, owned and handled by Lorraine Groshans. Joe is pictured here being awarded his second best in show by Judge David Doane. *Klein*

was bred to Ch. Nicholas Siberius (by Vigow of Romanoff II ex Alcyone Delvos) to produce the first two Loral champions: Alpha Nicholai and Alpha Sverkai. Arlekeen was bred to her son Nicholai producing Loral's Bakarska Vodica who was bred to Ch. Petrikov Midas of Sunbarr (by Wotan Krasnoje Selo ex Alicia of Sunbarr Ranch) for two litters. The first contained Ch. Loral's Electra Zorka and the second contained Ch. Loral's Gusòdar C.D. owned by Bob and Cynthia Berglund and Ch. Loral's Galena C.D. owned by Georgia Finch. Loral's Gavril Volkov from the second litter was taken to Portugal by Graydon Hough becoming the first champion Borzoi of record in that country.

Electra was bred to Ch. Trezor Ivan to produce the Loral "I" litter which contained the following Loral champions: Iossif Ivanevitch (Joe), Ivan Ivanevitch and Iskra Ivanovna C.D. all retained by the Groshans; Ivanda Ivanovna owned by the Cossack Kennels; Igor Ivanevitch owned at Pennylane by Carol and Elaine Misko; and Iristo Ivanevitch C.D.X. owned by Chere Fuessel. Joe was the Borzoi the Loral Kennels will always be best remembered for as he was a top winning Borzoi for six years before he died just short of eight years of age with many groups, bests in show and specialties to his credit. The Trezor Ivan—Electra breeding was repeated to produce Ch. Loral's Nadezhda kept by the breeders and Ch. Loral's Nika Timofe owned by Mrs. Alvin Neiberg.

Ivan was bred to his grandmother Vodica and the resulting litter contained Loral's Laska Ivanovna and Ch. Loral's Larissa Ivanovna. Laska was sold to Jim and Mary Tilton as a foundation bitch for their Northwind Kennels in Wisconsin. She was bred to the Ch. Northwind's Duncan of Dana Dan to produce Ch. Northwind's Dodie of Dana Dan and Ch. Northwind's Silver Moonspark. Larissa went through a series of owners in Florida finally ending up with Betty Berstrom who finished her and then bred her to Ch. Lenindav Ali Khan of Malora (by The Raven of Malora ex Medea of Malora) owned by David Kapral and Leonard Houman to produce Ch. Larissa's Pequena Muchacha. In 1970 the black and white Larissa was best of breed at the national Borzoi specialty in Philadelphia. The breeding of Larissa and Ali Khan was repeated by Betty to produce the champions with the Larissa prefix: Granoso owned by Marilyn Meyer, Zast Joshka Kahirah owned by Beth Everett and Elegante Hijo kept by Betty. Josh was shown by teenaged Beth to his championship and an enviable record including several groups and a best in show. Hijo followed in his dam's footsteps by winning best of breed at the national specialty in Philadelphia in 1975 as well as winning several groups and best in shows in rather limited campaigning under the capable hand of Dick Vaughn. In 1979 he again took the breed at the Philadelphia national specialty from the veteran class.

Left: **Ch. Loral's Iskra Ivanovna CD and Ch. Loral's Mudrei Sava CD, both bred at Loral. Iskra was owned and trained by Debra Loral Groshans, Mudrei by Lorraine Groshans.**

Above— A headstudy portrait of **Ch. Loral's Larissa Ivanovna with her daughter Ch. Larissa's Pequena Muchacha and son Ch. Larissa's Elegante Hijo, all owned by Bette Bergstrom in Florida.**

Ch. Larissa's Elegante Hijo, bred and owned by Bette Bergstrom, is shown handled by Dick Vaughn to best of breed at the 1975 BCOA National Specialty in Philadelphia under Judge Tom Stevenson. *Ashbey*

Electra was bred to her son Ivan to produce Ch. Loral's Quiet Thunder kept at Loral, Ch. Cossack Questa Glory of Loral going to Cossack and Loral's Quintessa C.D. owned by Jim Heard.

Iskra bred to Ch. Loral's Mudrei Sava C.D. (by Joe ex Ch. Loral's Kari Kostenov) produced Ch. Pillow Hill Orzaba of Loral C.D. owned by Thomas Jessie in Illinois and Ch. Loral's Oulitza owned by Pennylane. In the repeat breeding was Ch. Loral's Svetland owned by Patricia Smith. Iskra bred to Gusodar produced Ch. Loral's Urahna Khan and Ch. Loral's Sporting Field Ulova both kept at Loral, and Ch. Loral's Ultima Sorva owned by Jeanne Volosin and Tom Oehlslager.

Loral's Charisma of Sunbarr (by Malora's Bryan of Sunbarr ex Zanosa II of Sunbarr), a black and white bitch, was purchased from Sunbarr in 1970. In her first litter by Joe she produced Ch. Loral's Royal Charisma sold to Patricia Murphy as a foundation bitch for her Oaklara Kennels and Ch. Loral's Royal Ransom sold to Timothy and Sharon Robinson in Minnesota for their Street Kennels. For her second and third litters Charisma was bred to Joe's full brother Nika to produce Ch. Pillow Hill Taccoa of Loral co-owned by Lorraine with Tom Jessie, Ch. Loral's Talaironda sold to Joe Lashley and Nate McCannon in Georgia and Ch. Loral's Vanya Nikovitch sold to Carol and Joyce Levine and their Lejoy Kennels in Ohio.

The red and white Nadezhda was bred to the Dutch import Piotr Illjitsch van Borjoshka (by Eros v Borjoschka ex Moja v Borjoschka) owned by Jack and Jean Vandongen in Canada. This Loral litter contained: Ch. Loral's Whistle in the Dark kept by Loral, Ch. Loral's Wish Upon a Star owned by Harriet and Gary Goldner in Ohio, Can. Ch. Loral's Wizard Magic owned by Jan Brigadier of Adrienne Kennels in Washington and Can. Ch. Loral's Whirlaway of Pennylane owned by the Miskos. For her second litter Nadezhda was bred to Loral's Windswept Stargazer (by Joe ex Ch. Kaoc's Katerina of Windswept C.D.) to produce the multi-group winning Ch. Loral's Zachran of Volodea owned by Jeanne Volosin at her Volodea Kennels.

In 1974 Ch. Laba's Arimsky (by Piotr Illjitsch van Borjoschka ex Willolea Moonglow Tsepa) was purchased from Jean Vandongen in Canada. He finished his championship early the next year and won the first of many hound groups his first time out as a special at 15 months under the guidance of handler Jim Rathbun. During the next few years Rim added many specialty, group and best in show wins to his record. Rim's half-brother Whistle also established a record listing many specialty and group wins plus a best in show on his way to Canadian title.

Rim was bred to Ulova to produce Ch. Loral's Yves Korsakov owned by Jane Maddox and Ch. Loral's Yekatrina co-owned by Ed Brooks and

Ch. Loral's Royal Ransom owned by Tim and Sharon Robinson at their Mulberry Street Kennels in Minnesota.

Winner of many groups, specialties and a best in show, Ch. Loral's Whistle in the Dark is shown being handled to best of breed at the 1980 BCDV Specialty by Michael Hagen under judge Mary Nelson Stephenson for owner Debra Loral Groshans. *Ashbey*

103

and Al Groshans. Whistle bred to Ulova's litter sister Ulissa produced Ch. Loral's Brodyago of Aesir co-owned by Adrienne Baylin and Leonard Stapen. Taccoa was bred to Urahna Khan to produce the black and white bitch Ch. Pillow Hill Arlekeen of Loral retained at Loral.

Kathy O'Connell's Kaoc Kennels in Massachusetts produced many fine sighthounds including Borzoi during the 1960's. Much of her breeding was done in conjunction with William Woodley's Wilolea Kennels in New York. Among Kathy's several champions were Wilolea Nuryiev of Kaoc, Wilolea's Maeve of Kaoc and Kaoc's Rhises of Ekselo. Rhises rates a place among that select group of bitches who have won hound groups. When Rhises was bred to Ch. Loral's Iossif Ivanevitch, she produced in her first litter for owner Ellen O'Lesky and her Ekselo Kennels: Ch. Syroco's Serpico of Ekselo owned by Toni Coppola, Ch. Larissa of Ekselo retained by Ellen, Ch. Ekselo's Czarina Sophia for co-owners Carol O'Leske and Evelyn Hisoire, Ch. Jadetree's Jessie of Ekselo owned by Joe Taylor and Ch. Diamond Lil of Ekselo owned by Cathleen Flanagan.

Mr. and Mrs. Leslie Kaufman of Huntingdon Valley, Pennsylvania brought out a very fine bitch in the summer of 1956 that they had bred in their Med-O-Land Kennels. This was Ch. Med-O-Land's Petrova (by Nananhal's Bistri ex Zanoza of Topau) owned by Burton N. Axe of Philadelphia. Petrova was best of breed at the 1958 BCOA specialty show taking the breed from the classes. To prove that she was indeed worthy of that win, she repeated the best of breed win at the same specialty two years later.

James Barr of Thiensville, Wisconsin, whose business connection with the Perk Dog Food Company afforded him many years of experience with animals and animal nutrition, maintained his Sunbarr Kennels on a 300 acre spread originally laid out as a silver fox ranch. Dogs bred by Jim were named with Sunbarr or Sunbarr Ranch as part of their registered names. There was no significance as the which was used; the choice was based solely on how the name looked or sounded with one or the other. At the height of the Sunbarr operation, the number of Borzoi at the kennels ranged from 100 to 200. Jim planned and executed several breeding programs based on various American lines as well as dogs imported from England, Scotland, Holland and Germany.

In 1958 Jim imported the white and black bitch Solo of Barnaigh (by Ch. Reyas Romancer ex Chinchilla of Barnaigh) from Mrs. McNeil in Scotland. In 1959 he imported five Borzoi from Charlotte Zabel in Germany all sired by Int. Ch. Polongai Porchai Krasnoje Selo: littermates Helios v Bergland and Hoheit v Bergland (ex Charis v Bismarckturm), the red and white Ilja v Bergland (ex Enke v Bergland), the white and gray

Ch. Jadetree's Jesse of Ekselo, bred by Ellen O'Leske and owned by Joe Taylor, is shown here being awarded her finishing points by Judge Carol Duffy. *Gilbert*

Ch. Med-O-Land's Petrova, owned by Burton Axe, bred by Les Kauffman, was best of breed at the BCOA national specialties in 1958 and 1960.

bitch Grafinia v Bergland (ex Mariska) and the self-black male Wotan Krasnoje Selo (ex Walhall's Eliwajar). In 1962 Jim and Mary Taviner imported the sable and white bitch Shelbor's Anadyomene (by Ch. Arnorinski of Greenhaven ex Regas Sapphire of Borrowska) bred by Mrs. B. Hargrave in England. In 1968 Sunbarr imported the self-black bitch Ch. Barnaigh Voronoff Bielko (by Runskoff Ivanovich ex Ch. Ruth of Fortrouge) bred by Mr. and Mrs. T.E. Heller.

All of these imports were combined with lines from American kennels as well as with other imports in other American kennels. In a few cases, additional dogs were added that had been imported by others. One such dog was Lasky of Ukrainia (by Boris of Ukrainia ex Wendylon of Yadasar) imported by Dr. Todd Sterling from breeder Dorothy Dudley in England. Due to lack of space at his home, Dr. Sterlin sent Lasky to Sunbarr.

One of the litters that brought fame to Sunbarr was the "B" litter named after saints. Almost any pedigree that contains Sunbarr traces back to one or more from that litter. The Malora imported Bright of Barnaigh was bred to Ilja v Bergland to produce Malora's Blaise of Sunbarr and littermates similarly named: Bede, Beatrice, Bianca, Barnabas, Beata, Bryan, and Benedict. Bede was bred to Hoheit v Bergland to produce two of my favorite Sunbarr champions Tammogin of Sunbarr and Elain-Ward's Katawba v Sunbarr.

Sunbarr has had a distinct influence on the foundation of many kennels particularly those in the Midwest. Just to name a few: Nightsong Kennels of Joyce Brandin, Oaklara Kennels of Pat Murphy, Elain-Ward Kennels of Elaine Konwent, Vala Rama Kennels of Charles and Grace Conally, Bon-Ton Kennels of Cynthia and William Smith, Goldhof Kennels of Clarence and Pauline Eldred, Dana Dan Kennels of Paul and Ardietta Thompson, Bokara Kennels of Richard and Shen Smith and the Del-Jer Kennels of the Rooneys. And of course, the influence of Sunbarr on the Trezor, Loral and Sirhan lines cannot be denied as in each case one of the greatest litters produced at each kennel was directly due to the influence of a Sunbarr background.

Claire Anderson Klemmedson established the Kashan Kennels during the late 1950's. She owned Ch. Swanlake Eric of Kashan (by Kimita Kazan of Malora C.D. ex Swanlake Kasma of Malora) bred by the Swanlake Kennels in Minnesota. She also owned Ch. Sunbarr Melanie of Kashan (by Ilja v Bergland ex Jagasa v Bergland) bred from the German imports of the Sunbarr Kennels. Although she owned Ch. Ramadi of Sunbarr Ranch (by Ch. Tobolzkoi Krasnoje Selo ex Solo of Barnaigh) only a short time before he died, he had tremendous influence on the breed through his two champion sons out of Ch. Trezor Alupka—the great producing Ch. Trezor Ivan and his litter brother Ch. Trezor Ramadi of Vala Rama.

Charles W. Miller Jr. of Deerfield, Illinois became active in the Borzoi fancy during the 1950's when he purchased two hounds imported from Europe by Dr. Hans J. Mueller, a professor at the University of Chicago. Mr. Miller gave the dogs the freedom of his Lazy M Ranch in Elkhorn, Wisconsin and the care and exercise they received there developed the male into an outstanding show winner and top producing stud by the name of Ch. Tobolzkoi Krasnoje Selo (by Int. Ch. Polongai Porchai Krasnoje Selo ex Kaskade v Silberhof) bred by J.H.M. Van Der Molen in Holland.

Bernie Begley bought Loral's Elena (by Ch. Petrikov Midas of Sunbarr ex Loral's Bakarska Vodica) as a foundation bitch for his Berbeg Kennels in Ohio. Later he bought Sunbarr's Andriusha (by Beau Geste of Sunbarr ex Sophia of Sunbarr Ranch). The breeding of these two produced Ch. Berbeg Shalira. A breeding of Shalira of Ch. Sunbarr Berbeg Kashek Pasha (by Romulus of Sunbarr ex Patricia of Sunbarr) produced Ch. Berbeg Odette Odile for Jeffrey and Lynda Rissman's Vilovia Kennels at which they already housed Ch. Joseph Alexander Austerlitz (by Bonzeki of Shondar ex Loral's Janda Alexandra). Bernie bred Patricia of Sunbarr (by Beau Geste of Sunbarr ex Shelbor's Anadyomene) to the Canadian Dutch import Piotr Illjitsch van Borjoschka to produce Ch. Berbeg Govoroushka of Rakar owned by Ted Ralls and Peter Kartye in North Carolina.

The Warhill Kennels of Harry M. Ferguson and William W. Shepard were located in Cincinnati, Ohio and they were the most active during the late 1950's. They bred their Kotlas of Mettler Hobby Farm to Ch. Jaguar Jehan of Malora (by Barinoff Ambassador ex Lucky Lady of Barnaigh) to produce their first champions Warhill's Amber Roi and Warhill's Mountain Topaz owned by Calvin Perry (better known in Whippet circles today). Amber Roi was bred to Warhill's Myrthe of Malora to produce Ch. Warhill's Countess of Kolomna and Ch. Warhill's Khazar Khan C.D. owned by Jo Ranz. Warhill purchased Ch. Trezor Donitz of Warhill (by Ch. Jaguar Jehan of Malora ex Ramadan Koraleva Chevry) from Russell Everhart. Donitz was a multi-group placer before he was a year old and finished his championship at 15 months. Myrthe was bred to Donitz to produce Ch. Warhill's Donskoy kept by Warhill, Ch. Warhill's Elegance sold to W.H. Sampson and Ch. Warhill's Europa sold to Jo Ranz were sired by Donitz out of Sasha of Sharramoor. Warhill imported Ch. Borco's Blitz in 1962 from Louis Mennen in Holland. Later when the Warhill Kennel was disbanded, Blitz went to the Volga Kennels in California.

The Kostenov Kennels of Byron and Louenna Avery started in 1961 in Maryland but soon moved to the rural countryside of Vermont. Their first Borzoi was Haljeans Lily Sabina v K. Being limited to 25 letters for

Ch. Tammogin of Sunbarr (by Malora's Bede of Sunbarr ex Hoheit v Bergland) was bred by Jim Barr and then owned and finished by Martha Denton in Tennessee.

Ch. Kostenov Barrymore was bred by Kostenov and co-owned by Louenna Avery and Mark Berkel. *Ashbey*

her name didn't allow for the full spelling of their kennel name in her registered name. Sabina was bred by Mrs. Whisler of the Haljeans Kennels, her sire being Haljean's Flame and her dam Haljean's Mystery.

Before the move to Vermont, Byron and Louenna bought the white bitch Elmuer Zoi Tamihof (by Yelmorb Korchak ex Ch. Walhof Fraun) from Violet Elmer. She was bred after earning her championship to Ch. Loral's Alpha Sverkai (by Ch. Nicholas Siberius ex Arlekeen of Frontier). The litter was due after the move to Vermont. However, finding that their new home could not be occupied immediately, the Averys were forced to take up temporary residence in one room in a local motel. It was there that their first litter of three was whelped. Two of these were Ch. Kostenov Peer Gynt owned by Joan and Michael Carusone and Ch. Loral's Kari Kostenov owned by Lorraine Groshans.

Shortly after finally moving into their new home, the Averys bought Kostenov Phoenix of Twin Elms (by Ch. Tamazar of Twin Elms ex Bellina of Belzami). He was bred to Sabina to produce Ch. Kostenov Algernon Moncrieff, Ch. Kostenov Alexandrai of RRR and Ch. Kostenov Cecily Cardew.

Ch. Gwejon Zagreus of Kostenov (by Ch. Tersai of Gwejon ex Ch. Belka of Gwejon) was purchased from the Pinettes. When Cecily was bred to Zagreus, she produced Ch. Kostenov Kean who finished with group placings from the classes and was one of the very few self-blacks ever to place on the annual list of top ten Borzoi. A full brother to Kean is Ch. Raphael Wilson of Kostenov.

A breeding of Cecily to Ch. Sweet William de Foret (by Ch. Count Alexander of Cordova ex Ch. Bachelor's Forest Walnut) produced Ch. Kostenov Barrymore co-owned by Louenna and Mark Berkel. When Barrymore was bred to Marber's O'Tiffany of Loral (by Ch. Loral's Mudrei Sava C.D. ex Ch. Loral's Iskra Ivanovna C.D.), the result was Ch. Marber's Lady Liza Jane who was shown in Texas with breed wins and group placements from the classes. Barrymore was bred to Cecily's daughter Kostenov Leocadie Gardi with Ch. Tolstoy von Kostenov and Ch. Suntar Istilik of Kostenov as the result.

Cecily was bred to Kean producing Can. Ch. Kostenov Kemp. Obviously, Cecily is considered one of the better producing bitches at Kostenov.

At about the same time the Kostenov Kennels had its beginning, Priscilla Sanner in Westminster, Maryland bought her first bitch, also from the Haljeans Kennels, to start her Petrikov Kennels. This bitch was Kostenov Lorelei L'Ondine (by Haljean's Omar Khyyam ex Haljean's Queen of Sheba) and was always Priscilla's favorite Borzoi. Soon after Lorelei's purchase, Priscilla acquired Petrikov Midas of Sunbarr and

The favorite of the Kostenov Kennels, the self-black Kostenov Horatio owned by Byron Avery.

Two typical Cossack Borzoi: multi-group and specialty winner Ch. Cossack's Aristotle in the foreground and his daughter Ch. Cossack Glory's Gossamer.

110

showed him to his championship. Midas was by Wotan Krasnoje Selo out of Alicia of Sunbarr Ranch. He was appropriately named being a self-gold. Ch. Petrikov Boreas the Wind, a self-red sable male, was added to the Petrikov Kennels when he was acquired as a stud puppy from the breeding of Midas to Saskia of Tac-Mar (by Ch. Sundance of Malora ex Prekrasnie Frank of Tac-Mar). Priscilla also bought Anastasia of the Hunt (by Ivan Bunin ex Loral's Alpha Zanoza) bred by Eli Fleisher.

Lorelei was bred to Haljean's Flame (by Ch. Amurat v Merdody ex Haljean's Moonlight of Malora) to produce Ch. Petrikov Tascha of Helicon owned by Harry Ohlinger and Jeff Campbell as the foundation bitch for their Cossack Kennels. Then Lorelei was bred to Boreas to produce Ch. Petrikov Siva. Anastasia was bred to Midas to produce Ch. Petrikov Zeus.

About this time Priscilla married George Lineker and the kennel was moved to Tampa, Florida where several additional litters were bred. When George received orders for a transfer to Japan, all of the dogs except Zeus had to be placed elsewhere. Several were put out on breeding terms so that Priscilla could pick up again upon her return to the States, Midas was sent back to Sunbarr so that he could continue to be used at stud and several were sent to the Cossack Kennels in Maryland including Boreas who was used there to sire their first litter.

Harry Ohlinger had never had much experience with dogs when he went to buy a Borzoi for his partner Jeff Campbell at the Petrikov Kennels. When he selected Petrikov Tascha of Helicon, he wasn't even sure how to put her in the car to take her home. Priscilla calmed Harry's fears and placed the puppy carefully in the car and sped them on their way. It didn't take long for Harry to do a complete turnaround, to learn to love Borzoi and to handle in the show ring with the best of them. In fact, he is considered by many one of the top owner-handlers in the East now. In due time Tascha finished her championship and produced the first litter for the Cossack Kennels sired by Ch. Petrikov Boreas the Wind.

In 1967 Harry and Jeff purchased the lovely white and gold Loral's Ivanda Ivanovna (by Ch. Trezor Ivan ex Ch. Loral's Electra Zorka) and quickly added another champion to their kennel. Shortly thereafter Tascha was bred to Ch. Loral's Iossif Ivanevitch, Ivanda's litter brother, to produce the Cossack champions Aramis, Aristotle, Aphrodite and Adriana.

Aristotle added much glory to the history of Cossack with his outstanding show record of several groups and specialty best of breeds. He was bred to his dam to produce Ch. Cossack's Dostoevsky. Out of Ivanda he produced his best in show son Ch. Cossack's Echo co-owned with Harry Boteler and Ch. Eminence of Cossack owned by Carol Schiro. Bred

Carrying on the Cossack tradition is Ch. Cossack's Intrepid winning the breed with his owner Harry Ohlinger and judge J. Council Parker. *Gilbert*

Zaratove of Sunbarr and Ch. Cergewna Is Slonowaja were the first two Borzoi owned by Bruna Henry. A litter from these two started the Volga Kennels and included the well known Ch. Vronsky of Volga.

to his litter sister Aphrodite, Aristotle sired Ch. Cossack's Filigree and Ch. Cossack's Frivilous Fawn going to Jane Maddox's Korsakov Kennels as a foundation bitch.

In 1971 the black and white bitch Cossack Questa Glory of Loral (by Ch. Loral's Ivan Ivanevitch ex Ch. Loral's Electra Zorka) was purchased and she also earned her title of champion with winners points at the national specialty. Glory was bred to Aristotle to produce Ch. Cossack Geoffroy St. Hilair and Ch. Cossack Glory's Gossamer. Gossamer was the futurity winner of the BCOA in 1974 and also winners bitch at the national specialty the same day. Gossamer was bred to Ch. Crescent's Arctic Glacier (by Ch. Loral's Iossif Ivanevitch ex Ch. Crescent's Vamp of Tamarisk) to produce the two Cossack champions Intrepid and Imarra, the latter being owned by Mary E. Vile.

Genevieve Pitcock met Ch. Zvezda Petrovna of Alpine in 1955 a few weeks before Petrovna whelped her first litter by Mythe Ivanoff of Alpine. Genevieve chose the only bitch in the litter Yermak's Ekaterina as the foundation for her Van Strom Kennels. Tina finished her championship by the age of two years and was then bred to Marbob's Romulus of Malora to produce eight puppies. From this litter Genevieve kept a black masked red bitch Ninotchka of Van Strom later to become a champion. Nina produced only one litter and that by Vrozyat Alpine Tartar Prince. Ekatrina of Van Strom from the first litter was sold to Marguerite Benson in New York who bred her to Ch. Duncan's Shandan of Lazy Acres to produce Ch. Justour Ricochet and Ch. Lazy Acres' Druscella both going to Florida. Genevieve was very active in work for the Borzoi Club of Northern California. Both the club and the breed lost a very fine leader when she lost her life in a plane crash in 1977.

Bruna Henry's first Borzoi was Zaratove of Sunbarr (by Zandor of Malora III ex Gay Toinette of Malora). Later Bruna acquired the especially lovely red and white Swiss bitch Ch. Cergewna Is Slonowaja (by Int. Ch. Batruk v.d. Hatz ex Int. Ch. Natascha des Essertons). The breeding of these two Borzoi in 1962 put the Volga Kennels on the road to renown as the litter contained Ch. Vronsky of Volga and Varenka of Volga. Vronsky was the big winner of the kennel winning many specialties and best in shows.

Vladinoff was bred to his litter sister Varenka producing the top winning Ch. Mogadan of Volga owned by Bruna and Mr. and Mrs. Nathan Reese, and Ch. Marinsky of Volga kept by Bruna. Vronsky produced many champions including Ch. Ivanov of Volga (ex Sascha Duchess Narischkin) owned by Mr. and Mrs. Reese. Ch. Rogdai of Volga and Ch. Russack of Volga were also sired by Vronsky out of his litter sister Valeska of Volga as was Gail McRae's Ch. Markova's Kashaan of Volga. Bruna

Ch. Vronsky of Volga was bred, owned and handled by Bruna Henry. He won several groups, bests in show and specialties and figured prominently in the Volga breeding program.

Three daughters of Ch. Vronsky of Volga: litter sisters Yana of Volga and Ch. Yasna of Volga (ex Ch. Nadja of Volga) and Ch. Bielka of Volga (ex Valeska of Volga) all bred and owned by Bruna Henry.

Dorothy Carter

Ch. Mogadan of Volga, bred by Bruna Henry and co-owned with Nathan and Gloria Reese, was top winning Borzoi in 1973 with many groups and bests in show to his credit. *Ludwig*

Ch. Karina's Arcurov Yevanovitch was bred by Aud Karin Edmondson, owned by Mr. and Mrs. Nathan Reese and handled by Corky Vroom. *Bergman*

bred many litters of very fine Borzoi but was extremely selective as to the placement of her puppies and the use of her studs. In 1975 Ch. Wellthorne's Tilosky was imported from England (by Keepers Michael Angelo ex Wellthornes Kalinca) bred by Ann Thornwell. Tilosky was co-owned by Bruna and Ron and Dyane Roth.

Gloria Reese of Los Angeles, California must be mentioned here. While she and her husband Nathan did not engage in the breeding of Borzoi, they did much to further the interests in not only Borzoi but also Doberman Pinschers and Greyhounds by extensively campaigning top members of each breed across the country. Both Mogadan and Ivanov mentioned about were top winning Borzoi—Mogadan in 1973 and Ivanov in 1974. Gloria's Greyhound bitch Punky (Ch. Aroi Talk of the Blues) was top winning dog (all breeds) for 1976 and 1977. Currently being campaigned in the Borzoi ring is a Vronsky grandson Ch. Karina's Arcurov Yevanovitch (by Yevtushenko of Volga ex Myretta of Karina).

George Hinkle and William Reddick established their Kostroma Kennels in Philadelphia about 1968. Bad luck seemed to plague them at first with their Borzoi, but with the acquisition of Varushka Tarnoff of Kostroma fortune began to smile. Soon thereafter the kennel was moved to the lovely stone farmhouse in Bucks County in Pennsylvania. Varushka (by Ch. Galand's Alexander ex Ch. Tarnoff's Suzee Samovna) bred by Carol DiGioacchino was soon sporting a champion title. She was bred to Ch. Loral's Ivan Ivanevitch (by Ch. Trezor Ivan ex Ch. Loral's Electra Zorka) producing Ch. Petrov of Tarnoff retained by George and Bill and Ch. Tarnoff's Pasha P'Yesna going to Varushka's breeder Carol. Kostroma acquired Tusnaja of Volga (by Int. Ch. Vronsky of Volga ex Anushchka of Volga) and bred her to Ch. Rogdai of Volga (by Vronsky ex Valeska of Volga) to produce Kostroma's Svetana of Volga and Kostroma's Serov of Volga. Svetana was bred to Ch. Majenkir Serafix Siberius (by Ch. Majenkir Apollonian Tsar ex Shadybrook Swan of Wilolea) to produce Ch. Kostroma's Chekov owned by Joan Hack of Fox Run Kennels, Ch. Kostroma's Costya of Vanaya owned by Dan and Jill Baxter and Ch. Kostroma's Czarina. Varushka was bred to Serov to produce Kostroma's Afimya and Kostroma's Anisimov both of which earned their titles in Michigan after the kennel was moved there in 1976. When George and Bill relocated in New Jersey, the breeding and exhibiting at Kostroma was drastically curtailed. Bill's time after that was taken up by judging.

The Kry-Lyesa affix was used by Mrs. Irmgard Thompson in New Jersey starting with her first Borzoi Ch. Alexandra Kry-Lyesa (by Kazak of Don ex Ch. Liza of Don). Alexandra was bred to Ch. Nicholas Siberius producing Ch. Zarina Kry-Lyesa kept by Irmgard and Ch. Nicholas

Ch. Majmnkir Apollonian Tsar sitting beside his brother Ch. Majenkir Sverkai Snow Stag CD. These two top producing studs were bred and owned by Karen Staudt.

Ch. Chudak of Romanoff, bred by Louis Murr and owned by Irmgard Thompson, is shown here winning best of breed.
Gilbert

Siberius O'Dellmead going to his sire's owner Grace Dusenbury. Irmgard purchased Ch. Chudak of Romanoff from Louis Murr in 1964. Zarina was bred to Chudak to produce Ch. Nikki Kry-Lyesa of Chudak, Ch. Krasnaya Kry-Lyesa, and the two group placing bitches Ch. Balalaika Kry-Lyesa and Ch. Kukla Kry-Lyesa. Kukla was bred to the German import Istwan von der Solitude owned by Lydia Suchoff to produce Kym Kry-Lyesa and Ch. Kia Kry-Lyesa in 1973.

The grace, beauty and balance of the Borzoi quite naturally attracts the eye of the artist so it is not surprising that many such talented people become involved with the breed. One of them is Karen Staudt who extended her talent to that of a breeder of fine Borzoi in her Majenkir Kennels first located in Brooklyn, New York; then Staten Island and finally to its lovely rural location in Stewartsville, New Jersey. The first Majenkir Borzoi and first champion was the white bitch Ch. Tanya Majenkir of Kalevala C.D. (by Ch. Nicholas Siberius ex litter sister Snow Princess). She was bred to Ch. Chudak of Romanoff (by Ch. Vigow of Romanoff III ex Ch. Tatiana of Alpine) to produce Ch. Cognac of Fox Glen sold to Audrey Mulligan and Majenkir Alicia Alexandra. Bred to Ch. Conamor Count Tauskey C.D. (by Ch. Chudak of Romanoff ex Ch. Hasu's Elena of Conamor C.D.) Tanya produced the two outstanding top producing studs at Majankir, Ch. Majenkir Sverkai Snow Stag C.D. and Ch. Majenkir Apollonian Tsar (from two litters a year apart), also Ch. Majenkir Cassimer, Ch. Majenkir Snow Seiga and Ch. Majenkir Kristal Fawn. Alicia, the daughter from the Chudak litter, was leased back and bred to Snow Stag to produce Ch. Majenkir Asta sold to Robert Harvey, Int. and Ger. Ch. Majenkir Durak sold to Capt. W. and H. Pierce, Ch. Majenkir Gyrfalcon, Ch. Majenkir Hoflin Gossamer sold to Donald Hoflin and Ch. Majenkir Katya of Mare's Head sold to Joann Geiss. Gyrfalcon followed in his sire's image winning specialties and groups. In addition, he easily earned his field championship at lure coursing.

Snow Stag was used by Majenkir to produce several champions and also used by many other breeders with equal success. Phyllis Castells bred her Venga Djevoika of Sunbarr to him to produce Ch. Snow Stag's Djovoika C.D. sold to John Czech and Pedro Diaz as a foundation bitch for their PJ Kennels in Florida. Loral's Astra of Khazar (by Ch. Loral's Iossif Ivanevitch ex Loral's Zizanie of Aristoff) was bred to Snow Stag to produce Ch. Fenn Hills Tarka Soubrette owned by Barry Ellison. For Alfred Edlin's Ridgeside Kennel, out of Ch. Ridgeside Smoke Cloud, he sired the Ringside champions Ice Capade owned by Leslie Guberman and later sold to the Beowolf Kennels, Snow Cloud, Alexander Borodin owned by Barry Ellison, and Sir Prize Package. Out of Robert Zion's French bitch Tapia des Mariettes came Ch. Dimitri of Cream Ridge. From Ch.

Ch. Mikhail of Woodhill, bred by Clarence DeCraene, was owned first by Nellie Hilsmier and then sold to Dean and Louise Heaton as their first Borzoi.

Ch. Majenkir Gyrafalcon and his sire Ch. Majenkir Sverkai Snow Stag CD were bred and owned by Karen Staudt. Both are top producers and winning showdogs with specialties and groups.

Birchwood's Vonka of Majenkir came the Majenkir champions Valcon of Tara owned by Deborah Tarentino, Vikki Valeska owned by Pat Murphy and Vikki of Valleymede owned by Joanne Bogaty. Judy Harris of the Arista Kennels in Florida bred her Ch. Jarva of Rancho Gabriel (by Ch. Rogue of Rancho Gabriel C.D. ex Margail's Vivace) to Snow Stag producing Ch. Arista's Majenkir Jill co-owned by Karen Staudt and Betty Denman and Ch. Arista's Jarvas kept by Judy. Ch. Majenkir Kristal Fawn bred to her brother produced Ch. Majenkir Siberian Sorvan owned by Douglas and Mary Marvel. Ch. Rakar's Czar of Baymar (by Snow Stag ex Beryozka of Twin Elms) was sold to Peter Kartye and used by him as a foundation stud for his kennels in North Carolina.

Apollonian Tsar also was a top producer with a long record of champion offspring. Judy Harris sent her Ch. Serenade of Rancho Gabriel to Pollo and produced Ch. Arista's Scherzo. Nathan McCannon and Joe Lashley sent their Ch. Loral's Talaironda (by Ch. Loral's Iossif Ivanevitch ex Loral's Charisma of Sunbarr) to him producing Ch. Prince Basil of LaMac, winner of a national specialty as we have seen before in this chapter. Betty Denman sent her foundation bitch from her Astafiev Kennels Ch. Majenkir Pastel Portrait (by Snow Stag ex Shadybrook Swan of Wilolea) to Pollo producing her Ch. Astafiev Majenkir Masterpiece who was finished from the bred by exhibitor class as was his daughter Ch. Astafiev Charadai (ex Ch. Arista's Majenkir Jill). James Heard's Ch. Cathcade Reflection bred to Pollo produced Ch. Agridor's Alisa Astarte. Linda Mitchell's Windswept Effervescence bred to Pollo produced Ch. Timohir Aurora.

Karen purchased two bitches both of which produced very well for the kennel. These were the litter sisters Shadybrook Swan of Wilolea and Shadybrook Found Beauty (by Ch. Sirhan Kaissack ex Ch. Baguette Duncan) bred by Joan Carusone and William Woodley. Both were bred to Snow Stag and Pollo. Swan and Snow Stag produced the Majenkir champions Tolstaya Sherst and Pastel Portrait. Swan and Pollo produced the Majenkir champions Birchwood Vonka, Serafix Siberius, Tsarina Tsuzy, Ms of Dragonflite and Taras Shevchenko. Beauty bred to Snow Stag produced Moonfrost and Katya Krilatka both Majenkir champions the latter owned by John Czech and Pedro Diaz. Moonfrost was bred to Gyrfalcon to produce Ch. Majenkir Moonfalcon. Beauty and Pollo produced Ch. Hoflin's Apollo Don Hoflin owned as a foundation bitch by Glen Downey in Canada and Majenkir Grand Noble. Ch. Majenkir Wotan of Foxcroft, the group and specialty winning dog owned by Angela San Paolo, was produced from a breeding of Grand Noble to Tsuzy.

Gyrfalcon's stud record is almost an equal to his two kennelmates Snow Stag and Pollo. Bred to Don Hoflin's Ch. Velox Eryn he sired Ch. Aaronoff Belina of Calypso and Ch. Aaronoff Belitzar of Troykov. Bred to Kathy Davey and E. Abello's Ch. Sardonyx of Cordova he sired Ch. Kharma's Touch of Class. Bred to Jim and Joyce Gibson's Ch. Olga's Tenna of Fosteria he sired Ch. Tbilisi's Petrushka and Ch. Tbilisi's Pavlamishka Tsuzie. Bred at Majenkir to Tsuzy he sired Ch. Majenkir Artizan. H. Cowan and Nancy Rosenzweig sent their Ch. Countrybar's Barefoot Contessa to Gyrfalcon to produce Ch. Troykov Noble Thunderbird.

In general, Majenkir specializes in white Borzoi as Karen admits to preference for the white Borzoi. However, whether with or without color, Majenkir Borzoi have been a force to reckon with in the show and producing records to date.

In the 1960's the Bachelor's Forest Kennels of Joanna and David Abraham was established with littermates Ch. Bachelor's Forest Redwood and Ch. Bachelor's Forest Walnut (by Ataman of Kai-Lyn ex Haljean's Marina). The kennel name was taken from a development where they originally lived and the original intention was to use tree names as part of the names of their dogs. After moving to a more rural setting all that changed. The kennel name then became de Foret. They purchased Rena Sorvan of Rancho Gabriel (by Ch. Rogue of Rancho Gabriel C.D. ex Ch. Pocahontas of Rancho Gabriel). Walnut was bred to Ch. Count Alexandr of Cordova to produce Ch. Sweet William de Foret who in turn sired Ch. Kostenov Barrymore and Ch. Sasha Tigrero de Foret. The Walnut daughter Ch. Felicia de Foret was bred to Redwood to produce their Ch. Sumo de Foret. Rena was bred to Redwood to produce Ch. Mango de Foret. Walnut was sent to California to be bred to Ch. Ranchitos Silversheen (by Kasoss of Twin Elms ex Russell's Naughty Princess) which produced Ranchitos Camellia de Foret going to Audrey Dodson and Ecco de Foret going to Nancy Shaner MacLean.

Dean and Louise Heaton established their Cordova Kennels in Annapolis, Maryland. Their first Borzoi was Ch. Mikhail of Woodhill. Mikhail was bred to Loral's Alpha Yurochka to produce Ch. Loral's Cherneela Sanya owned by the Marshann Kennels and the dog that was to be renamed Kolchak V, the mascot of the Wolfhound Regiment in Hawaii. He was bred to the McCluskey's Ch. Sascha of Baronoff and it was from this litter that Louise picked her foundation bitch who was to establish an outstanding record both in the show ring and in the whelping box. This bitch was the red and white Ch. Cordova Mishka of Baronoff. In six litters she produced 18 champions including the following: Ch. Cordova's Cameo Carenya and Ch. Cordova's Camisado (by Ch. Bronze Falcon of Woodhill), Ch. Count Alexandr of Cordova and Ch. Cossack Andrei of Cordova (by Ch. Tersai of Gwejon); the Cordova champions Stefan Ivanov and Staritza (by Ch. Cossack Andrei of Cordova); the Cor-

Ch. Cordova Mishka of Baronoff was bred by the McCluskeys at their Baronoff Kennels and owned by Louise Heaton as the foundation bitch for her Cordova Kennels in Maryland. In six litters Mishka produced 18 champions. She is shown here winning the BCOA national specialty at Trenton in 1967 under Judge Julia Shearer. *Gilbert*

dova champions Tassandra, Tisha, Tovarich C.D., Tamara (by Ch. Galand's Alexander); and in the repeat breeding the champions Milova, Majeschka, Misha and Mendeleev; the Cordova champions Pegasus and Paasha (by Ch. Sirhan Poraschai). Although Louise bred her other bitches and those she co-owned with Francoise Einstein rather successfully, the breedings of Mishka are those that proved most productive and those that made the kennel name of Cordova well known during the eleven years (1961-72) it was in existence.

Nelshire is a kennel name associated with both Borzoi and Italian Greyhounds of quality. Eileen Nelson first had a bitch from Ristovia, Ristovia's Shahzara Ciona. She then bought the bitch to become her first Borzoi champion Tisha of Cordova. Shahzara was bred to Ch. Mendeleev of Cordova, a full brother to Tisha to produce Ch. Nelshire's Porta-Geist. Tisha was bred to Ch. Sorvan of TamBoer producing Ch. Nelshire's Milayna Makhaylia. Ch. Majeschka of Cordova was purchased and she also was bred to Sorvan to produce Dimitri v Gathonn, a champion proudly owned by Jonnie Gathings. A Dimitri and Tisha breeding produced the furturity winner Nelshire's Cameo Careyna.

Dr. Alfred Edlin established his Ridgeside Kennels in New Jersey with Ch. Galand's Tamara of Cordova C.D. (by Ch. Galand's Alexander ex Ch. Cordova Mishka of Baronoff) as his foundation bitch. He also bought Ch. Czar, litter brother of Alexander, from the Galand kennels. His first litter from these two was quite successful including as it did Ch. Ridgeside Prince Witcoff C.D. and Ch. Ridgeside Smoke Cloud C.D. Smoke Cloud was bred to Czar's litter brother Ch. Galand's Baronoff to produce the two bitches Ch. Ridgeside Toasted Honey and Ch. Ridgeside Burnt Sugar owned by Carol and Cabanne Smith. When Honey was bred to Ch. Majenkir Sverkai Snow Stag C.D., she produced Ch. Ridgeside Icecapade, Ch. Ridgeside Smoke Cloud, Ch. Ridgeside Alexander Borodin and Ch. Ridgeside Sir Prize Package. The sable marked bitch Majenkir Robed in Ermine was obtained from the Majenkir Kennels and bred to Prince Witcoff to produce Ch. Ridgeside Golden Brandy and Ch. Ridgeside Witcoff Power. When she was bred to Ch. Majenkir Gyrfalcon she produced Ch. Ridgeside Eve of Ermine.

At first located in Maryland, Nancy MacLean (formerly Shaner) established the Conamor Kennels which were moved later to Ohio. Her foundation bitch was Ch. Hasu's Elena of Conamor C.D. (by Haljean's Flame ex Ch. Sunday of TamBoer). She also owned Elena's sister Ch. Hasu's Marina of Conamor. Elena was bred to Ch. Chudak of Romanoff (by Ch. Vigow of Romanoff III ex Ch. Tatiana of Alpine to produce her outstanding Ch. Conamor Count Tauskey C.D., Conamor Christoff Cade sold to Dennis and Cherry Jones, and Ch. Conamor Sir Alex of

Dirona sold to Helen Langner. Nancy obtained Ch. Conamar Chantilly de Foret (by Ch. Ranchitos Silversheen ex Bachelor's Forest Walnut) from the Abrahams. She was leased by the Pennylane Kennels of the Miskos and bred to Count Tauskey to produce for them Ch. Pennylane Brother of the Wind. Ch. Conamor Gay of Colonial Acres was bred to Conamor Ecco de Foret to produce Ch. Conamor Czar Khan sold to Dick Blandford. Gay was later sold to the Joneses. Before that, however, she was bred to Ch. Lejoy Carol's Vodka to produce Ch. Lejoy Conamor Carol's Charles.

Pennylane Kennels of Carol, Elaine and Helen Misko in Pittsburgh, Pennsylvania picked as their first Borzoi the red and white dog that was to become Ch. Loral's Igor Ivanevitch (by Ch. Trezor Ivan ex Ch. Loral's Electra Zorka). Igor was bred to JoWag's Czarina of Ristovia from which the Miskos took three puppies to become Ch. Pennylane's Kristof Demetri sold to Penny Sommers, Ch. Pennylane's Darling Maggie and Ch. Pennylane's Sacha Igorjevitch. Loral's Royal Tiara (by Ch. Loral's Iossif Ivanevitch ex Loral's Charisma of Sunbarr) was purchased, bred to Igor, and produced Ch. Pennylane's Chateaugay. As we have seen above, Ch. Conamor Gay of Colonial Acres was leased for her litter containing Ch. Pennylane Brother of the Wind. The Miskos owned several other Borzoi that were finished: Ch. Loral's Oulitza (by Ch. Loral's Mudrei Sava C.D. ex Ch. Loral's Iskra Ivanovna C.D.), Can. Ch. Loral's Whirlaway of Pennylane (by Piotr Illjitsch van Borjoschka ex Ch. Loral's Nadezhda), and Rancho Gabriel Santa Inez (by Perchoten Bojar ex Ch. Rosia Dosa of Rancho Gabriel).

The Cathcade Kennels of Dennis and Cherry Jones of Richmond, Maine took its name from their first Borzoi Conamor Christoff Cade (by Ch. Chudak of Romanoff ex Ch. Hasu's Elena of Conamor C.D.). Cade sired their most outstanding Ch. Cathcade Curio (ex Shadybrook Ladi of Wilolea) and his litter brother Ch. Cathcade Cato sold to Nadine Eaton and Rene Chicoine. One of their winning bitches was a daughter of Curio (ex Ch. Majenkir Asta) Ch. Yasnayas Cathcade Kassatka co-bred by Robert Harvey and Karen Staudt. Her litter sister has also done some fine winning including some group placings, Ch. Yasnaya's Silva owned by Robert Harvey and shown by Dennis Jones. A Curio son Ch. Cathcade Bannik was bred by Mary Haigh out of her Ch. Conamor Cirena (by Conamor Christoff Cade ex Cable's Ronya) and co-owned by her and Dennis. Bannik like his father was a best in show winner.

In Miami, Florida Paul and Francoise Einstein started their Kalinka Kennels with the two bitches Ch. Staritza of Cordova (by Ch. Cossack Andrai of Cordova ex Ch. Cordova Mishka of Baronoff) and Ch. Tassandra

Ch. Loral's Igor Ivanevitch, the first Borzoi owned by the Pennylane Kennels of Carol, Elaine and Helen Misko in Pittsburgh, Pennsylvania.

Ch. Pennylane Brother of the Wind, bred and owned by Pennylane Kennels, is shown here winning points under Judge Garland Bell.

Klein

of Cordova (by Ch. Galand's Alexander ex Mishka). They also owned Ch. Toya of Baronoff Staritza bred to Toya produced Ch. Kashtanya of Kalinka. Tassandra bred to Ataman Andreevich Tom Catna yielded Ch. Ivana of Kalinka; bred to Ch. Conamor Count Tauskey she produced Ch. Kalina's Tiranka of Cordova. Toya bred to Solveig of Rancho Gabriel produced the first Kalinka champion Komar of Kalinka. Komar bred to Ch. Anastasia Nataskavitch Rama produced Ch. Count Basil of Kalinka. Paul purchased Ch. Kazan of Cordova and bred him to Natasha of Hollow to produce Ch. Krilat of Kalinka. Kashtanya was bred to Ch. Paasha or Cordova (by Ch. Sirhan Poraschai ex Ch. Cordova Mishka of Baronoff) to produce the Kalinka champions Kira and Katrina. In the early 1970's the Kalinka hounds were split between the Miami location and a new location in Maryland. Kalinka Borzoi were shown in both locations by Paul and Francoise.

Ch. Kira of Kalinka was sold to Ann Dill in Ocala, Florida for her Kumasan Kennels at which Ann also housed Ch. Conamor Lady Krista of HiHope. Krista was bred to Ch. Majenkir Taras Shevchenko to produce Ch. Kumasan's Cortada and Ch. Kumasan's Jasa. Cortada was bred to Ch. Astafiev Majenkir Masterpiece to produce the Kumasan champions Astafiev Cream Puff and Shadow of Astafiev. During the last few years Ann's energies have been directed more towards improving the excellence of her Borzoi and Salukis in lure coursing.

Although Edward Abblett's first Borzoi was a white male from Helen Colstad's Perchinoff Kennel, his preference has always been for the black hounds. He obtained the black Cindar Deacon of Aristoff (by The Night Hawk of Malora ex Kismet of Malora) and bred him to the dark blue marked bitch Loral's D Valhalla of Aristoff (by Ch. Loral's Alpha Nickolai ex Arlekeen of Frontier) producing the bitch owned by Diane True finishing her championship with two specialty wins — Ch. Sasha of Aristoff. Deacon's litter sister Whirling's Cricket of Malora was bred to the black and tan Vrozyat's Alpine Tartar Prince to produce Ch. Dark Duel of Aristoff, Ch. Berengeria of Aristoff, Ch. Loral's Yermak of Aristoff and Ch. Hardwicke Blazer of Aristoff. Yermak went to the Loral Kennels in Pennsylvania while the other three were retained by Aristoff in California. Two black and white bitches purchased by Ed were the littermates Ch. The Don's Zephora of Malora and Ch. Malora's Sparkle of the Don. All of these dogs and bitches were the start of the Aristoff Kennels.

Aristoff Kennels never housed more than a few Borzoi at a time as most of the bitches were farmed out on co-ownerships. Innumerable champions carry the Aristoff affix but those most remembered are those that came later after the purchase of Ch. Sirhan Poraschai from Audrey

Ch. The Don's Zephora of Malora was owned and finished by Edward Abblett and then sold to Yvonne Kall as the foundation bitch for her Kall of the Wild Kennels in California. *Ludwig*

Ch. Kall of the Wild's Zandor, the top winning Borzoi in 1970, was bred and owned by Yvonne Kall. He is shown here with his handler Yvonne Chashoudian and Judge Winifred Heckmann. *Bennett*

Benbow. Poraschai sired many litters out of Aristoff bitches as well as many others. In 1971 and 1972 Poraschai was the top winning Borzoi in this country. Many of his sons and daughters have done almost as well. The bitch Utka Alexander was bred to him by Karl and Elly Bonsack to produce among others Ch. Tambura's George von Berghof, Ch. Nikki Casandra von Berghof, Ch. Alexis Kosak von Berghof and Ch. Morningstar Mir von Berghof. George was top winning Borzoi for 1975 and 1976. Bred to Ch. Marvita's Ashani Phantom Lake, Poraschai sired the specialty winning white bitch Ch. Wildwood's Diva of Phantom Lake C.D.X. owned by John and Melinda Codling. The Phantom Lake Kennels in Washington produced many Poraschai champion sons and daughters as we shall see later. He also sired the black and white brace of Ch. Illyaan of Aristoff and Ch. Kureyakyn of Aristoff owned by Ron and Dyane Roth, a brace with a record of seventeen best brace in show wins. Carol Marshall bred her Ch. Katya Snow Maiden of Wilolea to Poraschai to produce among others Ch. Slavina of the Moorlands, Ch. Kamyenskya of the Moorlands, Ch. Koopava of the Moorlands, Ch. Ludmilla of the Moorlands. Other kennels using Poraschai to produce well for them were Rising Star, Cordova, Tamarisk and Phantom Lake.

Rosemary Gregg in Maryland purchased Crescent's Vamp of Tamarisk from the Tamarisk Kennels of Florence and Adrian Brian in Arizona out of a breeding of Poraschai to Ch. Kalinka of Aristoff. This breeding also produced Ch. Gang Buster of Tamarisk and Ch. Danilova's Gelert of Tamarisk. Vamp also became a champion and was soon thereafter bred to Ch. Loral's Iossif Ivanevitch producing Ch. Crescent's Arctic Glacier and Ch. The Crescent's Zarbo. Glacier has been used by many kennels to produce several champions. My favorite is the bitch Ch. Sundown's Charisma (ex Ristovia's Lady Tiffany) bred and owned by Nancy and Furman Joye.

Yvonne Kall established her Kall of the Wild Kennels in California. Her foundation bitch was purchased from Aristoff, Ch. The Don's Zephora of Malora. This bitch was bred to Ch. Vronsky of Volga producing Ch. Kall of the Wild's Zandor and Ch. Kall of the Wild's Zamora. The Van Roeckels bred their Ch. Locksley Hall's Clarionette to Zandor to produce Ch. Vanka's Czisse Kahlbah owned by Bob and Gene-Ann Bloomberg. Zandor was bred to his dam Zephora to produce Int. Ch. Kall of the Wild's Replica owned by Marvin and Sterra Maslin. Zandor was top winning Borzoi in 1970. Zamora was bred to the English import Ch. Dillon of Matalona (by Keepers Michael Angelo ex Krasa of Matalona) to produce Ch. Kall of the Wild Black Hawk. Zamora was bred to her brother Zandor producing Ch. Kall of the Wild's Dianna and Kall of the Wild's Dione owned by Florence and Phyllis Meyer.

Ch. Tassandra of Cordova and Ch. Kazan of Cordova were bred by Louise Heaton and co-owned with Paul and Francoise Einstein.

Ch. Crescent's Artic Glacier, owned by Rose Gregg, and his daughter Ch. Sundown's Charisma, owned by Nancy and Furman Joye, are shown winning best of breed and best opposite sex under Judge Lorraine Groshans. *Gilbert*

The Jobi Kennels of Joanne Jelke in Houston, Texas bred many litters in the mid to late 1960's heavily linebred on English Reyas stock. In the early 1970's Joanne started breeding small Borzoi averaging 24 inches in height, breeding down from standard-sized stock. Some, of course, are still standard size as witness the Beata's Red Sunbarr's son by Jobi Copper Fire; he is the best in show dog Ch. My Lil Tuff Salty Dog owned by Joyce Mabry.

In 1960 Tau-Ceti of Hethivar (by Ch. Yermak's Rurick ex Ch. Alta of Alpine) was sold by Marge and Sid Cox to Audrey Dodson as the foundation bitch for her Ranchitos Kennels. Five years later Audrey purchased Ch. Ranchitos Silversheen (by Kasoss of Twin Elms ex Russell's Naughty Princess) and he did very well for her winning groups and specialties. Silversheen bred to Lois Cooper's Srinagar Kolotta of Aristoff C.D. sired the lovely self-black Ch. Ranchitos Nisa of Chulista. Bred to Ch. Bachelors Forest Walnut he sired Ranchitos Camellia de Foret. Camellia bred to Ch. Forzando Taras of Olympus produced Ch. Ranchitos Blue Paint. Bred to Ch. Sirhan Poraschai she produced the large striking Ch. Ranchitos P.J. (standing for Poras Junor of course) and the lovely Ch. Ranchitos Gypsy Rose Val Yet owned by Jean and Harold Lau. Gypsy Rose bred to PJ produced the white bitch Ch. Ranchitos Veronica Val Yet. Poraschai was also used on the bitch Ranchitos Manzanita Jill (by Silversheen ex Ranchitos Zanita de Foret) to produce Ch. Ranchitos White Debutant owned by the Laus and Ch. Ranchitos Darling Donna kept by Audrey.

Chester and Irene Bukwaz started their Buks Kennels in Michigan with Mikhailovna of Mich-Burg (by Michael of Whiskey Run ex Negra of Twin Elms) in 1959. At first Chester and Irene had no intention of showing or breeding although they were interested in obedience training. However, as so often happens, one thing led to another and in 1960 Chester decided to purchase the gray-brindle and white male Sunbarr Bengal Lancer (by Haljean's Tarquin of Malora ex Zanosa of Whiskey Run Hill). Lancer quickly earned his breed championship and also earned a C.D.X. obedience title. The breeding of Lancer and Nina produced Ch. Buk's Ben Nilance C.D., Ch. Buk's Torance Nalkim C.D. and Ch. Buk's Susan O'Grady C.D. Nalkim was bred to Yehudi (by Ch. Jaguar Jehan of Malora ex Jerel's Amber Dawn) producing three beauties: Ch. Buk's Renata C.D., Ch. Buk's Roxanne and Ch. Buk's Shadow U.D. Lancer was bred to Roxanne producing Ch. Buk's Viveca of Perrito C.D. and Ch. Rishar Nataczha of Perrito C.D. Irene had always admired Ch. Trezor Ivan so it was quite natural for her to purchase his son Ch. Trezor Lancer

Ch. Ranchitos PJ, bred and owned by Audrey Dodson, is shown winning the stud dog class as the 1978 BCNC Specialty under English breeder judge Reginald Basset. *Langdon*

Ch. Ranchitos Gypsy Rose Val-Yet and her daughter Ch. Ranchitos Veronica Val-Yet with owners Harold Lau and Audrey Dodson and Judge Kay Finch. *Francis*

132

of Buk's (ex Trezor Eudoxia) in 1966. He was a group winner that might have gone on to bigger and better things if it hadn't been for the debilitating effects of heartworm infestation and treatment. He did sire two outstanding litters. Bred to Nataczha in 1970 he sired Ch. Buk's Arrow U.D., Ch. Buk's Calliope U.D., Ch. Buk's Catherine C.D., Ch. Buk's Omar of Nayra C.D.X., Buk's Shafeek C.D. and Buk's Shafica C.D. the last named owned by Doug and Mary Marvel as a foundation bitch at their Marvel Kennels where they also owned Ch. Majenkir Siberian Sorvan C.D. (by Ch. Majenkir Sverkai Snow Stag C.D. ex Ch. Majenkir Kristal Fawn). In Trezor Lancer's second litter (ex Nataczha) were Ch. Buk's and Fox Run El Toro U.D. and Buk's and Fox Run Genie C.D. Ch. Buk's Calliope U.D. was bred to Buk's Sambar of Fox Run to produce Buk's R Penelope C.D. winner of the 1978 BCOA award for obedience. The Buk's record in both breed and obedience is truly an outstanding one. Chester and Irene have earned a place of honor for themselves in Borzoi history.

David and Violet Ristau started their Ristovia Kennels in Warren, Pennsylvania in the 1950's combining Hensy Hobby Farm stock with Frontier. One of their first bitches was Brizhi of Frontier (by Safga of Grador ex Barishnya of Frontier). Bred to Komar of Frontier she produced Ristovia's Quicksilver and Ristovia's Prince Igorsky. Both of these males were bred to basically Sunbarr bitches producing Ch. Ristovia's Felwood Boja (Quicksilver ex Tara of Holly Grove) and the bitch Ch. Ristovia's Countess Tina (Igorsky ex Sunbarr's Sonya of Kirklea). The breeding of Tina and Silver produced a number of champions including Ch. Ristovia's Raskoli Baroness, Ch. Ristovia's Tsarevna Sheeba (foundation bitch for Arthur and Mary Neal's Tsarevna Kennels), Ch. Ristovia's Prince Komar, Ch. Ristovia's Czar of Zencor (owned by Asa and Karen Mays), Ch. Ristovia's Baron Dmitri (owned by Doris Ludy), and Ch. Ristovia's Mikola Voroshilov (owned by Steve Baxter). The breeding also produced the bitch Ristovia's Lady Tiffany going to Nancy and Furman Joyce's Sundown Kennels in Virginia. Tiffany was bred to her brother Dmitri to produce Ch. Sundown's Darius for the Joyes. Bred to Ch. Cossack's Aristotle (by Ch. Loral's Iossif Ivanevitch ex Ch. Petrikov Tascha of Helicon) she produced Ch. Sundown's Buccaneer and Ch. Sundown's Czarina. For her third litter, the Joyes bred Tiffany to Ch. Crescent's Arctic Glacier (by Ch. Loral's Iossif Ivanevitch ex Ch. Crescent's Vamp of Tamarisk) to produce the bitch Ch. Sundown's Charisma who finished going best of winners at the 1978 national specialty after placing in the group at the age of ten months.

The Zencor Kennels of Dr. Asa Mays and his wife Karen began with the acquisition of Ch. Baroness Inessa El Saba (by Ch. Akim Saba of Wolfschmidtzoff ex Queen Rurick), a group placing bitch. She was bred to Ch. Ristovia's Czar of Zencor for two litters which were of high quality making her a top producing bitch for five champion get three of which have had group placings from the classes. Three of the five that were retained at Zencor are Ch. Zencor Charlemagne, Ch. Zencor Catherine the Great and Ch. Zencor's Ahnidja. When Ahnidja was bred to Ch. Cossack's Aristotle (with Thomas and Marie Smythe as co-breeders), she produced Ch. Utkinton Zencor Alyta for Zencor and Ch. Utkinton Ajax of Zencor for the Utkinton Kennels of the Smythes.

Hugh James and Anna Bell Ungerleider shared a common interest in German Shepherd Dogs before they were married in 1961. After marriage, Anna switched her allegiance to Borzoi while her husband continued in Shepherds. Her first Borzoi Ch. Sunbarr's Anna Karenenya (by Haljean's Tarquin of Malora ex Zanosa of Whiskey Run Hill) was bred to Ch. Bronze Falcon of Woodhill (by Ch. Black Falcon of Twin Elms ex Ch. Tanya of Ladoga) to produce champions Sergei, Nicholas, Maxim, Anatol, Alexander and Anastasia, all of Windy Hill. Anastasia was shown extensively by her owner and accumulated an enviable record including specialty and group wins. She joined that small but elite group of Borzoi bitches that have won best in show, and she had two such wins. In 1966 Anna imported from England Ch. Zomahli Evolgo (by Zomahli Byasha ex Ch. Zavist of Carradale) bred by L. Pearson and K. Prior. The Windy Hill Kennels were brought to the attention of all nationwide as Anna campaigned Evolgo. He finished his American championship with group wins from the classes and went on to pile up an outstanding record of 124 best of breed, 110 group placings and 13 bests in show. By the time he was retired he had champion titles in England, United States, Bermuda, Canada and Mexico plus an international championship. He was top winning Borzoi in this country for 1967, 1968 and 1969. Anna's travels campaigning Evolgo were almost beyond belief. She thought nothing of showing on Saturday in Michigan or Indiana and then hopping a plane with Evolgo to show in Mississippi or Louisiana on Sunday. Unfortunately, Evolgo was never home long enough to sire more than a few litters. Sunbarr's Domini of Windy Hill was purchased specifically for breeding to him. The bitch Vala Rama's Lure of the Fflame was leased from the Conallys and bred to Evolgo producing among others Ch. Vala Rama's Jewel of Windy Hill and Ch. Vala Rama's Janda of Windy Hill. Anna died in 1970, Evolgo shortly thereafter and the kennel was soon dispersed. Anna's husband Jim applied for AKC approval to judge Borzoi and has been serving the breed in that capacity since then.

Ch. Trezor Lancer of Buk's, owned by Chester and Irene Bukwaz, being awarded best of breed by Judge Lorraine Groshans on his way to group first. *Booth*

Ch. Anastasia of Windy Hill, a group and best in show winning bitch, was bred, owned and handled by Anna Ungerleider. She is shown here going up under Judge Haskell Schuffman. *Conlon*

Ch. Cossack's Frivolous Fawn, a group winning bitch bred by C. Campbell and H. Ohlinger, was owned and handled by Jane Maddox in West Virginia. She is shown here with her owner and Judge Charles Herendeen. *Booth*

Int. Ch. Zomahli Evolgo, imported by Anna Ungerleider, was the winner of 13 bests in show in this country becoming top winning Borzoi in the U.S. for 1967, 1968, and 1969. *Frank*

136

The Korsakov Kennels of Jane Maddox started in West Virginia with the purchase of Ch. Loral's Matvey C.D.X. The first bitch was Ch. Cossack's Frivalous Fawn (by Ch. Cossack's Aristotle ex Ch. Cossack's Aphrodite) a group winner and placer. Fawn was bred to Matvey to produce the two bitches Ch. Korsakov Antigone owned by Debbie Littleton and Ch. Korsakov Altay Alesksei owned by Suzan Wilder. Another bitch added to the kennel is Ch. Loral's Yves Korsakov (by Ch. Laba's Arimsky ex Ch. Loral's Sporting Field Ulova). Fawn has also been bred to Ch. Crescent's Arctic Glacier and Ch. Aurora's Fun 'n Fancy of Lohee (by Ch. Lohee's V'Indra Bounte ex Butte Hills Nonnie). Yves was bred to a Matvey son (ex Andrevia Tolstoy of LaMac) Andrew Benzarr of LaMac.

The Stillwater Kennels of Kathe and Charles Tyson started in Florida and then moved to Tennessee. In addition to their Ch. Sunbarr's Cavalier of Dana Dan (by Malora's Bede of Sunbarr ex Sobrina of Sunbarr Ranch), the Tysons purchased a number of Sunbarr bitches after the Sunbarr Kennel was dispersed. One that they finished was Ch. Stillwater's Frost of Sunbarr (by Romulus of Sunbarr ex Deserie of Sunbarr). They also owned Ch. St. Just Krillut of Sirhan (by Ch. Sirhan Porchai ex Ch. Sirhan Raskolnika) and Ch. Vala Rama's Color Me Blue (by Ch. Vala Rama's Phoenix of Sunbarr ex Ch. Vala Rama's Funny Girl).

Although they have produced many colors in their Borzoi, Ardietta and Paul Thompson are rather known for the lovely soft silver-blue brindle colors on their Dana Dan hounds. The foundation bitch in 1964 was Ch. Baroness Bianca of Dana Dan (by Ch. Blaise II of Sunbarr ex Ch. Barefood Contessa of Dana Dan). Their first winning dog was Ch. Sunbarr Lancer of Dana Dan (by Sunbarr's Night Watch ex Malora's Beata of Sunbarr) with a best in show to his credit. From a breeding of Lady Edycia of Sunbarr (by Malora's Blaise of Sunbarr ex Ginka of Sunbarr) to Lancer, the Thompsons obtained their 1976 MBC Specialty winner Ch. Edycia's Adonis of Dana Dan. A breeding of Lancer and Bianca produced another specialty winner owned by Gregory and Prudence Key, Ch. Ilya Murometz of Dana Dan.

In Illinois, near the Wisconsin border, are the Nightsong Kennels of Henry and Joyce Brandin. Although Joyce dreamed of owning a Borzoi all through her childhood, it was not until 1964 that she purchased her first two: Ch. Nightsong Thor of Sunbarr (by Wotan of Sunbarr Ranch ex Andante of Sunbarr Ranch) and Ch. Nightsong Alix of Sunbarr (by Malora's Bede of Sunbarr ex Zanosa of Sunbarr Ranch). From a breeding of these two came the group winning self-black brace later exported to South America: Ch. Fflame's Sabre Dancer and Fflame's Thunderball.

Ch. Nightsong Thor of Bunbarr is shown with owners Henry and Joyce Brandin winning the veterans class at an MBC Specialty under English breeder-judge Eileen Ruggles. *Booth*

The Nightsong foundation bitch Ch. Nightsong Alix of Sunbarr is handled here by Henry Brandin with Judge Earl Adair. *Ritter*

Nightsong next purchased a silver and white bitch from Audrey Benbow to be named Ch. Sirhan Kara of Nightsong (by Ch. Sirhan Kaissack ex Ch. Sirhan Katya). Kara was bred to Thor to produce Ch. Nightsong Casanova, Ch. Nightsong is Happiness and Ch. Nightsong Bellhound.

Thor was also bred to Bob's Samantha (by Sunbarr's Tristan ex Malora's Bianca of Sunbarr Ranch) to produce the group winning Ch. Dalusha owned by Carol Stell and Betty Halesky of the Debonaire Kennels in Illinois. Another group winner was the mahogany and white male Ch. Aries Bernard Thor sired by Thor for owner Bente Opsahl.

Alix was bred to the English import Lasky of Ukrainia (by Boris of Ukrainia ex Wendylon of Yadasar) to produce Ch. Nightsong Black Orpheus, Ch. Nightsong Narcissus and the group winning Ch. Debonaire Darius O'Nightsong owned by Debonaire. Another bitch going to Debonaire was Ch. Debonaire Dominique (ex Fflame's Diana the Huntress) a top producer. Her litter brother was Ch. Silde Nightsong the Assassin, a specialty winner in 1974, owned by Dede Diehl.

Since Joyce felt she was doing so well with crossing English lines with the original Sunbarr, she then tried several English imports. Several seemed quite promising but did not live to produce. She then imported two puppies from Eileen Ruggles, Ch. Matalona Nightsong Hawk and Matalona Nightsong Robin. She also imported the bitch Racingold Diana (by Dougal of Matalona ex Racingold Minuet), a self-black.

A few miles south of Nightsong are the Oaklara Kennels of Pat Murphy. Her two foundation bitches were Afebra of Pillow Hill (by Ch. Loral's Iossif Ivanevitch ex Loral's Apache of Marshann) bred by Tom Jessie and Ch. Loral's Royal Charisma (by the same sire ex Loral's Charisma of Sunbarr) bred by Lorraine Groshans. Charisma was bred to Ch. Hollingdahl Ivan of Silde (by Ch. Nightsong Thor of Sunbarr ex Nightsong Andalusia) to produce an outstanding first litter which yielded the following champions with the Oaklara prefix: Aaron, Augustus, Antina and Alexis. Afebra was bred to Ch. Nightsong is Happiness (by Ch. Nightsong Thor of Sunbarr ex Ch. Sirhan Kara of Nightsong) producing Ch. Oaklara's Baree Sergai. Alexis was bred to Bristol Creme to produce Ch. Oaklara's Fyodore, Ch. Oaklara's Fantabulous Fred and Ch. Oaklara's Felicitations.

The Bokara Kennels of Richard and Shen Smith in Michigan first commanded attention with the winning of their Ch. Nightsong A Debonaire Dandy (by Ch. Debonaire Doremus of Silde ex Debonaire Deverie). The foundation bitch at the kennel was Ch. Vanessa of Rising Star (by Ch. Sirhan Poraschai ex Ch. Blythe Spirit of Rising Star) in 1973 bred by Nadine Johnson. Vanessa was bred to Ch. Sirhan Kaitar (by Ch. Sirhan

Ch. Hollingdahl Ivan of Silde, the sire of Oaklara's first litter of four champions, is shown here winning the points under Judge Frank Booth. *Olson*

Ch. Oaklara's Bristol Creme, a group winner bred and owned by Pat Murphy in Illinois, is shown here with handler Dick Cooper and Judge Herman Cox. *Olson*

140

Kaissack ex Ch. Sirhan Pleshka) to produce Ch. Bokhara's Bangalor of Rai-Mar owned by Ray and Marcia Trottier, the multi-group winning bitch Ch. Bokhara's Belladonna kept by the Smiths and Ch. Bokhara's Bresitka co-owned by K. Prince. Dandy bred to Vanessa produced Ch. Bokhara's Play It Again Sam. The Smiths imported Ch. Francehill Diamond Ring (by Ch. Sadko of Colhugh ex Ch. Francehill Diamond Lil). Ring was bred to Sam producing a nice litter, but soon thereafter died in a kennel accident.

In May of 1980, Shen and Richard purchased the cream and white Utkinton Ajax of Zencor (by Ch. Cossack's Aristotle ex Ch. Zencor's Ahnidja) from Tom Smythe with Tom retaining co-ownership. Within the next three months Ajax had finished his championship with a Best in Show from the classes plus another Best in Show and seven group placings becoming a new star at Bokhara.

Oklahoma is the home of the Duncan Kennels of Dwyer and Helga Duncan. Their foundation bitch in 1951 was Artemis and Huntress Del Vos (by Atlas ex Princess Sylvia of Millvale). Artemis was bred to Count Boris Patri (by Winjones Pavlin) to produce a litter of nine. The bitch Ballerina Duncan and dog Ch. Otto Duncan were retained. The other seven puppies and Artemis were given to a Kansas woman. Otto was also given away as a pet after finishing his championship. One of the seven given away became Ch. Barin Boriski, sire of Ch. Gregory of Twin Elms and Ch. Volney of Twin Elms among others.

Ballerina was never shown but she was a superior pet and hunter. Bred to Ch. Pushkin of Seacroft (by Dark Hazard of Malora ex Haljean's Mystery) she produced Ch. Taranto Duncan and Ch. Ballet Duncan. Bred to Ch. Moon Hawk of Malora (by Winjones Paskoss ex Ch. Zelda Shaun of Malora C.D.) she produced equally well. Moon Hawk was bred to Sunbarr Dark Angel of Malora (by Malora's Blaise of Sunbarr ex Twilight of Sunbarr Ranch) to produce the white dog for which this kennel is best remembered by most people — Ch. Adage Duncan C.D. Ballet was bred to Adage to produce Ch. Shandan Duncanof Lazy Acres sold to Pat Lovelace. After her second litter, Ballerina was sold to a Colorado wolf-hunter.

The Moon Hawk-Ballerina litter produced Blagueur Duncan and Ch. Prima Ballerina Duncan C.D. Also in the litter were Ch. Baguette Duncan and Ch. Misty Duncan. Blagueur sired Ch. Coquette Duncan becoming the mainstay in the breeding program. Coquette and Adage produced Ch. Fandango Duncan, Ch. Haughty Duncan and Ch. Naughty Duncan C.D. Coquette bred to Ch. Bimbelot Duncan (by Blagueur) produced Ch. His Highness Duncan who in turn sired Ch. Wichita Duncan. It is felt by the

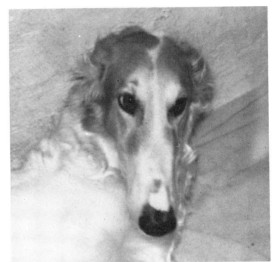

Ch. Coquette Duncan, bred and owned
by Helga and Dwyer Duncan, was considered one of their finest brood bitches.

Ch. His Highness Duncan, bred and owned by Helga and Dwyer Duncan, is considered by them as coming closest to
their ideal Borzoi. *Twomey*

142

Duncans that Blagueur has been the most potent stud of their breeding program passing on the characteristics they most desire.

Many of the linebred Duncan Borzoi have served as showdogs, racing hounds on a Greyhound track, obedience trialers and companions. All animals in the breeding program come from a multifaceted selection. The linebreeding carried on has been a concentration of the characteristics of Moon Hawk as in the pedigrees of the current generation of hounds he appears 40 times in nine generations. Duncan appears in the pedigrees of many of the major kennels. Pure Duncan has gone to Rurik, Deblar, Tuff, Nagel, Lazy Acres and Arnolf.

The kennel of Suzanne Hallberg in Kansas was known for the first few years as Bountiful and then changed to Arnolf. Her foundation bitch was Loral's Janda Alexander (by Ch. Loral's Yermak of Aristoff ex Ch. Loral's Kari Kostenov). Janda was bred to Ch. Zolotoi Volni of Twin Elms (by Ch. Barin Borisky ex Ziada of Twin Elms) to produce Ch. Bountiful's Vassily Alexis owned by Kristy Harris and Ch. Bountiful's Erik the Red. Erik was bred to Nightsong Starfire to produce Ch. Arnolf Alexander of Domaj. Suzanne purchased the bitch C.H. Hot Pants Duncan (by Ch. Bimbelot Duncan ex Ch. Coquette Duncan) and she was bred to Alexander to produce Ch. Arnolf's Roman Cavalier. Hot Pants was bred to Ch. Laba's Arimsky to produce Ch. Arnolf's Olga, Ch. Arnolf's Yuri Gagarin and the especially lovely red and white Ch. Arnolf's Leaping Lena who won best of breed over specials at only eight months of age and finished at 14 months with a total of four breed wins over specials.

The Rising Star Kennels have been located in Texas and Alaska and are currently in Colorado, but they are known in all parts of the country. Owners of the kennel are Nadine and Louis Johnson. Nadine started with two American-bred bitches in 1966 but in spite of loving them dearly decided that she wanted to start her breeding program with the best possible stock. She contacted an uncle who was then president of the Brussels' Federation Cynologique Internationale (FCI) to ask his advice on locating superior quality Borzoi. From his suggestions, Nadine contacted Madame d'Arbelles who had bred Borzoi for over 40 years in France under the kennel name Morton Hall. Two bitches were purchased: Int. Ch. Q'Blietzka des Balalaikas (by Ch. Kamenetz of Morton Hall ex Oasis du Bois de Fontenelle) and Q'Ariana d'Ymanville (by Otchame Kamenovitch de Morton Hall ex Olika d'Ymanville).

Blietzka bred to Ch. Llebasi Prince O'Lutolf (by Ch. Akim Saba of Wolfschmidtzoff ex Sascha Duchesse Narishkin) produced Mex. Ch. Balderan of Rising Star, Can. Ch. Sascha of Rising Star, Belg. Ch. Boris of Rising Star and Ch. Balzac of Rising Star. Ariana, though not a cham-

Can. and Am. Ch. Blythe Spirit of Rising Star was bred, owned and handled by Nadine Johnson at her Rising Star Kennels.
Bennett

Int. Ch. Kazan of Rising Star, a winner in the shows and as a stud dog for breeder-owner Nadine Johnson.

144

pion herself due to an injured foot, became the more important of the two from whom all Rising Star Borzoi are now descended. Her litter by Prince O'Lutolf yielded Can. Ch. Mishka of Rising Star, Mex. and Am. Ch. Rising Star's Ghost Dancer C.D., Ch. Blue Diamond of Rising Star, and Ch. Blythe Spirit of Rising Star.

Blythe Spirit was bred four times and is the dam of the following champions: (by Ch. Sirhan Poraschai) Ch. Vanessa of Rising Star, Ch. Voychek of Rising Star and Ch. Vega of Rising Star; (by Can. Ch. Mishka of Rising Star) Int. Ch. Kazan of Rising Star and Int. Ch. Karisma of Rising Star; (by Ch. Nightsong A Debonaire Dandy) Ch. Mazurka of Rising Star and Ch. Mishka A of Rising Star.

Kazan has established a proud record as a producer as well as a show dog. This three time specialty winner has sired the following champions: (ex Ch. Vega of Rising Star) Ch. Toolik of Rising Star, Ch. Melody Tonsina of Rising Star, Can. Ch. Tatellina of Rising Star, Ch. Fazan of Rising Star and Ch. Fabian of Rising Star; (ex Can. Ch. Francehill Party Piece of Jonwin) Ch. Waco of Rising Star, Ch. Wind 'n Fire of Rising Star and Ch. Wabash of Rising Star.

In Georgia, Annette Foster has been breeding Fosteria Borzoi for several years. She is best known for Ch. Great Heart of Fosteria (by Ch. Keepers Romance) specialty winner and top winning Borzoi for 1973. Ch. Tanya of Wolfschmidtzoff was bred to Ch. Keepers Romance to produce Ch. Lady Romance of Fosteria. Lady was bred to Ch. Wolfschmidtzoff Rez Kelton to produce Ch. Lovers Natscha of Fosteria and Ch. Fosteria's Desiderata. A full brother to Lady Romance, Ch. Lord Saul of Fosteria also sported a C.D.X. degree.

The Willowview Kennels were established in Colorado by Douglas and Joyce Arns. The self-black, group winning Ch. Willowview's Shondar Eclipse (by Vrozyat's Alpine Chuda ex Ch. Sultana of Shondar) is probably the best known dog owned by this kennel. Eclipse bred to Ch. Rathrahilly Rose of Shondar (by Ch. Moonhawk of Malora ex Rathrahilly Misha) produced Willowview's Scheherazade who was bred to Wildwind's Flame of Willowview (of Shondar and Kostenov lines) to produce Ch. Willowview's Wildfire. Eclipse bred to Anavar of Pillow Hill (by Ch. Loral's Iossif Ivanevitch ex Loral's Apache of Marshann) produced Ch. Rimski's Shonadar owned by Jon and Penny Sommers.

The first Borzoi owned by Aatis Lillstrom was the self cream brindle Clouds Clouds Wish O'Twin Elms (by Ch. Duke Alexander of Twin Elms ex Zarka of Twin Elms). After their marriage Aatis and Ping moved to western Pennsylvania and bred Borzoi on their Windhound farm. They purchased Silk Will Smoke of Sunbarr (by Ch. Tammogin of Sunbarr ex

Malora's Beata of Sunbarr) and bred her to their original dog to produce Ch. Windhound's Belle Canto. Belle was bred back to her sire to produce the white Ch. Windhound's Cybele Cycle. In 1976, they imported Int. Ch. Amurat v d Zilverstrand (by Int. Ch. Alexander v d Emelenberg ex Int. Ch. Sirotka v d Sabatchnaja Izba) that they co-own with Jack and Jean Vandongen.

For many years the Pacific Northwest was populated by very few Borzoi and even fewer Borzoi breeders. This situation came to an abrupt end when Phyllis Brettell started buying and breeding Borzoi. Her lovely home located on Phantom Lake near Seattle has housed up to a hundred Borzoi, Afghans, Greyhounds, Salukis, Foxhounds and others at one time. Eventually her two daughters Helen Ybarra and Cecilia Barnett joined Phyllis in showing and breeding Borzoi. The kennel, quite naturally, took the name Phantom Lake.

In 1965 Phyllis bought Ch. Wesbrook's Tamazar (by Ch. Aynsley Serge ex Ch. Aynsley Nada) who finished rapidly infecting Phyllis with a bad case of show fever. Soon after that she purchased Natasha of Winmart (by Rodion of Van Strom ex Ramadan's Yermak Alyssa) and Ch. Zinaida of Aynsley (by Can. Ch. Alcides of Tyree ex Can. Ch. Aynsley Delia). Both bitches were bred, but Phyllis found that she didn't enjoy breeding, whelping and puppy care as much as she enjoyed the more mature dogs. She purchased several dogs from various kennels and finished most of them: Ch. Evoljunov of Kranjcevich (by Int. Ch. Zomahli Evolgo ex Ch. Shadowrock Laimant), Ch. Wesbrook's Ballet Russe (Tamazar's litter brother), Ch. Inca Jo-Ao of Vala Rama (by Ch. Vala Rama's Phoenix of Sunbarr ex Ch. Vala Rama's Pandora of Sunbarr), Ch. Aynsley Nada (by Can. Ch. Alcides of Tyree ex Can. Ch. Aynsley Delia), Ch. Marvita's Ashani Phantom Lake (by Aquilla D'Oro of Aurora ex Sunbarr Zula of Malora), Ch. Wesbrook's Tanya (by Ch. Aynsley Nikolai ex Can. Ch. Tyree Bellona), Ch. Phaedra of Vala Rama (by Ch. Trezor Ramadi of Vala Rama ex Ch. Vala Rama's Pandora of Sunbarr), Can. Ch. Sirhan Tamaroff (by Ch. Sirhan Wilolea Teryoshka ex Ch. Sirhan Pleshka), Can. Ch. Kelcrest Blue on Blue (by Ch. Vala Rama Color Me Blue ex Pele of Prekrasnaya), Can. Ch. Windy Hills Legacy Lenore (by Int. Ch. Zomahli Evolgo ex Sunbarr's Domini of Windy Hill), Tovaresh of Rising Star (by Ch. Kazan of Rising Star ex Ch. Vega of Rising Star) and Sunbarr Lilla of Malora (by Beau Gest of Sunbarr ex Sunbarr's Midnight Lace).

Ch. Valia of Phantom Lake (by Ch. Wesbrook's Ballet Russe ex Wesbrook's Tanya) was bred to Ch. Sirhan Poraschai to produce a multichampion litter of Ch. Comanche of Phantom Lake, Ch. Phantom Lake's

Am. and Can. Ch. Wildwood's Diva of Phantom Lake CDX, a lovely white bitch with a nice record in both the breed and the obedience ring. She was bred by Phyllis Brettell and owned by John and Melinda Codling. She is shown here winning best of breed at the 1976 BCOA Western Specialty under Judge Leo Murphy. *Bennett*

Ch. Eglon of Karistan, a multi-group winner, was bred and owned by Irv and Nancy Bonios. *Bergman*

Painted Falcon, Ch. Ybarra's Phantom Lake Apache, Ch. Skaya of Phantom Lake, Ch. Seine of Phantom Lake and Ch. Iroquois of Phantom Lake.

One of the few totally home-bred litters (by Ch. Toshi's Alexei of Phantom Lake ex Ch. Valia of Phantom Lake) produced Ch. Alexei's Xandu of Phantom Lake who was winners dog at the BCOA specialty in Seattle in 1976 at the age of seven months.

During 1978 the number of dogs at the kennel had to be drastically reduced with most of the breeding and exhibiting being done by Helen and Cecilia.

A bit east of Seattle, in Spokane, Washington are the Chulista Kennels of Lois Cooper. The foundation bitch was Srinagar Kolotta of Aristoff C.D. (by Cindar Deacon of Aristoff ex Locksley Halls Rodalinda). Kolotta was bred to Ch. Ranchitos Silversheen to produce Ch. Natalie of Chulista C.D.X.. Kolotta was bred to Ranchitos Brother of Millie (a Silversheen grandson) to produce Viktor of Chulista. Viktor and Natalie produced Wildrose of Chulista. Next Lois purchased Ch. Ranchitos Tally-Ho Chulista C.D. (by Ch. Sirhan Poraschai ex Ranchitos Manzanita Jill) from Audrey Dodson. Tally bred to Wildrose produced Paladin of Chulista. A breeding of Paladin to Natalie produced the best Chulista litter to date containing Ch. Chulista Sunrise Sunset and Ch. Chulista Song Song Blue, a specialty winning and group placing bitch.

The foundation bitch for the Lejoy Kennels of Joyce and Carol Levine in Ohio was Lejoy Carol Sascha of Twin Elms (by Ch. Yanoff of Twin Elms ex Talia of Twin Elms) who was bred to Ch. Trezor Ivan to produce Ch. Lejoy Carol's Vodka. Vodka was bred to Nancy McLean's Ch. Conamor Gay of Colonial Acres from which litter Joyce and Carol picked the puppy that became Ch. Lejoy Conamor Carol's Charles. Loral's Sunbarr Genie (by Malora's Blaise of Sunbarr ex Dezdra of Sunbarr Ranch) was leased by Lejoy and bred to Vodka producing among others Ch. Lejoy Carol's Nichol. Charles was bred to Nichol producing the puppy who finished at only ten months of age, Ch. Lejoy Carol's Boris Badinoff. In 1976 Joyce purchased and Carol later finished Ch. Loral's Vanya Nikovitch (by Ch. Loral's Nika Timofe ex Loral's Charisma of Sunbarr).

The foundation bitch of Gail Rathbun's Windswept Kennels in Waverly, New York was the self-gold Ch. Kaoc's Katerina of Windswept C.D. (by Ch. Wilolea's Nuryiev of Kaoc ex Kaoc's Treasure of Sunbarr). Buttercup, as she was called, was bred twice to Ch. Loral's Iossif Ivanevitch producing the specialty and group placing bitches Ch. Windswept's Favorite Angel and Ch. Windswept's Wicked Marguerita, Ch. Windswept Whim of Dorado, Ch. Windswept Lioubov-Burke, Ch. Wind-

Winners bitch class at the Philadelphia national specialty in 1972: Cossack Questa Glory of Loral (winners bitch) owned by J. Campbell and H. Ohlinger; Shandra of Cordova owned by J. Cole; Cathcade Charisma (reserve winners) owned by C. and D. Jones; Sardonyx of Cordova owned by L. Heaton; Crescent's Vamp of Tamarisk owned by R. and G. Gregg.

Winners dog class at the Philadelphia national specialty in 1978: Sirhan Palauskey II (reserve winners) owned by J. and A. Benbow; Sirhan Tytianko of Windrift (winners dog) owned by D. Beaumont; Mytarka Thingell Greycloak owned by M. McNeil; Windrift Scepter owned by J. and N. Reimer; Loral's Dmitri Durov owned by L. Groshans.

149

swept Shenandoah, Can. Ch. Windswept Dalusha Burke and Ch. Windswept April Love. Marguerita went to Harriet and Gary Goldner to become the foundation bitch of their Echovesna Kennels in Ohio. She was bred to Ch. Loral's Urahna Khan (by Ch. Loral's Gusodar C.D. ex Ch. Loral's Iskra Ivanovna C.D.) to produce Ch. A Giggle of Echovesna and Ch. Echovesna's A Black Russian. Echovesna also owns Ch. Loral's Wish Upon a Star (by Piotr Illjitsch van Borjoschka ex Ch. Loral's Nadezhda).

Irv and Nancy Bonios established their Karistan Kennels in California with the acquisition of the bitch Ch. Pupkah-Luv of Aristoff (by Aristoff's Kyber of Jobi ex Ch. Malora's Sparkle of the Don). They soon thereafter bought Ch. Springbank Sarno (by Reyas Marquis ex Reyas Tonya) bred in England by Mrs. V. Sayre in 1966. The following year they imported Ch. Zomahli Gordey (by Ch. Black Diamond of Enolam ex Zomahli Nayada) bred by L. Pearson and K. Prior in 1967. A few years later they imported two bitches: Magic Glitter of Enolam (by Ch. Black Diamond of Enolam ex Francehill Martini of Enolam) and Ch. Keepers Melissa (by Ch. Michelangelo ex Falconcraig Ksarina) bred by Mrs. M. Malone and Mrs. J. Bennett-Heard respectively.

Sarno was bred only seven times but he produced eleven champions some of which were: Ch. Gregorian of Karistan and Ch. Karistan's Sarno of Hundaar (both ex Pupkah-Luv), Ch. Eglon of Karistan (ex Windy Hill's Fancy Tassy), and Ch. Morgyanna of Aristoff (ex Sherdon's Desiree of Aristoff). Bred to Sunbarr's Ebony Girl of Windy Hill (by Lasky of Ukrainia ex Orel of Sunbarr), he sired Karistan's Sarnoette. Gordey bred to Velox Gratsea of Karistan produced Ch. Karistan's Kashmari of Iam.

Irv and Nancy bred Melissa to Sirhan Wilolea Teryoshka (by Ch. Adage Duncan C.D. ex Springett Sheer Vanity) producing Ch. Karistan's Winter Ash, Ch. Karistan's Picasso and Ch. Karistan's Pegasus. Both Eglon and Pegasus established enviable show records for Karistan. The team of Eglon and Nancy created a picture of grace and beauty specially noted for the great rapport between hound and handler. Pegasus was sent east to live with Dick and Lynn Hlavin.

The foundation bitch of the Borogove Kennels of the Hlavins in Ohio was Bo-Mick's Desire of Borogove (by Ch. Sunbarr Berbeg Kashek Pasha ex Ch. Lejoy Bo-Mick Tanya) purchased in 1972. Desire was bred to Ch. Loral's Mudrei Sava C.D. (by Ch. Loral's Iossif Ivanevitch ex Ch. Loral's Kari Kostenov) producing Ch. Borogove's Azov Jasha, group placing Borogove's Azov Nikolenka and Borogove's Azov Miloska in 1973. In 1974 Lynn purchased the dog who became Ch. Karistan's Kazhan (by Ch. Karistan's Pegasbs ex Karistan's Kenya). Miloska was bred to Kazhan to produce Ch. Borogove's Czar Dimitri. A few years later Borogove was able to obtain both Pegasus and the English import bitch Ch. Tsarina of Enolam (by Ch. Petroff of Enolam ex Francehill Martini of Enolam) from the Karistan Kennels.

Ch. Chulista Song Sung Blue, bred and owned by Lois Cooper in Washington, is shown here winning her first points from the bred-by-exhibitor class handled by eight year old Jane Cooper under Judge Kurt Mueller. *Bennett*

4

History of the Borzoi in Other Countries

THE BORZOI BREED took the first step on the road to international recognition when the first one left Russia about the middle of the 17th century for a new homeland. From that day on, travelers returned with Borzoi they acquired during their journeys to their various native lands where they established kennels and formed breed clubs until these hounds are known now in all countries of the world. Due to language barriers, different methods of recording data, the inaccessibility of certain authentic records, and political situations which impose strict censorship on all information coming from a few countries, it is difficult to obtain a complete picture of the breed in all foreign lands. The facts presented here may give no more than a bird's eye view, but they are offered in the belief that this is better than no view at all.

Canada

Our northern neighbor Canada has had Borzoi registered with the Canadian Kennel Club since the end of the 19th century. In 1900 there were two dogs and three bitches registered, and in 1901 five dogs and four bitches were registered. Some of the first were imported by John G. Kent in Toronto, Ontario from General Boldareff's kennels in Russia.

During the next few years there were at least a half dozen individual breeders and exhibitors entering the Borzoi fancy. However, the great up-surge in interest came in 1907 when O.A. Zuercher in Ontario purchased

152

the three year old Valley Farm bitch Vintka II (by Bistri of Perchino ex Catherine the Great). She was an outstanding show specimen and when bred to Kopchic O'Valley Farm gave Mr. Zuercher his Ch. Czar of the Brook in 1908. Also in 1908 Mrs. M.C. O'Brien in Manitoba imported two Valley Farm hounds, Prenor and Bazar O'Valley Farm, and Mrs. Helene Barry imported Colne Bellina from the same source. These three hounds formed the American strain in Canadian Borzoi. Mrs. O'Brien, Mr. Zuercher and Dr. E.A. Harrington were considered the leaders in the breeding and exhibiting of Borzoi in Canada during those early years.

Mrs. Murray Hendrie in Alberta joined the Borzoi fancy in 1914 when she imported Valeska (by Ch. Kopchic O'Valley Farm ex Tama O'Valley Farm) from her breeder P. Colvin in Toledo, Ohio. In 1914 and 1916 two imports from Mrs. Vlasto's English kennels went to Hugh Nickle in Kingston, Ontario. These were Knave of Addlestone (by Ch. Ramsden Rajah ex Zenia) and the exceptional white and brindle male Petrofski of Addlestone (by Ch. Trumps of Addlestone ex Czarina of Addlestone). Petrofski was sold to Mr. A.V. Webley in 1918 for his Tolstoi kennels in Toronto, and in 1920 he was resold to the Canadian Romanoff Kennels of Mrs. Janet Patterson.

With the opening of the Tolstoy Kennels in 1919, Borzoi popularity reached a new high in Canada with 104 registrations the following year due in large measure to Mr. Webley's enthusiastic participation in all phases of Borzoi activity. He was the breeder of the famous Morvich of Tolstoi (by Ch. Johnston's Krilenko ex Zafftra of Romanoff). At only nine months of age Morvich soared from the novice class to best of breed at the 1922 Westminster show in New York judged by J. Bailey Wilson. In 1924 he returned to Westminster as a champion to repeat the best of breed win.

The Romanoff Kennels of Mrs. Janet Patterson in Brantford, Ontario were rapidly forging ahead at this same time. Ch. Petrofski of Addlestone, his daughter War Baby (ex Zola II), Boris Romanoff and Lizka Henrietta (by Almaz of Spring Farm ex Georgeville Olga) all played major roles in building the reputation of this kennel until it became the most widely known of all in Canada.

Two of Mrs. Patterson's early achievements in 1919 were Ch. Lady Romanoff and Ch. Neva Romanoff (both by Boris Romanoff ex Lizka Henrietta although from different litters). Then followed Ch. Romanoff Lasky (by Pertzoff O'Valley Farm ex Lady of Romanoff) in 1922, a prized stud in Mrs. Cluxton's Glenwild Kennels in the States; Romanoff Rasputin (by Borloff ex Roma of Romanoff); and Ch. Romanoff Peterhof (by Bolivia of Glenwild ex Kisamis of Kingswood) in 1923. Mrs. Patterson owned Baby Orloff (by Ch. Orloff of Tolstoi ex War Baby), littermates Borloff and Ch. Nazimova (by Ch. Johnson's Krilenko ex War

Ch. Nicholas of Melnikoff, whelped in 1928, bred and owned by Frank Allin in Toronto.

Orloff of Melnikoff (by Ch. Nicholas of Melnikoff ex Veda of Orloff) pictured at 17 months.

Baby). Ch. Nazimova and Ch. Romanoff Peterhof were both gold medal winners at the 1926 Sesqui-Centennial in Canada. The fine Borzoi of Romanoff were legion. Only a few of the best remembered are mentioned here.

Fred Ubelacker in Stratford, Ontario used Romanoff stock to start his Volga Kennels in which he bred a noteworthy winner in Volga Debroski (by Romanoff Kanduit ex Romanoff Anisia).

Mr. E.M. Burke of Lambeth, Ontario joined the fancy in 1923 when he imported the Dutch dog Bessberk's Fenella O'Valley Farm (by Boldareff du Zwaenhoek ex Arsinoi Nikolskoi) by way of the United States to his Vaski Kennels. Later he purchased more Borzoi from Valley Farm to add to his luxurious kennels which boasted among other features a large heated swimming pool for the dogs. He was an active breeder and exhibitor for about eight years.

Mr. J.A. McLaughlin in Montreal, Quebec, based his Agatestone lines on English imports that included Butterfly of Barnaigh (by Gordey of Addlestone ex Talmina de l'Ermitage) in 1931. This bitch was bred by Mrs. Vlasto but exported by Mrs. McNeil of Scotland which explains the name. When Mr. McLaughlin bred her to Ivan of Agatestone, she produced Krassai of Agatestone who in turn sired Canadian and American Ch. Radziwell Valdai of Glenwild found in the Mogedo line and the early Vala Rama line in the United States.

The Marlboro Kennels of Mr. M.B. Zwicker in Halifax, Nova Scotia imported foundation stock from the Haywra and Shay English kennels. The imports included Nona of Shay (by Ripley Perfection ex Olga of Haywra). Nona was registered with the Canadian Kennel Club as Marlboro Nona of Shay. The Marlbora hounds enjoyed the unique distinction of being trained for all types of winter sports including sled work.

Frank Allin of Toronto, Ontario became interested in Borzoi in 1922. By carefully mating dogs that possessed the lines of Ch. Bistri of Perchino, his ideal, he obtained the first champion in his Melnikoff Kennels, Ch. Nicholas of Melnikoff (by Bozo Khotni ex Alda Jeritza). The breeding of Nicholas to Veda of Orloff owned by Florence Kilby produced Ch. Orloff of Melnikoff that was said to resemble the original Bistri of Perchino.

During World War II, Mr. Allin was in the Canadian Army. Shortly before his return in 1946, the Borzoi he had counted on using as a stud to re-establish his kennels had been destroyed. Mr. Allin died a few years later, but the Melnikoff line still exists through the Malora line in the United States.

Two other Canadian bloodlines frequently found in Malora pedigrees are those created by Mrs. Florence McKibbin of Toronto

155

through her Rubinoff Babe and Mrs. Wilhelmina Dunham of Bronte, Ontario through her Wil-Dun's Grand Duke Alexander. Since Alexander was sired by Kount Korda of Malora out of Sandra of Glenwild, he might better be classified as Canadian-American.

Early in 1954 Mrs. V.M. Martinson of Marysville, New Brunswick imported to her Tyree Kennels Kuban's Kuzma (by Curio of Fortrouge ex Kuban's Mantilla of Yof) bred by Mrs. Reed in England.

About the same time Mrs. Olive Dewsbury of Locust Hill, Ontario added Borzoi to her Dewsa Kennels with Ch. Dewsa Boreas Secundus (from the Canadian Romanoff line) in 1954 and a bitch from Andrew Cunningham's Frontier Kennels in Buffalo, New York. She bred these two and the ensuing litter was eagerly purchased by hunters and ranchers in Canada. Mrs. Dewsbury continued to breed fine Borzoi for several years. After her death in 1961, her son Fred Dewsbury established his own Duchenka Kennels in Rockwood, Ontario.

The Sirhan Kennels of Audrey Benbow outside Montreal started in 1960 as far as Borzoi were concerned. The kennel name was originally chosed as one appropriate for the Salukis kept at the kennel which has since housed many assorted breeds, mostly sighthounds.

The first Borzoi added to the Sirhan Kennels was American and Canadian Ch. Topaze (by Sasha's Sensation ex Alcyone Delvos). In 1959 Yelmorb Natasha of Sirhan (by Ch. Yelmorb Kolchak ex Walhof Fraun) was purchased from the Bromleys in New York. A linebreeding of Natasha to Topaze produced the bitch Am. and Can. Ch. Sirhan Almaz.

The foundation bitch at Sirhan was Am. and Can. Ch. Antigone of Tyree (by Can Ch. Kuban's Kuzma C.D. ex Can. Ch. Prunella of Fortrouge). In 1964 Antigone bred to Topaze produced Kaissack, Tatyana and Govorushka all bearing the Sirhan affix and Canadian and American championships. Also in the litter were Can. Ch. Sirhan Katya and Can. Ch. Sirhan Borya.

Kaissack established an outstanding reputation both as a stud dog and as a show dog bringing the Sirhan name to prominence on both sides of the border. In Canada he won best in show as did his sister Tatyana. In 1967 at the Midwest Borzoi Club's specialty at Detroit, he won winners dog and as one of his trophies he won the puppy offered by Sunbarr who became Sirhan Podar of Sunbarr (by Malora's Bede of Sunbarr ex Kaskade of Sunbarr Ranch).

Kaissack bred back to his dam Antigone sired Can. Ch. Sirhan Sokolka and Am. and Can. Ch. Sirhan Raskolnika. When Sirhan Yelena was bred to him, she produced Am. Ch. Sirhan Yuri and Can. Ch. Sirhan Yegorovna. A brother-sister mating of Kaissack and Katya produced Am. Ch. Sirhan Kara of Nightsong going to Joyce Brandin in Illinois. Can. Ch.

156

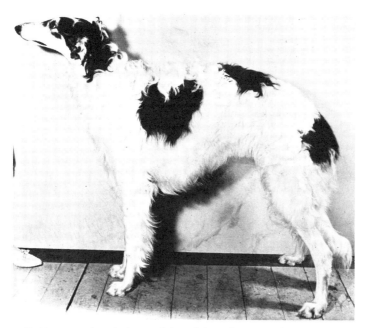

Ch. Topaze, a foundation stud dog of the Sirhan Kennels of Julian and Audrey Benbow.

Can. and Am. Ch. Sirhan Kaissack, pictured at 12 years of age but showing the winning form that won the winners' points at several American specialties.

157

Piotr Illjitschf van Borjoschka, imported from Holland by Jack and Jean Vandongen. Although never shown and bred only a few times before he died, he had an impact on the breed through several of his offspring.

Can. and Am. Ch. Sirhan Porchai, bred and owned by Julian and Audrey Benbow in Quebec. Porchai was a top winning Borzoi in Canada while his litter brother Poraschai was establishing the same record in the United States. *Bixler*

Svetlana of Sirhan (by Springett Copper Harvester ex Sirhan Sasha) bred to Kaissack produced the Canadian champions Sirhan Galuzina and Sirhan Galasha. Kaissack bred to Ch. Sirhan Pleshka sired Ch. Sirhan Kaitar; bred to Sunbarr's Balvoniza he sired Ch. Sirhan Kolpitza and Ch. Sirhan Korovka.

Podar bred to Tatyana produced the Sirhan American and Canadian champions Poraschai, Porchai, Pobedim, Pleshka and Polya; also the Sirhan Canadian champions Petrushka and Prokhai. The first named three males won great recognition. Porchai was retained by Sirhan and established himself as one of Canada's top Borzoi with many best in show wins in Canada. Pobedim and Poraschai went to California. Poraschai was co-owned by Edward Abblett and George Root. He was piloted to top Borzoi in the United States for 1971 and 1972 winning many specialties and bests in show. He was bred to numerous bitches from many kennels as we have seen in a previous chapter with many sons and daughters winning impressive records in their own right.

Katya bred to Podar produced the Sirhan champions Polivanoff II, Palauskey II, Pushkina II and Papotchka II. This last named dog was sent to Brazil where he added a championship in that country. Pushkina went to Jon and Nancy Reimer's Windrift Kennels in Indiana.

Porchai bred to Ch. Sirhan Raskolnika owned by Mesdames Stehr and Hawkins sired Ch. St. Just Wanja retained by the breeders although boarded and shown by Kishniga Kennels, and St. Just Yuzak owned by Jack and Jean Vandongen. Yuzak bred to Petrikov Moria of Far Fields (by Ch. Trezor Ivan ex Ch. Petrikov Enyo of Far Fields C.D.) in 1973 by Sidney Barber's Kamzor Kennels sired Ch. Kamzor Nimzovitch and Ch. Kamzor Nureyev for daughter Stephanie Hanes and her Belitzar Kennels.

Katya bred to Porchai produced Ch. Sirhan Zingaro and best in show winner Int. Ch. Sirhan Zyganka. Porchai was bred to Am. and Can. Ch. Tehrsha of Birchwood (by Kaissack ex Ch. Majenkir's Cognac of Fox Glen). The first litter had the best in show winning bitch Brazilian Ch. Sirhan Moskintchka and Am. Ch. Sirhan Miloshlavskaya sent back to Cognac's breeder Audrey Mulligan in New Jersey. The second litter yielded Ch. Sirhan Iskra and Ch. Sirhan Ilagin.

Sirhan also imported additional stock among which were Ch. Sirhan Nagradka of Sunbarr (by Sunbarr's Holy Moses ex Nedra of Kashan) bred by James Barr in Wisconsin and Ch. Black Watch of Fortrouge (by Whist of Fortrouge ex Bianca of Fortrouge) bred in England by Betty Murray. Nagradka bred to Katya sired the Sirhan champions Nijinsky, Nazarov, Nochenka, Nadezhda and Natasha. Black Watch bred to Petrushka sired Ch. Sirhan Czartoryski.

The breeding activities at Sirhan have now been limited as Audrey

Benbow applies her considerable knowledge of the breed to judging in both Canada and the United States.

Jack and Jean Vandongen's Bordonsky Kennels in London, Ontario has been noted primarily for its Dutch imports including Canadian Ch. Ethos vom Troybhiko and Canadian Ch. Kalinka vom Troybhiko in the late 1960's. In 1973 Jean imported Piotr Illjitsch van Borjoschka (by Eros van Borjoschka ex Moja van Borjoschka) whose outstanding son Am. and Can. Ch. Laba's Arimsky was sold to the Loral Kennels in Pennsylvania. In 1976 the Vandongens purchased Int. Ch. Amurat v d Zilverstrand (by Int. Ch. Alexander v d Emelenberg ex Int. Ch. Sirotka v d Sabatchnaja Izba) that they co-own with Aatis Lillstrom in the States.

Another small but important recent Borzoi kennel in Canada is the Lanel Kennels of Laura Nel in Edwards, Ontario. The foundation bitch at Lanel is Can. Ch. Catherina de Borodin (by Can. Ch. Sully de Bolshoy ex Can. Ch. Kalinka de Bolshoy). She was bred to Ch. Laba's Arimsky to produce the Lanel champions Alasha Arimski, Anyakira Arimskova, Aurelia Arimskova, Aninushka Arimskova, Ambra Arimski and American Ch. Alexei Arimsky of Loral-Lanel.

The most recent Canadian Borzoi kennel of note is the Kishniga Kennels of Dr. Richard Meen and Dr. John Reeve-Newson of Campbellville, Ontario. In 1972 they leased Ch. Sirhan Raskolnika from Eva Stehr and bred her to Podar at the Sirhan Kennels. This produced the Kishniga "A" litter of 13 puppies of which three became Canadian and American champions and six earned their Canadian titles. Included in the litter, all bearing the Kishniga prefix, were Poh Ardagan, Amneris, Anisette, Antonia Willa, Anna and Gallant Anubis.

Ruby de Bolshoy was obtained from Mr. and Mrs. Paul DeRyche. This red and white bitch was by Ch. Sirhan Rugay of Wilolea out of the Belgian import Strela de la Polianka (by Troyka v Borjoschka ex Bljetska v Troybhiko). Ruby was bred to Ch. Kishniga's Gallant Anubis to produce the Kishniga "D" litter the star of which was the striking red and white Am. and Can. Ch. Kishniga's Desert Song known at home and to the show world as Moustache. This dog's record includes 45 Best in Shows (17 American), number one Borzoi in Canada 1976-1977, number one dog all breeds in Canada in 1977, number one Borzoi and number six dog all breeds in the United States in 1978. The handsome team of Moustache and Dick had indeed caught the eye of the dog fancy on both sides of the border.

Ch. Kishniga Dalgarth, the black and white litter brother of Moustache, achieved fame as the top Canadian Borzoi in 1975. In 1978 he was sold to Ron and Dyane Roth in California who then arranged for the

Can. and Am. Ch. Kishniga's Desert Song, bred and owned by Dr. Richard Meen and Dr. John Reeve-Newson, shown winning one of his many bests in show while he established himself as a top winning Borzoi in both Canada and the United States. He is shown here with his owner Dr. Meen and Judge Edith Hellerman. *Alverson*

services of Edd Abblett to show the dog in the States. With several specialty, group and best in show honors, Dalgarth was top winning Borzoi in the United States in 1979 and 1980.

Holland

Borzoi have thrived in Holland for many years and much of the credit for their popularity is due to Mr. J.H.M. van der Molen of Limburg province, owner of the oldest Dutch kennel in existence until recently and known by the name of Krasnoje Selo. Mr. van der Molen was one of the founders of the Borzoi Club in Holland and served as its president for 15 years. He had Borzoi all his life and his collection of information and portraits of the breed is second to none. He met many of the old Russian Borzoi breeders when they fled to Paris after the Russian Revolution. They had a great deal in common to discuss as Mr. van der Molen's foundation stock descended from the Perchina hounds.

To start at the beginnings of Dutch Borzoi history, we must list Louis Dobbelman, reputed to have had the largest Borzoi kennel in Holland before the turn of the century. After he married he started his kennels with Ch. Atman II of Perchina said to have been one of the best exported from Russia at that time. Mr. Dobbelman was well known in Borzoi circles on the continent and held a dominant position in the breed for over 20 years.

The Gerlia Kennels founded in 1900 by Henry van Haaren in Nijmeugen operated successfully for about ten years. Most of his basic stock stemmed from the Perchina importations of Mr. Cuvelier's French kennels. The history of Dutch Borzoi would not be complete without mentioning van Haaren's Ch. Sergei Gerlia (by Ch. Fasolt ex Ch. Lebedka Gerlia) although he bred many others.

The end of World War I found Mr. and Mrs. van der Berkoff's Bessberk Kennels among those with a world-wide reputation for excellence. They began with German imports such as the self-black Ajax von Sachsenwald (by Chack Bielaja ex Ch. Isma Beresina) from Richard Kallmeyer, Ch. Segai Freisia Pascholl from Frau Else Mann, Arsinoi Nikolskoi and Aliaska Nikolskoi from Mrs. von Bessel and other hounds from Frau Dr. Wegener. Bedin Achotnik (by Ch. Almadin Nikolskoi ex Planza Pascholl) was exported to England. Other Bessberk Borzoi went to the United States with the great majority to Valley Farm including Bessberks' Cresta and Bessberk's Fenella O'Valley Farm both later resold to Canadian breeders.

During the second World War it was a struggle to keep livestock of any kind in prime breeding condition ready for normal peacetime pur-

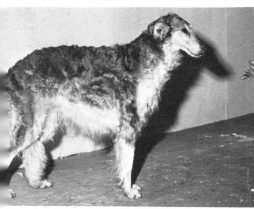

Ch. Sergei Gerlia, son Ch. Fasolt out of Ch. Lebedka, whelped in 1904 at the Gerlia Kennels of Henry van Haaren in Holland.

Dutch Ch. and Int. Ch. Annuschka van Lentevreugde, a red and white daughter of Ch. Cilly Charley van Vredewold, bred by J. van Bloomendall and owned by A. Staffhorst in Holland.

Borcos Blitz, bred by Louis Mennen, was exported to the United States where he was first owned by the Warhill Kennels in Ohio and then the Volga Kennels in California.

Int. Ch. Troyka van Borjoschka, one of the most outstanding Borzoi on the continent during the 1960's, was bred by Mr. and Mrs. Van Kessel and owned by C. Mattheeuwsen in Holland.

suits. How the Dutch people managed to feed Borzoi during those years, when food to keep themselves alive barely existed, we may never learn. However, there must have been another "finger in the dike" some place for the fine show entries that turned up shortly after the end of the war were adequate proof of the ingenuity of these people and their love of animals. One example of such quality in 1945 was Int. Ch. and Dutch Ch. Babka Bletska Krasnoje Selo (by Stepnjakov's Nicolai ex Farlee v Karamasov) bred by Mr. van der Molen and owned by Mr. W.J. Staffhorst. This white and gray bitch was winner at the 1951 *Sieger* show in Germany.

Mr. M.J. Boer started his Vredewold Kennels at Leek at the end of World War II. Two of his noted Borzoi were Ch. Cilly Charley van Vredewold and Cilly van Vredewold. When Charley was bred to Ch. Sonja v Vredewold, she produced the bitch Ch. Sonja's Alfridy v Vredewold. Many of these closely bred Vredewold dogs went to Louis Mennen of Asten. Mr. Mennen bred Alfridy's Clown v Vredewold (by Ch. Sonja Iwan v Vredewold ex Ch. Sonja's Alfridy v Vredewold) to Int. Ch. Clown's Japke v Vredewold. One of the sons, Am. Ch. Borco's Blitz, after earning a Dutch *Kampioen-Schapsprijs* (junior champion) in 1962 was sold to Harry Ferguson and William Shepard of Warhill Kennels in Cincinnati, Ohio and subsequently sold to Mrs. Bruna Henry in California.

The Vorenoff Kennels of Jo Heller have produced several international champions. Some Vorenoff Borzoi have been exported to the United States and Canada. American Ch. Vorenoff Kyril Tolkaia C.D. (by Tolkai von Bergland ex Inushka v d Sabatchnaja) went to the Kristull Kennels in Texas. Vorenoff imported many Borzoi from the English Fortrouge Kennels among which was Ch. Ruth of Fortrouge. Ruth was bred to Ch. Runskoff Ivanovitch to produce Ch. Barnaigh Vorenoff Bielka which was sent to Mrs. McNeil in Scotland.

Mr. and Mrs. Van Kessel have the Borjoschka Kennels. While they breed and show rarely, dogs from their kennel have had a definite impact on the breed especially in the United States. They owned the bitch Josha Wilkaja who was bred to the beautiful Kosak Alexander owned by C. Mattheuwsen of the Troybhiko Kennels. An outstanding litter of five was produced which was split between the two kennels. Borjoschka kept the two bitches Anushka and Muschka van Borjoschka. Anushka was bred to Iwan v d Zilverstrand (by Marushka's Petrov v Sjeco ex Tasha of Fortrouge) to produce Eros van Borjoschka. Eros was bred to Muschka to produce Moja van Borjoschka. Moja bred back to her sire Eros produced among others Piotr Illjitsch van Borjoschka who was exported to Canada.

Troyka van Borjoschka from the Kosak-Josha litter went to the

Troybhiko Kennels of C. Mattheeuwsen under whose guidance he became one of the most outstanding Borzoi on the continent in the late 1960's, easily earning his international championship as well as other honors. Troyka was bred to the great producing bitch Nadja is Slonawaja to produce Int. Ch. Ljasko van Troybhiko, an outstanding winner following in his sire's footsteps in the early 1970's. Troyka was bred to the American bitch Ch. Whirling's Celeste of Malora (by Sunbarr Hercules of Malora ex Sunbarr Atlanta of Malora) to produce well for the Rancho Gabriel Kennels in California who later imported a Troyka son Ch. Perchotin's Byankaj Gabriel (ex Tanjuscha von Bergland).

Belgium

Mr. G. van Muylem's Ziesenghen Kennels in the town of the same name provided foundation stock for many German kennels, his Ch. Oydesse de Ziesenghen being in the pedigree of one of Germany's greatest studs Ch. Rurik Ural. Mr. van Muylem was a contemporary of Joseph B. Thomas Jr. of the Valley Farm Kennels in the United States, and for some time the two men waged a heated battle in *Chasse et Peche*, the Belgian canine journal, over the respective merits of Russian-bred Borzoi favored by Thomas and English-bred Borzoi favored by Mr. van Muylem. Mr. Thomas issued a challenge to Mr. van Muylem with stakes of 5000 francs a side in gold or plate, the challenge remaining open until April 1, 1905. Mr. van Muylem, being no April Fool, never accepted that challenge.

Apparently not all Belgian breeders followed the same breeding programs as Mr. van Muylem. Gustave Beernaerts purchased Ch. Ugar Perchino from the Grand Duke Nicholas and this was the start of the Zwaenhoek Kennels near Ghent. Adding to the beauty of the surroundings of the estate is the statue of a group of three life-sized Borzoi the Baernaerts commissioned sculptor Merculina to create in a nearby park. They are supposedly replicas of Mazeppa de l'Etoile, Moudjick du Ziesenghem and Ch. Lebrodka. Lebrodka was imported from the Woronzova Kennels in Russia.

Ch. Bolderoff du Zwaenhoek (by Ajax von Sachsenwald ex Priska Pascholl) was one of Europe's leading studs during the 1920's. Ch. Helga du Zwaenhoek (by the French Ch. Volga du Nord) was another outstanding hound bred by the Baernaerts. Helga's litter brother Ch. Hettman du Zwaenhoek was sold to Baroness Sloet, resold to a German breeder and sold again to Czechoslovakia. The Zwaenhoek affix may be found in extended pedigrees of American, Canadian, French, English and German Borzoi. This kennel had many dealings with the Valley Farm Kennels in the United States, leasing and purchasing several dogs from them. In 1925 the lovely Zohra du Zwaenhoek (by Bolderoff du Zwaenhoek ex Kolpitza du Zwaenhoek) was sent to Valley Farm.

The first World War took its dreadful toll of this magnificent kennel, but a gallant comeback saw Zwaenhoek host to about 100 Borzoi at one time during the 1930's. After Mr. Baernaerts' death the hounds were dispersed.

Postwar reconstruction took precedence over all other forms of endeavor, so Borzoi activity was at a standstill for many years after the second World War. This was so until Mrs. Robert Deckers in Antwerp imported Int. Ch. Zomahli Birovitch and Belgian Ch. Zomahli Anyushka both bred by Lillie Pearson in England. This established Mrs. Deckers' Bagdad Kennels. The two imports made records by winning their Belgian championships undefeated. Birovitch was also a consistent hound group winner. When he died in 1955, the Bagdad kennel was closed.

France

Two of the prominent early Borzoi kennels in France were l'Etoile and Nord both situated in northern France. L'Etoile was owned by Auguste Caron and is best remembered for its Mazeppa de l'Etoile (by Nenagladni of Perchina ex Tamara Gabrien). The Nord Kennel was owned by Mr. Cuvelier and was based on Russian imports. Lihody Perchina was one of them. The Nord affix is represented in American, German, Belgian and Dutch pedigrees through Ch. Wartha du Nord and Ch. Volga du Nord both purchased by the Zwaenhoek kennels in Belgium. It appeared in French pedigrees up to 1929 although this kennel was another casualty of the first World War.

After that l'Ermitage owned by Mr. and Mrs. Henri Teissonniere of Alex flourished until 1944. During the same time Mme. d'Autryve operated the Macon Kennel in southern France which existed for about the same length of time as l'Ermitage. Mme. Guy Deloupy's Tcherkowitch Kennels at Toulouse and Col. and Mme. de Clerck's Sourkovitch Kennels were founded on l'Ermitage and Zwaenhoek bloodlines. Both Mr. Tessionniere and Col. de Clerck held the office of president of the French Borzoi Club. Many of the names of the better dogs produced by these kennels have been obscured by the passage of time. However, l'Ar-Vro-Goz Kennels owned by Mme. Jouan La Roche developed bloodlines that appear often in American pedigrees through the brood matron Ch. Warona de l'Ar-Vro-Goz.

In the 1960's the most notable Borzoi winning in France was Ch.

Ch. Charly von Silberhof, bred in Germany by Frau Dr. Schaef, was exported to Holland where he was used extensively and successfully at stud.

Several Morton Hall Borzoi bred and owned by Mme. A. d'Arbelles: Ozo Kazanova de Morton Hall, Natieva Kamenova de Morton Hall, Ch. Oteiva Kazanova de Morton Hall and best in show winner Ch. Kamenetz Pascovitch de Morton Hall.

Kamenetz Pascovitch de Morton Hall bred by Mme. A. d'Arbelles. Several of his grandsons and granddaughters were exported to the United States.

Germany

The Perchina Kennels of the Grand Duke Nicholas furnished the basic breeding stock used by the first German Borzoi breeders. In 1911 and 1912 Dr. Paul Wegener of the Ural Kennels in Chemnitz imported Asmody, Asmaley, Armavir and Ptitachka Perchina. These hounds had great influence on the breed throughout all of Europe.

Richard Kallmeyer of Berlin established his Sachsenwald Kennels which housed among others Ch. Isma Beresina (by Ch. Bedin Alexandroff ex Ch. Mara Slava). Isma had been bred by J. Stumpf at his Beresins Kennels in Marbeck. Herr Kallmeyer is perhaps best known for his translation from the Russian of "The Perchino Hunt" by Dmitri Walzoff which appears in the English translation as the last part of Winifred Chadwick's book *The Borzoi* first published in Great Britain in 1952.

Frau Eva Rug had the Slava Kennels in Munchen and was the breeder of the 1910 German Grand Champion bitch Mara Slava (by Ch. Rurik Ural ex Zenia Moja Goordost). Frau von Bessel had the Nikolskoi Kennels in Lexowshof and is best remembered for Arsinoi Nikolskoi which was sent to Valley Farm. The Alexandroff Kennels in Augsburg belonged to Frau E. Lackner whose two greatest Borzoi in 1911 were the dog Ch. Bedin Alexandroff and the bitch Ch. Tigra Alexandroff, and in 1912 the champions Ugo Alexandroff and Razza Alexandroff. Richard Dix was quite inactive both in the German Borzoi Club and the combined sighthound club, the Windhund Association. His Bielaja Kennels were located in Weimar and his first champion was Carima Bielaja in 1921. The kennel continued to prosper until World War II.

Frau Else Mann had the Pascholl Kennels in Sponhalz. She bred and exported to Valley Farm in 1922 Asmaley Pascholl. Frau G. Sinkel had the Frisia Kennels at Krefeld. Together the two ladies formed a partnership using the suffix Frisia-Pascholl which was quite apart from their separate breeding arrangements. Under the partnership they produced the 1922 Grand Champion Sergai Frisia-Pascholl, a repeat winner in 1924 under the Bessberk colors.

Veterinarian Frau Dr. Schaaf owned the Silberhof Kennels in Freiberg which fell behind the Iron Curtain. The kennel was established in 1925 but was closed in the early 1950's. A severe bombing during the war destroyed most of the Silberhof dogs. Col. and Mrs. Dean E. Ryman of

Virginia brought several Silberhof dogs back to the States when they returned in 1952 from a six year tour with the U.S. Army in Germany.

The Bergland Kennels of Frau Hanne Muller in Assenhausen was a very large Borzoi establishment in postwar Germany after its beginnings in 1936 with some of Dr. Wegener's and Rasswet hounds: Ch. Granat Ural (by Ch. Amurat Alers Ural) and two bitches Rasset's Liebe and Rasswet's Freue both of which died before producing anything for the kennel. Soon thereafter Frau Muller bought Cora Ismailoff who was bred to Granat to produce Ch. Kismet v Bergland to become the foundation bitch for Mrs. Julia Curnow's English Woodcourt Kennel and Ch. Kryill v Bergland. The Barnaigh Kennel in Scotland used Yerres v Bergland to produce several outstanding bitches two of which went to the Malora Kennels in America. Terry DeCraene in New Jersey purchased Colby v Bergland (by Quick v Bergland ex Ch. Japis v Bergland) in 1952 soon to be followed by the purchase of Djumber v Bergland, Fandango v Bergland and Golem v Bergland. Frau Muller died suddenly in 1959 and the kennel was dispersed shortly afterwards. It is believed that James Barr in Wisconsin imported the last Bergland dog — Ch. Helios v Bergland.

Australia and New Zealand

Dr. Charles Ryan imported the first known Borzoi in Australia. With the aid of Mr. de Passek, the Russian Consul at Melbourne, he bought Orloff and Katrina from the Czar's Imperial Kennels about 1898. He bred the first Australian litter from them, one of the puppies going to Cecil Ryan in Tasmania.

The next Borzoi activity as far as can be determined occurred after the first World War with imports arriving from the Nevarc and Bransgore Kennels in England. These went to the Beaulieu Kennels which provided basic stock for the Sarova Kennels in New Zealand.

During the period between the two World Wars the following kennels flourished: Petrograd, Volga, Rooskaya, Regal, Atlas and Perchina.

Miss Maisie Huddleston established her Perchina Kennels at South Geelong, Victoria prior to World War II although the name of the kennel was adopted after the war. She purchased her foundation stock from the Regal Kennels in Victoria with bloodlines stemming from the English Bransgore dogs. Her first producing bitch was Countess Olga of Regal. Distemper destroyed the stock Miss Huddleston managed to breed during the war, and her first import after the war, Dignity of Rydens, died enroute. This did not put an end to the kennel as a purchase was soon made of Ch. Braznik of Atlas, Czarina of Atlas and Ch. Aurora of Atlas from

Miss Maisie Huddlestone's Perchina Borzoi in Victoria, Australia. At her left is Ch. Aurora of Atlas, the other two are her seven month old puppies Perchina Mazeppa and Perchina Elegance.

Ch. Romanov Raina Rebecca and her owner Jon Skiller. This red and white bitch was best in show at the Borzoi Club of NSW championship show in 1976.

the Atlas Kennels of Charles Venable of Myrtlebank, Victoria. Ch. Aurora produced three litters with several of the puppies earning their championships. The Kuban bloodline was added to Perchina with the importation of Zanikoff of Kuban who sired two of Aurora's litters. In the early 1960's Maisie visited Canada, the United States and England returning with Avonisky of Greenhaven (by Ch. Arnorinski of Greenhaven ex Menthe Golden Clou of Greenhaven) bred by Mrs. Harrison and a Boran daughter Saycha of Fortrouge (ex Carlotta of Fortrouge) bred by Betty Murray. Avonisky, known to all as Bim, established an enviable show record for Maisie and remained her favorite — a real companion and friend.

Robert A. Hewlett of Attunga in New South Wales bred Borzoi for a few years immediately after World War II in his Wyaralong Kennels using Atlas dogs almost exclusively. Mrs. E.K. Dixon in Victoria opened her Elwill Kennels with Woodcourt hounds imported from England, adding the Atlas bloodline later. She remained active in the breed until about 1954.

After World War II, Miss Dorothy Robertson, later to become Dorothy Mercuri, in Queensland entered the Borzoi world with Atlas, Wyaralong and Elwill bloodlines in her Boronova Kennels. She showed Wyaralong Wonder (by Ch. Atlas Archimedes ex Atlas Illona) and Elwill Ballerina (by Ch. Prince Peter of Atlas ex Ch. Penza of Woodcourt) to their championships.

In 1953 Mrs. Mercuri imported Winones Kalinka (by Mazeppa Brazhnikoff ex Winjones Astral), a bitch sent out in whelp from Mrs. Chadwick's kennel in England. Kalinka produced five puppies enroute on the ship Clan MacDonald. From that litter came the best in show winner Ch. Boronova Brastus. Winjones Otmena and Winjones Naglaty accompanied Kalinka on that trip. In 1954 Mrs. Mercuri imported two more from Mrs. Chadwick: Winjones Zakla of Carradale and Chanctonbury Mirth. In 1956 Mrs. Mercuri discontinued breeding and exhibiting, but her son Peppi then increased his interest in the breed becoming the youngest and most prolific breeder/importer in Victoria.

The Nova Zambla Kennels owned by Mr. and Mrs. Castor in Sydney shared the show ring spotlight with Boronova. Mrs. W.S. Young exported Reyas Rydens Malina in whelp to Ch. Eglon of Rydens to Nova Zambla. Malina not only earned her Australian championship but also won several best in show awards.

Since that time in recent years there have been many active kennels in Australia. From Mrs. Frazer's Elfield Kennels in Perth, Ch. Elfield's Martov Marinsky and Ch. Elfield's Davaluri were sent to Carole Waldron's

Mindean Kennels. Elfield's Flight Master C.D. (by Ch. Elfield's Golden Fleece ex Ch. Elfield's Glad Tidings C.D.) was sent to California.

Mrs. M. Holmes has the Dolinoff Kennels. Mr. and Mrs. Brian Johnson operate the Yadasar Kennels. Miss Jenny Grimwood owned Ch. Levela Ilia, named Borzoi of the Year in 1974, at her Khorassan Kennels. At the Romanov Kennels of B. Gilbey and Jon Skiller reside the red and white bitch Ch. Romanov Rana Raskarla, Ch. Yadasar Count Romanoff and Ch. Romanov Raina Rebecca. Raina is a lovely red and white bitch who won best in show at the second championship show of the Borzoi Club of N.S.W. in 1977. Bruce Huntley-Snedden, at his Rusharn Kennels, has Ch. Boronoff By-Glori and the great winner Ch. Rusharn Yuseff. In 1975 he imported Ch. The Roysterer of Patrioona, a multi-best in show winner.

Scandinavia

Although the Borzoi, called *Rysk Vinthud*, was not a popular breed in Sweden during the first part of the 20th century, there were always a few to be found listed in every issue of the Swedish Kennel Club stud books signifying that a small but loyal group of fanciers did exist.

One of the first really good specimens was Ch. Eros imported from Austria in the 1920's. When mated to the German-bred Militza Godohoff, he sired the well known champions Tchaiky and Cyrano. Sharing the showring honors with him at that time was the bitch Ch. Lojka (by Ch. Blejslo ex Tachajka).

Shortly after 1930 many Danish-bred Borzoi appeared in the Swedish shows most of them being from German bloodlines. Chief among these was Wladislau Monasterium (by German Ch. Clon Ural ex Gazelle von Konugefort).

1936 saw Ch. Cyrano's son Tarzan of Braska finish his championship. Leaders at that time with him were Ch. Czarina of Trolliden and Ch. Natascha of Trolliden (by Ch. Tarzan of Braska ex Knjasthna Wergei). The Trolliden suffix was used by Leif Delin of Gayle. Ch. Czarina was the dam of such fine hounds as Ch. Bonnen's Fedja and Bonnen's Roviti. Roviti was the dam of Ch. Pekrow, Ch. Czarina, Ch. Nadja, Ch. Jana and Ch. Bonnen's Raja, this last one being one of the best dogs at the end of the 1940's and an exceptionally good sire. The Bonnen prefix was adopted by Dagmar Watz-Ohlsson in Stockholm.

During the 1950's Swedish breeders imported several Borzoi from England including Ch. Achilles of Woodcourt. In 1954 and 1955 Norsk Ch. Bandana of Woodcourt (by Ch. Apex of Woodcourt ex Anita of

Int. Ch. Kara-Kyralina de Norois, owned by E. Resko in Finland, was winner of the year in 1965 and 1966. This bitch also carried championship titles from Finland, Sweden, Denmark and Norway.

A kennel maid shows off three Barnaigh Borzoi for Mrs. K. McNeil: Ch. Onyx of Barnaigh, Olga of Barnaigh and their sire Ch. Winjones Ataman. The dam of Olga and Onyx was Astrakan of Barnaigh.

174

Woodcourt), Astor of Woodcourt and Diadome of Woodcourt were imported by Helga Wiklund of Hallstavik.

The best known breeders in Sweden in the 1970's have been Mrs. S. Hallquist of Ekhaga Kennels and Mrs. M.S. Wallner of Igoroff Kennels.

From 1930 to 1950 Denmark claimed some very outstanding Borzoi kennels. One familiar to Americans would be Midtfyn in Allestad owned by Marie Barlebo who bred American Ch. Midtfyn Boja imported to California by Mr. and Mrs. Harald Sundt.

As in Denmark, Norway is host to few Borzoi breeders. The oldest on record is Fritjof Asmot who bred Borzoi for about 26 years for hunting and show purposes. In 1914 Ramsden Romance and Ramsden Reindeer were imported from the Bormans' kennel in England. The breeding of these two produced the bitch Vanja av Ullebers.

Ireland

At one time there were four kennels in Ireland breeding and showing Borzoi: Moscow, Volga, Williamsford and Yof.

Mrs. Hafner began the Volga line with Tangmere dogs. In 1941 she purchased the bitch Ch. Williamsford April (by Bargany of Barnaigh ex Williamsford Actress). She followed this with breedings of this bitch into the Kuban line.

Many of the Borzoi from Miss Helen Foy's Yof Kennels went to the Kuban Kennels when she died, returning to their native country as it were for the Yof Kennels were founded on English stock. One of the main stud dogs at Yof was Tsigan Kuban (by Kuban's Almaz ex Kuban's Baba Yaga).

When Erma Denton, secretary of the Borzoi Club of America, made inquiries of the Irish Kennel Club concerning active breeders and exhibitors of Borzoi in Ireland during the 1950's, the reply from the Club Secretary Miss Maud Fox stated in effect that there were no Borzoi breeders in Ireland at that time and the only exhibitors at the Irish shows were from England. However, since that time several Borzoi have been imported including Ch. Ruth of Fortrouge imported by Mr. and Mrs. Wallis from the Dutch Vorenoff Kennels although originally bred in the English Fortrouge Kennels.

Scotland

In 1831 Duncan McNeil, who later became Lord Colonsay, is reputed to have imported the first Borzoi from Russia although it was many years later before the breed became well known in this country. Even in later

175

years, we find few breeders there, but these few seemed to compensate for scarcity of numerical superiority by the enthusiasm and excellence of their endeavors.

One of the first kennels was Brunton owned by Florence Forsyth-Caddell in Edinburgh. Ch. Zikovitch of Brunton brought honors to his kennel before World War II closed the kennel temporarily. The purchase of Ulick of Rydens who quickly earned his championship title under the hand of his new owner aided in the post-war revival of Brunton.

Another kennel active both before and after World War II was Barnaigh which was established in the 1920's by Mrs. Kathleen McNeil in Glasgow. The first Barnaigh-owned dog of note was White Hawk of Barnaigh (by Sparrowhawk of Addlestone ex Earlstown Exornation) bred by Miss Rigby. In 1926 Mrs. McNeil produced White Eagle of Barnaigh (by White Hawk of Barnaigh ex Mirza of Gelsia) and acquired Ch. Lady Luck of Barnaigh (by White Hawk of Barnaigh ex Arncliffe Tzaritzia). Lady Luck's daughter Ch. Miss Mazeppa of Barnaigh (by Ch. Mythe Mazeppa) earned her championship title at the Crufts Jubilee Show in 1936. The litter brothers White Falcon of Barnaigh and Kestrel of Barnaigh (by Podar of Notts ex Lady Luck of Barnaigh) were whelped in 1929 and proved their worth many times over as studs for Barnaigh and various English kennels. Several Barnaigh Borzoi were exported to the United States adding quality to several bloodlines there. The litter sisters Lucky Lady of Barnaigh and Lovely Lady of Barnaigh (by the German Menthes Yerres v Bergland ex Domino of Barnaigh) were sent to the Malora kennels. The bitch Bright of Barnaigh (by Ch. Reyas Romancer ex Olga of Barnaigh) was sent to the Sunbarr kennels and when bred to Ilja v Bergland produced the famous Sunbarr "B" litter.

Mrs. McNeil was the first Scottish person to show a Borzoi to a championship title and the first to judge the breed at a championship show. In 1936 she succeeded Kathleen, Duchess of Newcastle as President of the Borzoi Club of England.

England

Our English cousins were among the first to breed Borzoi on a large scale outside of Russia. The interest in England continues unabated to this day with entries at shows rivaling those at the larger American shows. In 1947 there were 255 entries at the Cheltenham Open Show, at the 1957 Crufts show there was an entry of 147, and at the 1952 Diamond Jubilee Show the entry was 144. Even allowing for the usual English practice of double entering, these are outstanding entries.

176

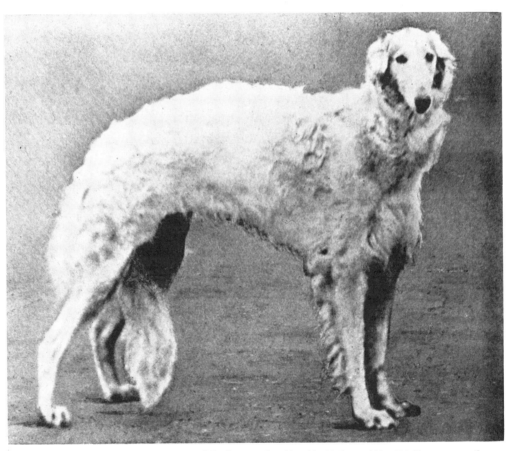

Ch. Miss Piostri (by Piostri ex Princess Rubikoff), owned and bred by Major and Mrs. E.L. Borman, was the first English Borzoi bitch to win best in show honors.

The pioneers in the Borzoi field were the kennels of Lady Innes-Ker and the Duchess of Newcastle mentioned in a previous chapter. In June 1897 Mrs. J. McIntyre registered Wulfruna. Mrs. McIntyre used as her kennel name the name of this first Borzoi and her kennels were located in Wolverhampton, Staffordshire. She also owned the Russian-bred bitch Militza (by Kharashi ex Malina). Two of her popular stud dogs were Wulfruna Velsk (by Velsk ex Nadeshda) and Wulfruna Meteor.

The Ramsden prefix of Major and Mrs. E.L. Borman of Ramsden Heath in Essex had its inception about the turn of the century with the acquisition of Skylark, Starlight, and Statesman with the last named dog becoming the first Borman champion. Mrs. Borman obtained Piostri (by Windle Earl ex Alston Queen) in 1902 from Sidney Turner and bred him to Princess Rubikoff (by Statesman ex Heloise) with Ch. Miss Piostri as the result. Miss Piostri was the first English Borzoi bitch to win best in show honors, was the winner of over 20 challenge certificates during her career, and was the source of most of the fine qualities found in the Ramsden strain. Two of her outstanding sons were Ch. Ramsden Rajah (by Ch. Ramsden Ranger) and his litter brother Ch. Ramsden Radient whelped in 1907. Another Borman champion at this same time was Ch. Kieff (by Fedia ex Ina). Kieff sired Ch. Strawberry King (ex Maid of Honour) for Mrs. Aitcheson.

The Ramsden kennel closed during the first World War when Major Borman returned to active duty. The Bormans planned to reopen when the war ended and imported Bedin Achotnik from Holland with that in mind. However, the dog died after siring only one litter. Both Major and Mrs. Borman died in 1932, but the bloodlines developed by them were destined to live on in the Addlestone dogs through the brothers Michael and Czar of Addlestone (by Ch. Ramsden Rajah ex Ch. Miss Piostri).

In 1901 Mrs. Philip Huth in Devon obtained the bitch Olga Lofki (by Lofki ex Xenia). This bitch was bred to the Duchess of Newcastle's Velsk to produce Michael Veloski, a most successful show winner and stud. He was the start of the Kestor Kennels. Mrs. Huth's first show ring appearance was with Michael in 1902; her last was in 1947 with Kestor Serge (by Zmaros of Bransgore ex Boriana of Bransgore).

Ch. Ramsden set a pattern of success for the Addlestone Kennels of Mrs. A.A. Vlasto in Bracknell, Berkshire in 1905 that endured throughout forty years of Borzoi activity. Two of her studs often credited with improving the quality of the breed were Sparrowhawk of Addlestone, who was not a champion but sired more champions than any other dog of that period, and Gornostay of Addlestone (by Podar of Notts ex Aureola of Llanfair).

The spacious exercising grounds of Addlestone, unused by Borzoi since the kennel closed in 1945, were again a background for their matchless beauty in 1952 when Mrs. Vlasto was hostess to the English Borzoi Club's Diamond Jubilee Show.

The beginning of the 20th century also witnessed the start of the Mythe Kennels of Miss Edith M. Robinson at Tewkesbury, later at Taunton. Her basic stock quite naturally at that period of Borzoi history stemmed from Russian imports but later included Ariane O'Valley Farm's famous daughter Templewood Rynda (by Gornostay of Addlestone) bred by Mrs. E. Laurie of Farnham Common in Bucks.

Some of the better known studs that carried the Mythe prefix were: Ch. Mythe Maxim (by White Elegance ex Mythe Volga), Ch. Mythe Ivanoff (by Ivan of Rebma ex Mythe Vaga), Ch. Mythe Mazeppa (by Gornostay of Addlestone ex Mythe Moya), Ch. Mythe Marinsky (by Ch. Mythe Mazeppa ex Ch. Mythe Marika), Ch. Mythe Marius (by Ivan of Rebma ex Mythe Moya) purchased by Mrs. McNeil as a foundation stud for her Barnaigh kennels in Scotland. A few of the outstanding Mythe bitches were Ch. Marinsky's litter sister Ch. Mythe Molva, Mythe Moya (by Mythe Maxim ex Mythe Marova), Ch. Mythe Petroushka (by Gordey of Addlestone ex Mythe Petrovna), Ch. Mythe Petchora (by Mythe Mazeppa ex Ch. Mythe Petroushka), Ch. Mythe Maelova (by Ch. Mythe Mazeppa ex Powdra Padinia) bred by Mr. Guy but owned by Miss Robinson.

When Miss Robinson realized she faced a terminal illness, she sold or gave away some of her favorite hounds to people who would provide good homes for them. Ch. Mythe Marinsky was sold to Mrs. Hanson who intended to take him to India along with Verba of Moskowa and Borzaya of Bransgore to start a kennel there. When Japan entered the war, the dogs could not be shipped so she had to abandon her plans. Ch. Mythe Marinsky and Borzaya went to Mrs. Jenkins' Moskowa Kennels at Folkestone where they became the sire and dam of Ch. Moryak of Moskowa in 1942. Then Mrs. Jenkins decided it would be best to part with Marinsky as his use as a stud at her kennels was severely curtailed by the war-imposed ban on travel. The dog was purchased by Mr. H.W. Higgins, and he lived the rest of his life as monarch of the Barinoff Kennels at Betchley in Bucks. Verba of Moskowa (by Baraban of Bransgore ex Ch. Brussilovna of Bransgore) was put in a boarding kennel by Mrs. Hanson, later going to the Barinoff Kennels where she and Marinsky produced Barinina of Barinoff in 1943 who in turn produced Mazeppa Brazhinoff (by Amber Elegance) in 1947 owned by Mr. G. Sarson in Leicester.

Mr. Arthur Craven in Manchester was the author of two dog books

Ch. Ivan Turgeneff in a painting by Maude Earle. The white and gold Ivan was a famous winner owned by the Duchess of Newcastle.

Ch. Mythe Mazeppa (by Gornostay of Addlestone ex Mythe Moya) bred and owned by Edith Robinson. He won 21 challenge certificates during his show career. *Fall*

Three of Miss Robinson's typical Mythe Borzoi: Mythe Moya (by Ch. Mythe Maxim ex Mythe Marova), Mythe Planza (by Gordey of Addlestone ex Mythe Petrovna) and Ch. Mythe Ivanoff (by Ivan of Rebma ex Mythe Vaga).

180

published about 1930: *The Borzoi As I Know It* and *Dogs of the World.* In addition to raising many fine Borzoi, both Mr. Craven and his wife were highly respected judges of the breed. One of the first litters of Borzoi bred in their Nevaro Kennels included an outstanding bitch who was a consistent winner until retiring at eight years of age with a record that included a best in show when she was a veteran. Nevarc Poschar Perchina (by Serdechni Bielaja ex Butterfly Ural) bred by Mr. P. Pechan in 1921 was imported by Mrs. Craven. He was a first class stud, show and racing dog known for having one of the finest heads ever seen on a Borzoi. Nevarc Distinction was exported to Australia where she won many honors in the show ring. Nevarc Perfection was sold to Mrs. James G. Dugdale of Hawkdale Kennels. An outstanding bitch retained by the Cravens was the sparkling Nevarc Bubbles (by Ripley Perfection ex Vaynor Gift).

During this same era the Ripley prefix, owned by Mrs. H. Ingham in Starbeck, Harrogate, came into being with Borzoi obtained from Ramsden when that kennel closed during the first World War. Mrs. Ingham also owned Ripley Perfection (by Apostrophe ex Ramsden Refrain). Mrs. Vlasto gave Mrs. Ingham a striking, almost all white, puppy that became Ch. The Gift. When this bitch was bred to Vaynor Dimitri, she produced Ch. Ripley White Marquis whose record included a best in show.

A small but important kennel registered in 1920 was owned by Bernard Timberlake in Harrogate. Haywra produced bitches that were tremendous assets to Mythe, Powdra, Bransgore and Canada's Agatestone kennels. Some of these bitches were: Marie of Haywra (by King of Diamonds of Addlestone ex Vaynor Perfection), Olga of Haywra (by Courageous ex Vaynor Perfection), Olga's litter sister Zia of Haywra, Lilya of Haywra (by Zanoza Peter ex Grainne of Haywra), Zara of Haywra (by Earlstown Exoriri ex Exoriria) and Ch. Felice of Haywra.

Mrs. H. Staple-Smith of Kent purchased Lilya of Haywra, bred her to Ch. Podar of Notts and from this combination chose her affex Powdra. In 1930 she added Mythe Petrovna (by Mythe Maxim ex Ruth Ellen of Haywra). Petrovna was bred to Gordey of Addlestone establishing a bloodline that lives on in American lines through some of Mr. Guy's exports.

One of England's greatest brood bitches was produced by Mr. J. Cramb's Llanfair Kennels at Hitchin in Herts when he bred Zara of Haywra to the self-red Dutch import Max to produce Ch. Aureola of Llanfair. She became a champion at 16 months and was reputed to be the first self-colored deep bronze-red Borzoi to attain that status. Her most famous son was Ch. Gornostay of Addlestone.

Mr. H.A. Thompson of York registered the Shay affix in 1923. He

Ch. Mythe Marius and a basketfull of his puppies.

Nevarc Distinction, bred by the Nevarc Kennels in Manchester, England, was sent out to Australia in 1925.

Ch. Brazhnik of Bransgore, a white and grey dog bred and owned by Mrs. Lucy Ginsgold, earned a spectacular show record including many bests in show.

Ch. Ballerina of Bransgore, bred and owned by Mrs. Ginsgold, one of the top English bitches, was a consistent best in show winner at Championship shows and also a producer of winning progeny.

was the breeder of the Duchess of Newcastle's Ch. Podar of Notts (by Chack Kozak of Shay ex Achotnik of Shay) and the owner of his sire Chack (by Podar von Baikel ex Blanda Achotnik).

Mr. Ernest Henry Guy's first kennel was at Reigate in the late twenties but was then moved to Taunton in Somerset. In lieu of a kennel name as part of the names of his Borzoi, Mr. Guy named his dogs after famous race horses. Ch. Felstead (by Mythe Novikoff ex Topsetta) was named after a Derby winner. One of his favorites was Ch. Blue Train (by Challenge ex Godiva). Blue Train and Ch. Fearless Lass were exported to Major Clark's Sleeping Bear Kennels in Michigan in the late forties. They both quickly earned their American championships also.

Another pre-World War II kennel — and one of England's finest — was Bransgore owned by Mrs. Lucy Gingold in Stockbridge, Hampshire. Although this kennel was not known for breeding the greatest number of Borzoi, the fact that its dogs were in demand in so many countries speaks for their quality. Mrs. Gingold exported Brynzga of Bransgore to Mrs. Chantler's Iskra Kennels in Louisiana. Blistai of Bransgore (by Ch. Gornostay of Addlestone ex Ch. Siegerin of Addlestone) went to New Zealand, and her litter brother Balagur of Bransgore went to Japan. In 1936 alone Mrs. Gingold sent a total of eighteen to Norway, Australia, India and New Zealand.

Siegerin of Addlestone (by Gordey of Addlestone ex Zavist of Addlestone) won her championship after going to Bransgore and was one of Mrs. Gingold's best brood matrons. Ch. Ballerina of Bransgore (by Gordey of Addlestone ex Sandra of Addlestone) was a consistent winner in 1934. Another of Bransgore breeding, Brussiloff of Bransgore (by Ch. Gornostay of Addlestone ex Ch. Cassia of Addlestone) sired many a champion although not shown himself due to a shoulder injury received while hunting hare. Ch. Brazhnik of Bransgore, litter brother of Blistai and Balagur, perhaps the most famous of all Bransgore hounds, won his challenge certificates in three consecutive shows and was a best in show winner for the first time of many before he was a year and a half old. Mrs. Gingold imported American Ch. Akuratni of Romanoff (by Ch. Vigow O'Valley Farm ex Zanoza of Recall) from breeder Louis J. Murr in 1935 to blend his bloodlines with those she had acquired previously.

The Carradale Kennels of Mr. H.A. and Miss S.A. Hawkin of Altrincham in Cheshire boasted over forty years of exhibiting Borzoi. They were among the few breeders surviving the rigors of World War II. Their Zavan of Carradale (by Ch. Zakar of Carradale ex Yomita of Carradale) won three challenge certificates in three consecutive shows to become the only pre-war Borzoi to win a post-war title. In 1954 Ch. Zerlina of Carradale was whelped (by Netheroid Zamba of Carradale ex Ch. Zadiah of Carradale). Zerlina was bred to Horst of Woodcourt to produce Ch. Zastro of Carradale owned by Mrs. O'Haire and Ch. Zarah of Carradale owned by Mrs. Malone. Zadiah was bred to Horst to produce Ch. Zia of Carradale going to Mrs. Curnow and Ch. Zavist of Carradale sold to the Zomahli Kennels.

The Rydens affix came to the fore after the World War II when Mrs. W. Stanley Young in Surrey purchased a puppy from Mrs. Lacy-Hulbert that became the renowned Rimski of Rydens (by Ch. Mythe Marinsky ex Mermain). Rimski was the sire of Ch. Antoinette (ex Olga of Lenoken) in 1944, Ch. Eglon (also ex Olga of Lenoken) in 1946, and Am. Ch. Bellona of Rydens (again ex Olga) in 1945 owned by Bill and Marion Woodcock in California.

Mrs. U.R. Reed's Kuban Kennels in Billericay, Essex opened before the war, drastically curtailed breeding during the war, then resumed at its close with her Mythe stock that formerly included Mythe Grishka (by Ch. Mythe Mazeppa ex Mythe Felia) and Kuban's Almaz (by Mythe Grishka ex Kestor Zmarouna) and Olga of Yof and Irish Ch. Maxim of Moscow. Olga was bred to Ch. Moryak of Moskowa thus adding Bransgore to her line. Her purchase of Barinina of Barinoff from Mr. Guy gave Mrs. Reed Kuban's Krillut when bred to Ch. Winjones Ermolai. Krillut was said to have been one of the best of the Kuban stud force.

Mrs. E.C.M. Harris in Cheshire obtained Velikaya of Addlestone (by Ruski Alexis Sylvanus ex Koporia Sollima) from Mrs. Vlasto in 1933 for a companion. Later she showed her successfully before breeding her thereby starting the Mantavani Kennels. This kennel was one of the few that was active during World War II. Mrs. Harris' first best in show winner was Marinoff Mantavani. Markina of Mantavani was exported to the United States and eventually reached the Alpine Kennels in California.

The saga of the Winjones Kennels really began in 1919 when the owner Mrs. Winfred E. Chadwick of East Horsley in Surrey purchased a Borzoi from the Ripley kennels, then two more from Addlestone in 1922. However, these two bloodlines and the descendants from them were destroyed by misfortunes that plagued the early days of this kennel. In 1945, Mrs. Chadwick, always partial to self-blacks, obtained Astrakan of Barnaigh (by Bargany of Barnaigh ex Sylph of Barnaigh) from the breeder Mrs. McNeil. Astrakan was a prized companion and brood bitch producing Winjones Ataman when bred to Kuban's Almaz. Ataman earned his championship title after being sold to Mrs. McNeil. Another Astrakan son Wihjones Janda (by Mazeppa Brazhnikoff) was sent to the United States when still a puppy to the kennels of Mary Taviner. Janda quickly became a champion and won the 1953 Borzoi Club of America Best of Breed Annual Award.

184

Mrs. Winifred Chadwick and her daughter Audrey with several Winjones Borzoi: Bistri, Ermolai, Dunyasha, Astrakan of Barnaigh, Int. Ch. Balvoniza and Kuban's Nadya.

With judges Mrs. T.A.M. Hill, Miss M.F. Laughrey and Mrs. A.A. Vlasto at the Borzoi Club's Diamond Jubilee Championship show in May, 1952 are the winners of the challenge certificates that day: Mrs. Chadwick's self-black dog Ch. Winjones Ermolai and Mrs. Bereford's red and white bitch Tessina of Yadasar (best in show).

Mrs. Chadwick with one of her lovely Winjones bitches
and Mrs. Beresford's Ch. Gay Cavalier of Yadasar.

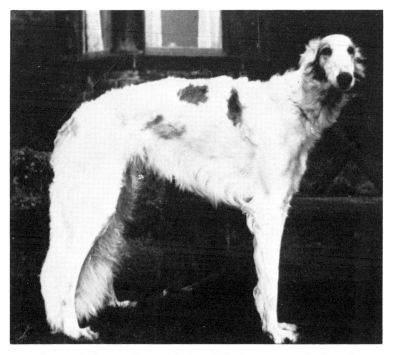

Zomahli Natasha, bred and owned by Mrs. Lillie Pearson, was the dam of many
noted Zomahli winners: Ch. Netheroyd Zomahli Alexey (11 C.C.), Belgian and Int.
Ch. Zomahli Anyushka, Int. Ch. Zomahli Birovitch, Ch. Zomahli Bistri (13 bests in
show), and Ch. Zomahli Almadin of the Barn (6 bests in show).

In 1954 a breeding of the lovely bitch Winjones Dunyashka to Valdaihills Jack Jinks produced the champions Winjones Razluka and Winjones Ritzar. Probably the best known of all the Winjones blacks was the self-black Ch. Winjones Ermolai. This isn't to say that Mrs. Chadwick bred exclusively for blacks by any means. Her lovely best in show bitch Ch. Winjones Lebediska was a rich red and white. Ch. Winjones Razluka was almost totally white and according to Mrs. Chadwick was her favorite. It was after his death in 1960 that the Winjones entries at the shows ceased although Mrs. Chadwick continued in other ways to support and promote the breed.

Mrs. Grace Beresford's Yasasar Kennels in Derby bred Borzoi for many years including many active years after World War II. Her stock was strongly based on Winjones Jiffy of Nenefen (by Kretchit of Kuban ex Orita of Marith) and Ch. Winjones Bolshaia (by Balalaika of Rydens ex Winjones Bistri). Her Terrina of Yadasar (by Zikovitch of Mantavani ex Sorokina of Mantavani) was best of breed at the 1952 Diamond Jubilee show out of an entry of 143. Also well known among her stud force was the lovely red and white Gay Cavalier of Yadasar (by Ch. Winjones Ermolai ex Ch. Winjones Bolshaia). In the early fifties, Mrs. Beresford exported Jonathan of Yadasar to France, Ivanda of Yadasar to Mary Taviner in Nebraska and Model of Yadasar of Robwood (by Wagner of Yadasar ex Tessina of Yadasar) to the Brewsters' Robwood Kennels in New York.

In 1966 Mrs. Beresford co-owned Ch. Tana of Yadasar (by Barthill Feodorovitch ex Ch. Iliad of Woodcourt) with Mrs. Tomlinson. A few years later the two ladies bought Ch. Petronella of Yadasar from Mrs. Harpur's Barthill Kennels. This bitch was bred to Ch. Wellthorne's Bronsky to produce Ch. Yadasar Robin Hood of Boranya and Ch. Yadasar Red Riding Hood of Boranya both sold to Mrs. Wolland.

The Zomahli Kennels in York is operated by Mrs. Lillie Pearson and her nephew Keith Prior. One of the most successful show winners after World War II was their Ch. Netheroyd Zomahli Alexey (by Ch. Maryak of Moskowa ex Zomahli Natasha) in the late forties. Another was Ch. Zomahli Nadia (by Gay Cavalier of Yadasar ex Lady Nadia of Aberwynd) bred by Mrs. D. Pugsley. The dog that did the most to create a favorable reputation for Zomahli was Ch. Zomahli Chernila (by Zeraph of Carradale ex Ch. Zavist of Carradale) with his all time record of 22 Challenge Certificates putting him one C.C. ahead of the previous record holder twenty years previously, Ch. Mythe Maxim. Jackie Bennet-Heard bred her Ch. Angelola of Enolam to Chernila to produce her Ch. Zomahli Keepers Doultuse.

The breeding of Zomahli Dyasha (by Zahedi of Carradale ex Ch. Zomahli Nadia) to Ch. Zavist of Carradale (by Horst of Woodcourt ex

Ch. Zadiah of Carradale) produced Int. Ch. Zomahli Evolgo who was sent to the Windy Hill Kennels of Anna B. Ungerleider in Kentucky after establishing an enviable record in England. Before export, Evolgo produced Ch. Zomahli Feleekan kept at Zomahli and Ch. Zomahli Forona (ex Zomahli Nayada) sent to Windy Hill also. Nayada was bred also to Ch. Black Diamond of Enolam two years later to produce Ch. Zomahli Gueroy and Ch. Zomahli Gratseeya both kept at Zomahli. From that same litter Zomahli Gordey was sent to Irv and Nancy Bonios in California where he earned his American championship. Zomahli Narida was bred to Gueroy to produce Ch. Zomahli Igrock; bred to Gordey she produced Ch. Zomahli Haroshyi sold to Mr. Barratt who took him to South Africa after he was bred by Miss Deane to Zomahli Iskra of Racingold producing Ch. Zomahli Nadesda, Ch. Zomahli Nachal and Ch. Racingold Yaska of Lanclare.

The Woodcourt affix appeared about 1945 when Mrs. Julia Curnow of Warningild, Sussex acquired Ladoga Vassily (by Mythe Grishka ex Kuban's Nadeja) from Mr. C.J. Graham and Olenka of Mantavani (by Marinoff of Mantavani ex Chernova of Mantavani) followed by Priska of Kuban (by Mythe Grishka ex Kestor Zmarouna) and Ladoga Stefan (by Kuban's Almaz ex Kuban's Baba Yaga). Later Woodcourt used Rydens' studs Rimski of Rydens, Balalaika of Rydens and Ch. Eglon of Rydens. Ch. Achilles of Woodcourt (by Ch. Eglon of Rydens ex Carrisima of Woodcourt) was exported to Sweden where he was best in show at Gothenberg. Penza of Woodcourt (by Ladoga Vassily ex Priska of Kuban) went to Australia to earn his championship there. Several others were exported to South Africa including Fleche of Woodcourt (by Horst of Woodcourt ex Nita of Rydens) owned by Mr. R. Sadler of Johannesburg.

In 1950 Mrs. Curnow acquired the German bitch Kismet vom Bergland. When Kismet was bred to Ch. Apex of Woodcourt she produced Ch. Emperor of Woodcourt and Ch. Ebony of Woodcourt. In 1960 Mrs. Curnow sold Ch. Iliad of Woodcourt (by Ch. Emperor of Woodcourt ex Ch. Zia of Carradale) to Mrs. Beresford.

Mr. Edgar Sayer in Northampton was the breeder of Borzoi bearing the Reyas prefix. Probably the best known was Ch. Reyas Romancer (by Reyas Mende ex Winjones Akulina). When Romancer was bred to Mrs. McNeil's Chinchilla of Barnaigh (by Menthe's Yerres v Bergland ex Domino of Barnaigh), Solo of Barnaigh was produced and subsequently sold to James Barr in Wisconsin. Also purchased by Mr. Barr was Bright of Barnaigh, another daughter of Romancer out of Olga of Barnaigh (by Winjones Ataman ex Natasha of Barnaigh). Probably the greatest number of Reyas exports to a single breeder in the United States went to Joanne B. Jelke's Jobi Kennels in Texas. The one to have the most impact on her breeding program was Ch. Jobi Reyas Rohan (by Reyas Rodin ex Donan Alexeyevna). Another Reyas male used by Mrs. Jelke fairly often and successfully was Ch. Reyas Rosandic (by Reyas Marquis ex Reyas Royalise).

Mr. Sayre bred several champions that were kept at his kennel that finished to their titles in the late fifties: Ch. Reyas Rubarto (by Dimski of Rydens ex Reyas Rosalia) and the littermates Ch. Reyas Sandra and Ch. Reyas Mischa (by Jonathan of Yadasar ex Reyas Rosalia). Ch. Reyas Joad of Fortrouge (by Rydens Rythm of Yvill ex Fleet of Fortrouge) was bred by Betty Murray, bought by Mr. Sayer, owned for a while by Jackie Bennett-Heard and then sent to India. Ch. Reyas Black Magic (by Aksakoff Marcovitch ex Reyas Rusalka) was sold to Mrs. Malone. Ch. Reyas Roberto (by Ch. Reyas Rubarto ex Am. Ch. Reyas Zoraya of Carradale) was owned by Mr. Yoeward. Ch. Reyas Ravenna (by Reyas Marquis ex Reyas Royalaise) was retained by the Reyas kennel but sold after Mr. Sayer's demise. The bitch Ledvedka Perchino was bred to Reyas Rainbow to produce Ch. Reyas Rainmaker retained by the Sayers and Ch. Springbank Reyas Raincloud sold to Mrs. Harpur and Ch. Reyas Raingirl sold to Don Robb in Michigan. When Ledvedka was bred to Reyas Rijeka she produced the bitch Ch. Reyas Moyana. Mrs. Sayer bred Reyas Tonya to Reyas Marquis to produce Springbank Sarno later exported to Don Robb, finished by handler Jerry Edwards and then sold to Irv and Nancy Bonios in California.

After he was sold by Mrs. Jenkins, Ch. Moryak of Moskowa's home was the Fortrouge Kennels of Miss Betty Murray, a veterinarian in Croyden. Among his get were Sabre of Fortrouge (ex Seidal of Hindham), Alexis of Swalescar (ex Marion of Lenoken), Bistri of Barinoff (ex Verba of Moskowa) and Zomahli Byadenko (ex Zomahli Natasha). Many of the Fortrouge Borzoi that were exhibited during the late fifties were aired by Ch. Eglon of Rydens.

In 1959 Miss Murray bred Francesca of Hindham to Ch. Reyas Rubarto producing Ch. Ruth of Fortrouge. Ruth went first to the Dutch Vorenoff Kennell and then to Mr. and Mrs. Wallis in Ireland. When the Russian Borzoi Boran arrived in England in the early sixties, Miss Murray bred Carlotta of Fortrouge to him for two litters from which came Ch. Matalona Sudarka of Fortrouge going to Eileen Ruggles, Ch. Zest of Fortrouge and Ch. Zircon of Fortrouge.

Miss Murray and Robin Searle co-owned the bitrch Springbank Lilli. This bitch was bred to Ch. Black Diamond of Enolam to produce Ch. Francehill Diamond Lil; bred to Ch. Zomahli Haroshyi she produced Ch. Francehill Pimlico. The Dutch-bred bitch Vorenoff Diane of Fortrouge bred to Ch. Gay Navaree of Matalona produced Ch. Black Jack of Fortrouge. In the mid-sixties several Borzoi were imported by Fortrouge from the American Sunbarr Kennels. One of these, Fortrouge Invader of Sunbarr was bred to Shelbor Natasha by Mrs. Hargrave to sire Ch. Shelbor Desirable.

Mrs. Jackie Bennett-Heard established the Keepers Kennels and built a reputation around her success with self-black Borzoi with lovely heads. Several Keepers Borzoi were exported to kennels in Holland, Canada and the United States. The foundation bitch of the kennel was Ch. Angelola of Enolam (by Reyas Ringer ex Reyas Black Magic) whelped in 1962. The three best known dogs from this kennel were: Ch. Keepers Michael Angelo (by Ch. Zomahli Chernila ex Anglola) later sent to Finland and litter brothers Ch. Keepers The Baron and Ch. Reyas Keepers Kwango. The latter two were sired by the Russian import Boran out of Anglola. Anglola, bred to Keepers Johnny Angel, produced Ch. Keepers Angeline Les Angels owned by Mr. Duckworth. Angeline was bred to Michael Angelo producing Ch. Skolwood Seraph. Baron sired littermates Ch. Keepers Baroness and Ch. Patrioona Keepers Bolshoi (ex Keepers Sardi). Mrs. Etheridge bred Rodvigal Moonflower to Baron producing Ch. Keepers Black Hawk which Mrs. Bennett-Heard sent to Spain.

A word about Boran would seem to be in order here. He was bred in Moscow by N.V. Vosnesensky in 1960. In 1964, Nikita Kruschev presented this black and white Borzoi to Sir Rùdi Sternberg who had arranged the first British agricultural show in Moscow that year. He was presented to Lady Sternberg and described as "the best dog in Russia." At that time he had reaped many Russian show honors including the grade of Excellent and a gold medal. His honors included competition not only in the breed ring but also in hunting trials and obedience trials. Although not shown in England, he did sire three litters which were considered outstanding and a great contribution to the breed movement in England. Mary Baeton of the Springhurst kennels in Green Bay, Wisconsin imported a Fortrouge-bred son of Boran, but since the American Kennel Club does not accept the Russian Stud Book, the dog could not be registered in the United States. Of course, this also meant that the dog could not be used at stud so his good qualities were unavailable to American breeders unfortunately. I visited at Springhurst shortly after he was imported and found him to be a very fine specimen of the breed both in general conformation and in temperament.

The Francehill Kennels were established by Robin Searle in the 1960's. In 1969 he finished the championship of Ch. Francehill Fairybridge Balinka (by Francehill Russian Cocktail ex Fairybridge Ballerina) bred by Mrs. Bailey and Miss Anthony in 1966. He co-owned Springbank Lilli with Betty Murray from which was produced Ch. Francehill Diamond Lil and Ch. Francehill Pimlico from two litters and registered in his name. Diamond Lil was bred to Ch. Sadko of Colhugh to produce Ch. Francehill Diamond Ring. Two other champions at Francehill are Ch. Francehill Joker (by Reyas Rodin ex Francehill Sweet Sherry) and the lovely red bitch Ch. Francehill Pantaloons (by Int. Ch. Alexie of Colhugh ex Francehill Mary Poppins).

The Barthill Kennels was begun by Mrs. Harpur. Lustre of Yadasar was bred to Aksakoff Marcovitch for two litters in the late 1950's. A puppy from each litter was sold to Mrs. McNeil's Barnaigh kennel in Scotland to become Ch. Barnaigh Barthill Red Rose and Ch. Barnaigh Barthill Marcovitch. After the death of Mrs. Sayer, Ch. Springbank Reyas Raincloud went to reside at the Barthill Kennels. In 1970 Barthill Amber Rose was bred to Barthill Nero to produce Ch. Petronella of Yadasar going to Mrs. Beresford and Mrs. Tomlinson.

Ch. Angelola of Enolam (by Reyas Ringer ex Reyas Black Magic) who produced so well for the Keepers Kennel was bred in 1962 by Mrs. Malone at her Enolam Kennels. From that same litter Mrs. Malone kept the two males Ch. Black Tarquin of Enolam and Ch. Black Diamond of Enolam. Black Magic was then bred to Reyas Rohan who was later exported to the United States to produce Ch. Petroff of Enolam. Bred to Keepers Michael Angelo she produced the bitch Ch. Black Limelight of Enolam. In 1967 Francehill Martini of Enolam was bred to Black Diamond to produce Ch. Magic Dust of Enolam exported to the United States and Ch. Domino of Enolam who was kept at Enolam. Martini was later bred to Petroff to produce Ch. Dark Enchantress of Enolam.

The Matalona Kennels of Mrs. Eileen Ruggles are at Maldon in Essex. Her best known stud was Ch. Gay Navaree of Matalona (by Matalona Babur of Rydens ex Ruth of Matalona). In 1965 Mrs. Ruggles obtained from Miss Murray the Boran daughter Ch. Matalona Sudarka of Fortrouge (ex Carlotta of Fortrouge).

Reg Bassett has done a considerable amount of successful breeding at his Colhugh Kennels during the last two decades. In 1967, he finished title on Ch. Grand Manner of Colhugh (by Lataband of Alesi ex Reyas Red Plume) bred by Mr. Berney. Mr. Bassett bred the bitch Annikka of Greenhaven to Grand Manner for three litters from which came Ch. Tina of Colhugh, Int. Ch. Alesei of Colhugh, Ch. Yalina of Colhugh, Ch. Sarclash of Colhugh, Ch. Colhugh Mia, Ch. Sadko of Colhugh and Ch. Colhugh Valla. Alesei was used by Mr. Barclay and Mrs. Anderson as a stud for their bitch Anastasia of Waycross to produce Ch. Wellthorne's Tilosky before he was exported to the United States to produce the bitch Ch. Colhugh Chrystal. During the same year Ch. Tina of Colhugh was also bred to Tilosky to produce Ch. Colhugh Oriole sold to Mr. Hill. Mr. Hill bred his Dimland Zerlina of Colhugh to Tilosky also in 1973 to produce Ch. Dim land Kohoutek of Colhugh. Mr. Basett used Kohoutek on his bitch Keepers Falling Leaves to produce Ch. Colhugh Blangers.

Ann Thornwell has been breeding Borzoi using the Wellthorne affix. In 1964 she bred her Galina of Matalona to Ch. Arnorinski of Greenhaven (by Marcellus of Fortrouge ex Winjones Radonga) to produce the bitch Ch. Wellthorne's Kalinca. Kalinca was bred to Ch. Gay Nevaree of Matalona to produce Ch. Wellthorne's Kitev in 1967. In 1969 she was bred to Int. Ch. Keepers Michael Angelo producing the brothers Ch. Wellthorne's Tilosky and Ch. Wellthorne's Bronsky. She kept Bronsky and sold Tilosky to Reg Basett who later exported him to the United States where he was co-owned by Bruna Henry and Ron Dyane Roth in California. Tilosky was bred to Lisa of Waycross by Mr. Barclay and Mrs. Anderson to produce Ch. Waycross Roksana and Ch. Stonebar Nicholenka.

Many of the English breeders of today are quite familiar to American breeders and fanciers as there has been much correspondence crossing the Atlantic as well as several exports. Several of these English breeders have been invited to judge at various American Borzoi specialty shows: Betty Murray, Eileen Ruggles, Reg Bassett, Ann Thornwell, Keith Prior, Robin Searle and Fred and Julia Curnow.

5

Borzoi Standards

WHENEVER A NEW BREED has been created, a need has arisen for a written description of the ideal specimen of the breed, a standard to which breeders refer when planning breeding programs and against which all dogs produced may be judged. While governing bodies devoted to the breed may have made changes from time to time, the Borzoi standard has remained basically the same for over three quarters of a century in the United States. The fancy has over the years improved the picture of the Borzoi but not always the functional qualities. Too often faults that are seen frequently gradually become a part of the breed and accepted. Those truly devoted to the breed must constantly strive to create dogs meeting the specifications laid down in the standard.

The standard for Borzoi was written to describe the type of dog which could most effectively course wolves and other large game over vast open land. Basically, the Russian, English, Canadian and American standards are the same. In each standard there may be a more detailed description of various features than in another, but the total in each case is the same. Probably the greatest difference worth noting is the description of toplines. The Russian standard requires a back "slightly arched forming a regular arch prolonged by the loins." Both Canadian and American standards call for a back "rising a little at the loins in a graceful curve". The English standard wants a "back rising in a graceful arch from as near the shoulder as possible....."

It behooves all students of the Borzoi to study and compare each standard included herewith. Semantics being what they are, individual experience being what it is, there may well be confusion on various points, definitions of various descriptive words and phrases. The next chapter will attempt to clear up some of this confusion, define some of the terms and more broadly interpret the description of the Borzoi which is the Standard.

The first Borzoi standard was adopted in the United States in 1903 and remained unchanged until 1940 at which time the disqualification for blacks and black-and-tans was deleted. On June 13, 1972 the American Kennel Club approved the revised standard below. The revisions to the 1940 standard included broadening the scope of the general description, including a section on gait, and eliminating the point scale in favor of a more realistic determination of the degree of importance of various faults.

The American Standard for Borzoi

GENERAL APPEARANCE—The Borzoi was originally bred for the coursing of wild game on more or less open terrain, relying on sight rather than scent. To accomplish this purpose, the Borzoi needed particular structural qualities to chase, catch and hold his quarry. Special emphasis is placed on sound running gear, strong neck and jaws, courage and agility, combined with proper condition. The Borzoi should always possess unmistakable elegance, with flowing lines, graceful in motion or repose. Males, masculine without coarseness; bitches, feminine and refined.

HEAD—Skull slightly domed, long and narrow, with scarcely any perceptible stop, inclined to be Roman-nosed. Jaws long, powerful and deep, somewhat finer in bitches but not snipy. Teeth strong and clean with either an even or a scissors bite. Missing teeth should be penalized. Nose large and black.

EARS—Small and fine in quality, lying back on the neck when in repose with the tips when thrown back almost touching behind occiput; raised when at attention.

EYES—Set somewhat obliquely, dark in color, intelligent but rather soft in expression; never round, full nor staring, nor light in color; eye rims dark; inner corner midway between tip of nose and occiput.

NECK—Clean, free from throatiness; slightly arched, very powerful and well set on.

SHOULDERS—Sloping, fine at the withers and free from coarseness or lumber.

CHEST—Rather narrow, with great depth of brisket.

RIBS—Only slightly sprung, but very deep, giving room for heart and lung play.

BACK—Rising a little at the loins in a graceful curve.

LOINS—Extremely muscular, but rather tucked up, owing to the great depth of chest and comparative shortness of back and ribs.

FORELEGS—Bones straight and somewhat flattened like blades, with the narrower edge forward. The elbows have free play and are turned neither in nor out. Pasterns strong.

FEET—Hare-shaped, with well-arched knuckles, toes close and well padded.

HINDQUARTERS—Long, very muscular and powerful with well bent stifles; somewhat wider than the forequarters; strong first and second thighs; hocks clean and well let down; legs parallel when viewed from the rear.

DEWCLAWS—Dewclaws, if any, on the hind legs are generally removed; dewclaws on the forelegs may be removed.

TAIL—Long, set on and carried low in a graceful curve.

COAT—Long, silky (not woolly), either flat, wavy or rather curly. On the head, ears and front of legs it should be short and smooth; on the neck the frill should be profuse and rather curly. Feather on hindquarters and tail, long and profuse, less so on chest and back of forelegs.

COLOR—Any color or combination of colors is acceptable.

SIZE—Mature males should be at least 28 inches at the withers and mature bitches at least 26 inches at the withers. Dogs and bitches below these respective limits should be severely penalized; dogs and bitches above the respective limits should not be penalized as long as extra size is not acquired at the expense of symmetry, speed and staying quality. Range in weight for males from 75 to 105 pounds and for bitches from 15 to 20 pounds less.

GAIT—Front legs must reach well out in front with pasterns strong and springy. Hackneyed motion with mincing gait is not desired nor is weaving and crossing. However, while the hind legs are wider apart than the front, the feet tend to move closer to the center line when the dog moves at a fast trot. When viewed from the side there should be noticeable drive with a ground-covering stride from well-angulated stifles and hocks. The over-all appearance in motion should be that of effortless power, endurance, speed, agility, smoothness and grace.

FAULTS—The foregoing description is that of the ideal Borzoi. Any deviation from the above described dog must be penalized to the extent of the deviation, keeping in mind the importance of the contribution of the various features toward the basic original purpose of the breed.

The Canadian Standard for Borzoi

HEAD—Skull slightly domed, long and narrow, with scarcely any perceptible stop, rather inclined to be Roman-nosed; jaws long, powerful and deep; teeth strong, clean and even, neither pig-jawed nor undershot; nose large and black.

EARS—Small and fine in quality, lying back on the neck when in repose with the tips when thrown back almost touching behind the occiput; raised when at attention.

EYES—Set somewhat obliquely, dark in color, intelligent, but rather soft in expression, never full nor staring, nor light in color, eyelids dark.

NECK—Clean, free from throatiness, somewhat shorter than in the Greyhound, slightly arched, very powerful and well set on.

SHOULDERS—Sloping, should be fine at the withers and free from coarseness or lumber.

CHEST—Rather narrow, with great depth of brisket.

RIBS—Only slightly sprung, but very deep, giving room for heart and lung play.

BACK—Rising a little at the loins in a graceful curve.

LOINS—Extremely muscular, but rather tucked up, owing to the great depth of chest and comparative shortness of back and ribs.

FORELEGS—Bone flat, straight, giving free play for the elbows, which should be neither turned in nor out; pasterns strong.

FEET—Hare-shaped, with well-arched knuckles, toes close and well padded.

HINDQUARTERS—Long, very muscular and powerful, with well bent stifles and strong second thighs, hocks broad, clean and well let down.

TAIL—Long, set on and carried low in a graceful curve.

COAT—Long, silky (not woolly), either flat, wavy or rather curly. On the head, ears and front of legs it should be short and smooth; on the neck the frill should be profuse and rather curly. Feather on hindquarters and tail long and profuse, less so on the chest and back of forelegs.

COLOR—Any color, white usually predominating, more or less marked with lemon, tan, brindle, gray or black. Whole-colored specimens of these tints occasionally appear.

GENERAL APPEARANCE—Should be that of an elegant, graceful aristocrat among dogs, possessing courage and combining muscular power with extreme speed.

SIZE—Dogs, average height at shoulder from 28 to 31 inches; average weight from 75 to 105 pounds. Larger dogs are often seen, extra size being no disadvantage when it is not acquired at the expense of sym-

196

metry, speed and staying quality. Bitches are invariable smaller than dogs, and two inches less in height, and from 15 to 20 pounds less in weight is a fair average.

Scale of Points

Head 12
Eyes 5
Ears 3
Neck. 5
Shoulders and brisket 10
Ribs, back and loins 15
Hindquarters, stifles and hocks 12
Legs and feet 10
Coat and feather 10
Tail. 5
Conformation and gait. 15

                                                            Total   100

The English Borzoi Standard

CHARACTERISTICS—Alertness, dignity, courage.

GENERAL APPEARANCE—Very graceful, aristocratic and elegant, combining courage, muscular power and great speed.

HEAD AND SKULL—Head long and lean; well filled in below the eyes. Measurement equal from the occiput to the inner corner of the eye, and from the inner corner of the eye to the tip of nose. Skull very slightly domed and narrow, stop not perceptible, inclining to Roman-nose. Head fine so that the direction of the bones and principal veins can be clearly seen. Bitches' heads should be finer than dogs'. Jaws long, deep and powerful; nose large and black, not pink or brown, nicely rounded, neither cornered nor sharp. Viewed from above should look narrow, converging very gradually to tip of nose.

EYES—Dark, intelligent, alert and keen. Almond shaped, set obliquely, placed well back but not too far apart. Eye rims dark. Eyes should not be light, round or staring.

EARS—Small and fine in quality; not too far apart. They should be active and responsive; when alert can be erect; when in repose nearly touching at the occiput.

MOUTH—Teeth even, neither pig-jawed nor undershot.

NECK—Clean, slightly arched; reasonably long; powerful. Well set on, free from throatiness. Flat at the sides, not round.

FOREQUARTERS—Shoulders clean, sloping well back, fine at withers, free from lumpiness. Forelegs lean and straight. Seen from the front, narrow like blades; from the side, wide at shoulder, narrowing down to foot; elbows neither turned in nor out; pasterns strong, flexible, springy.

BODY—Chest, great depth of brisket, rather narrow. Ribs well sprung and flexible; neither flat-sided nor barrel-shaped. Very deep, giving heart room and lung play, especially in the case of mature males. (It is from depth of chest rather than breadth that the Borzoi derives its heart room and lung play.) Back rising in a graceful arch from as near the shoulder as possible with a well-balanced fall-away. The arch to be more marked in dogs than bitches. Rather bony, muscular and free from any cavity. Muscles highly developed and well distributed.

HINDQUARTERS—Loins broad and very powerful, with plenty of muscular development. Quarters should be wider than shoulders, ensuring stability of stance. Thighs long, well developed with good second thigh. Hindlegs long, muscular, stifles well bent, hocks broad, clean and well let down.

FEET—Front feet rather long, toes close together; well arched, never flat, neither turning in nor out. Hind feet hare-like, i.e. longer and less arched.

TAIL—Long, rather low set. Well feathered, carried low, not gaily. In action may be used as rudder but not rising above level of back. From hocks may be sickle shaped but not ringed.

COAT—Long and silky (never woolly), either flat, wavy or rather curly. Short and smooth on head, ears, and front of legs, on neck the frill profuse and rather curly, forelegs and chest well feathered, on hindquarters and tail feathering long and profuse.

COLOUR—Immaterial. In the opinion of the Club a dog should never be penalised for being self-coloured.

SIZE—Height at shoulder: Dogs from 29 inches upwards; bitches from 27 inches upwards.

FAULTS—Short neck, coarse and big ears. "Dish-faced", coarse head, light or round eyes, straight shoulders, flat back, arch starting too far back, too narrow in front. Round bone, straight hocks, weak quarters, coarse coat, splay footed, too close behind, also lack of quality and lack of condition.

Head complete 15
      (eyes and ears included)
Neck 10
Shoulders and chest 15
Ribs, back and loins 15
Hindquarters, stifles and hocks 15

Total   100

The Russian Borzoi Standard

GENERAL APPEARANCE, TYPE OF CONSTRUCTION—Hound of great height, long racy build and strong. The height at the withers is of 70-82 centimeters (27¼ to 32½ inches) for males, about 5 centimeters (2 inches) less for bitches. The height at the withers is almost the same as that of the croup or hardly superior. The length index is about 105 for males, about 107 for bitches.

TEMPERAMENT—Quiet.

CHARACTERISTIC MOVEMENT—Until the game is raised, a not very fast trot; during the chase a speedy gallop in long, fleet leaps.

COLORS—White; sable of all shades; silver shaded sable, dark shaded sable; tan shade with black, muzzle and legs dark; grey, from ash-grey to yellowish-grey; brindled, sable or tan or grey with extended darker stripes; tan, black and all intermediary shades of these colors. Tan points are admissible but not desired. For dark-colored dogs, a black muzzle is typical as well as dark patches on the body. All colors can be either plain or spotted. The self-colored dogs are darker on the upper side, the color fading into a lighter shade towards the extremities, the belly and the hind part of the legs.

COAT—The hair is soft, wavy or in great curls. At the head and legs the hair is short. At the neck, on the back and on the breast, the hair is longer. The ornamental hair is most developed around the neck, at the lower part of the chest, the belly, the hind part of the front legs and the thighs. At the lower part of the tail it hangs in fringes; at the upper part of the tail, it is curly.

SKIN, MUSCLES, BONE—The skin is thin, elastic, without any loose cellular tissue underneath and without folds. The muscles are strongly developed, long. The bones are solid.

HEAD—Long, narrow, lean. The length of the muzzle is equal to that of the skull. The passage from the forehead to the muzzle is hardly noticeable. Seen from the side, forehead and upper line of muzzle form an almost straight line, very slightly convex. The skull is narrow, oval-shaped. The occipital hillock is well accentuated. The upper part of the skull is straight or receding.

MUZZLE—Narrow, straight, lean, with a slight hill towards the nose. The nose is black, over-reaching. The lips are thin, well stretched along the jawbones, with dark rims.

199

EARS—Small, delicate, narrow, pointed, set high, not very far apart, folded back along the neck, the tips very close together. When alert, the Psovaya Barzaya raises the ears on their cartilages, the tips sometimes falling over.

EYES—Large, the lids cut obliquely, dark brown or chestnut brown. The lids are black.

NECK—Long, slightly arched, well muscled, flattened laterally, set at an angle of 50-60° to the longitudinal axis of the body.

CHEST—Not broad, of narrow oval, reaching to the elbows and lower. The ribs are regular, getting shorter towards the rear part of the chest which goes sharply over to the belly.

WITHERS—Not pronounced.

BACK—Wide, muscled, slightly arched, forming a regular arch prolonged by the loins. This arch is more pronounced in males than in bitches.

LOINS—Strong, muscular, not accentuated.

CROUP—Long, wide, muscled, with a slight fall-down. The width between the hipbones must be at least 8 centimeters (3.2 inches).

BELLY—Sharply tucked-up. The passage from the false ribs to the belly is very accentuated.

FOREQUARTERS—Straight, lean, bony, muscled. Seen from the front the legs are straight and parallel. The shoulders are muscled. The bones are oval cut. The elbows are directed to the rear. The shoulder angle is of about 110-120°. The length of the forelegs is nearly equal to half of the total height at the withers. The pasterns are slightly bent.

HINDQUARTERS—Lean, bony, muscled. Seen from the back, the legs are straight and parallel. Seen from the side, they show well developed angles of the joints. They are wide standing and slightly pulled to the rear. The thighs are well developed with jutting-out muscles. The angle of the hock is lean, slightly rounded at the rear, the hocks are short, vertical.

FEET—Lean, narrow, of oval shape, with slightly arched toes. The nails touch the ground.

TAIL—Sabre or slightly sickle shaped, tapering, with heavy feathering. When the dog is quiet, the tail is hanging; when he is excited, it should not be carried above the topline of the back. Long. Pulled between the thighs, it should reach the top of the nearest hipbone.

Faults and Insufficiencies of the Psovaya Barzaya

GENERAL APPEARANCE, TYPE OF CONSTRUCTION—Too high on the legs, too long, short on the legs, height less than the given measures.

COLORS—Too sharply accentuated tan points; coffee-colored, speckled.

COAT—Dull, short hair, ruffled, little furnished; insufficient development of the hair at the thighs and of the feathering; hard, dense and equally distributed on the whole body.

HEAD—Pronounced passage from the skull to the muzzle; clumsy; too broad in cheeks; snipey muzzle; light colored nose.

EARS—Set low, too wide apart, not enough drawn back and close to neck, large, clumsy, with rounded tips.

EYES—Small, round opening of lids; light colored eyes; light lids.

NECK—Round, clumsy.

CHEST—Narrow, hollow, too broad.

BACK—Narrow, sunken, a saddle-back is a heavy fault. A flat back is a fault for males, an insufficiency for bitches.

CROUP—Narrow, insufficient.

BELLY—Not enough tuck-up. Too long.

FOREQUARTERS—Weak pasterns; close or loose elbows; out-turned feet; irregular, clumsy moving, signs of ricketts.

HINDQUARTERS—Cow-hocked; O-shaped; not enough accentuated angle of hock; too straight rear, too thick feet.

FEET—Spread toes; thick, round feet.

TAIL—Short, ring-shaped, carried high; not enough feathering.
All imperfections have to be considered as faults or insufficiencies, depending on the degree of their accentuation.

6
Interpretation of the American Borzoi Standard

General Appearance

Whenever a judge is faced with the problem of determining the degree to which he must penalize one or more of the faults observed in a dog upon which he is passing judgment, he will often solve that problem by asking himself the question "To what degree would this particular fault hinder the dog in fulfilling the breed's original function?" The introductory portion of the standard attempts to set forth this original purpose among other things. In the former standard (prior to 1972) this introduction did not appear as such, but a scale of points was included to indicate the relative importance of the various parts and actions of the dog.

Theodore Marples, editor of *Our Dogs* in England at the turn of the century, published a book *Show Dogs* in 1904 in which he describes all breeds of that era. One sentence he included on the Borzoi is worth quoting as it sums up the description of the Borzoi quite concisely. "The chief requirements of the Borzoi may be summed up in four words all beginning with 'S' — viz., size, speed, strength, symmetry."

I think that everyone would agree that one of the most important words used in describing an ideal Borzoi, a lovely piece of sculpture or even life itself, would be balance. This balance is an important consideration in head proportions, front and rear angulation, height to length ratios, etc. There is occasionally talk of making measurements part of the standard: e.g. the length of the head being equal to the length of the neck. However, when you get too caught-up in measurements and numbers, you tend to lose that necessary sense of balance. Balance is a key word in assessing the quality of an animal: balance between type and soundness, balance in overall proportions, balance between pretty and functional. Balance is something you see with your eyes and you feel with your hands. No tape measure will ever replace hands and eyes.

To me, the most important balance is the balance between type and soundness. This brings up the definition of type. Actually, this definition will vary from person to person. There are some who contend that type encompasses soundness, that type is all that is encompassed by the standard describing the ideal Borzoi. My own definition of type is narrower. I believe that type is the total of all the features, as described in the standard, that make a dog appear to be a Borzoi. Soundness is the correctly put-together parts of the dog coupled with the correct utilization of that structure for the breed. Therefore, using my sort of definitions, there must be a balance of type and soundness in the judging of an ideal Borzoi.

Just as there are degrees of soundness, there are degrees or differences in type. There is no one perfect Borzoi type as the interpretation of the standard in many areas is open to individual definition and interpretation due to semantics and at times personal preference. There are variations in type and all may fit very well within the framework of the standard. These variations may be noted also as representations of different bloodlines. Those people who have had long exposure to the breed are often easily able to identify the bloodlines or kennel from which a particular dog comes. One annoying tendency I find among Borzoi fanciers is the reference to a "national type" — an English type, a Dutch type, a German type. These same people would be the first to deny that there is only one American type. The truth, of course, is that there are varying types in every country where there are many breeders each breeding his own interpretation of the standard.

Even in old Russia there were several types, each being typical of the kennel or hunt by which it was developed. In 1930, N. N. Tschelischtscheff described types found in various Russian Hunts of earlier years in an article in the *Russian Hunting Journal.* Allowing for subjective opinion of dogs remembered from many years before the article was written, the types described by Tschelischtscheff are as follows:

PERCHINO. This was developed by H.I.H. the Grand Duke Nicholas and was divided into two groups — dark colored and light colored. The dark colored type had long, refined heads and were roman-nosed. Size averaged 30½ inches for males, eyes were dark, coats were wavy but not curly and not of great length, and bone was medium. The light colored type had the same type head without the roman-nose. They were the same in general height but were stronger with heavier bone.

OSEROFF. This type was mostly white or white with grey, the coats being close and curly. The head was roman-nosed and there was a definite angle to muzzle and skull rather than parallel planes as in the other types. The eyes were dark but somewhat round with bloodshot whites. (Very likely he was referring to prominent haws rather than bloodshot whites.) Size averaged about 30½ inches.

BOLDAREFF. This was a smaller type with size averaging 29 inches. The heads varied as to being roman-nosed.

TSCHELISCHTSCHEFF. This type was developed by the author of the article and was the largest of the types described, standing at 33 inches. (Was the author possibly playing the game of "bigger is better"?) The coats were wavy and mostly in light colors. The eyes were the same as in the Oseroff type, but the ears were very small and fine often being pricked when alert. These hounds gave the impression of great strength and represented the most ancient type.

SUMAROKOFF. These hounds would seem to be of the most undesirable type as judged by today's standards. The eyes were light and there was a lack of pigmentation in nose and eyelids. They were said to be sound in forequarters but unsound in hindquarters.

GEJEROFF. These hounds averaged 29 inches in height and included more of the darker colors — black, mahogany, several with black muzzles. The prevalence of light eyes in the darker heads did not create an attractive expression. The coats had length but often exhibited a coarse texture. These dogs were described as being fierce and often vicious.

BIBIKOFF. These were of small size and had coarse or wiry texture to the coats.

Dogs from almost all of these types were exported to countries outside Russia during the early years of the 20th century contributing to the variety of types found in all countries then and since.

One often sees extremes in Borzoi: the overly refined dog and the decidedly coarse dog, the camel-backed dog and the flat or even sway-backed dog, the coatless dog and the overly coated dog, the 29 inch male and the 36 inch male, the shy dog and the vicious dog, the thin (to the point of emaciation) dog and the grossly fat dog. There are even those breeders who maintain that the extremes have a place in a breeding program. Experienced, thoughtful breeders know that breeding one extreme to the opposite extreme is NOT the way to produce the more correct median. Black mixed with white in a breeding program does not in itself produce grey. The features as described in the standard are the preferable medians. Breeding the median features, or features varying only slightly to one side or the other of the median, is breeding to the standard and will bring results closest to the ideal Borzoi.

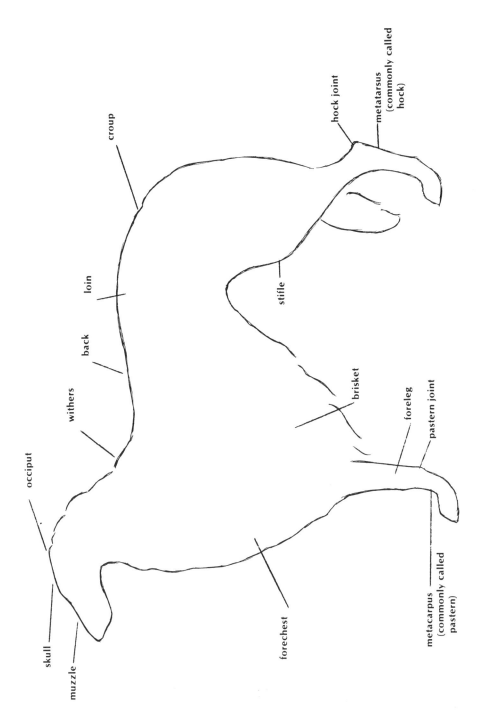

croup

hock joint

metatarsus
(commonly called
hock)

loin

stifle

back

withers

brisket

foreleg

pastern joint

occiput

skull

muzzle

forechest

metacarpus
(commonly called
pastern)

205

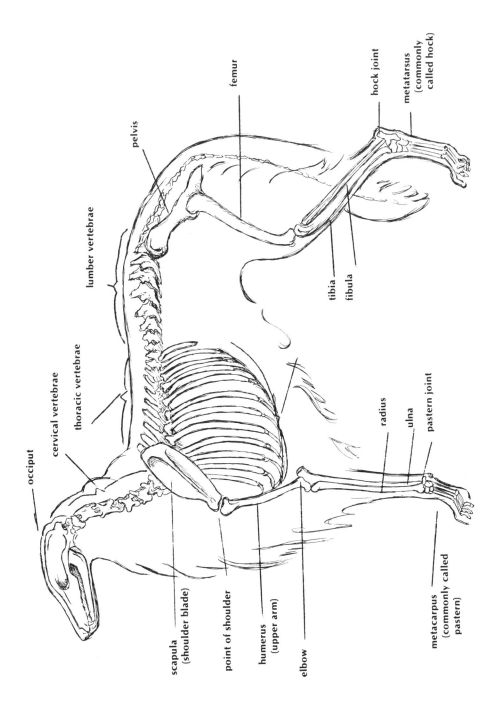

occiput

cervical vertebrae

thoracic vertebrae

lumber vertebrae

pelvis

femur

hock joint

metatarsus
(commonly
called hock)

tibia

fibula

radius

ulna

pastern joint

scapula
(shoulder blade)

point of shoulder

humerus
(upper arm)

elbow

metacarpus
(commonly called
pastern)

The wording of this introductory paragraph of the standard, headed "General Appearance," needs little further clarification. However, I do think a few words need to be said of the last sentence. In some breeds, especially smooth-coated breeds, there is little variation in structure and general appearance between dogs and bitches. In Borzoi there is often a great difference between the sexes, size and coat probably presenting the most notable differences. The standard requires that a male look like a male. By saying that he should be masculine without coarseness, the standard tries to emphasize that extra size does not mean bone too heavy or a skull too broad, both common features contributing to the undesirable coarse, heavy look. A bitch to look feminine should be a refined version of the male but not refined to the point of weediness or frailty. A champion male shown in best-of-breed classes, to be a winner, should present the picture of what is sometimes referred to as a "stallion hound" — totally masculine with an aura of majesty.

Many bitches finish their championships every year yet it is a rare owner who specials a bitch, even an outstandingly good one. Sometimes this is because the bitch is retired to the whelping box to make her impact on the breed from there. Sometimes it is because the bitch doesn't enjoy showing, doesn't have the right attitude for campaigning. But sometimes it is because the owner has the misguided notion that bitches never make it as specials, that bitches never get more than automatic best-of-opposites, that bitches are always discriminated against. Statistics can prove otherwise. Not every bitch champion, of course, can make the grade. But not every male champion can make the grade either. Just in the last several years or so with competition becoming stiffer all the time, two bitches have won best in show at all-breed shows: Ch. Anastasia of Windy Hill (with two such wins) owned-bred-handled by Anna Ungerleider, and Ch. Half Moons Patches owned by P. and D. Redding. Best of breed at several national specialties has been awarded to bitches in recent years: Ch. Med-O-Land's Petrova (twice) owned by Burton Axe and handled by Les Kauffman, Ch. Cordova's Mishka of Baronoff owned and handled by Louise Heaton, Ch. Wildwood's Diva of Phantom Lake C.D.X. owned and handled by John and Melinda Codling, and Ch. Loral's Larissa Ivanovna owned by Bette Bergstrom and handled by Dick Vaughn. Larissa proved she could excel in both the showring and in the whelping box. Three years after her national specialty best of breed, her son Ch. Larissa's Elegante Hijo was best of breed at the same national specialty. The ladies can do it!

Head

Heads of Borzoi generally represent the greatest variation in type, many correctly within the limits of the standard. After getting the first general impression of the overall dog, one usually notices the head next. Often it is the head that impresses the novice the most. The correct head, more than any other feature of the Borzoi, contributes to the look of elegance that is a MUST if a Borzoi is to BE a Borzoi.

The skull is somewhat ovoid having a distinct arched backskull due to the prominent occiput. Sometimes a Borzoi will lack this backskull and the skull will appear more wedge-shaped as in a Whippet or Greyhound. This, of course, is incorrect. Generally, the length of the head is in the range of eleven to thirteen inches although this must be in proportion to the overall size of the dog. It has been said that the head length, multiplied two and a half times, equals the height of the dog. The head must be balanced in length with the length of the skull equaling the length of the muzzle as measured from the tip of the occiput to the inner corner of the eye to the tip of the nose.

The planes of the head are important. In some types the skull and muzzle are in parallel planes, in others the muzzle is slightly angled down from the parallel in reference to the skull. (This would be similar to the old Russian Oseroff type mentioned earlier in this chapter.) In either case there is scarcely any perceptible stop, or "step" from one plane to the other at the juncture of the skull and muzzle. NEVER should there be a continuous convex curvature of skull running into muzzle (as in the Bull Terrier) which would be termed roman-headed. There were problems with this roman-headedness in the 1920's and 1930's but then it was almost bred out by conscientious breeders. In the 1950's it was rarely seen, but in the 1960's and 1970's a few were cropping up, an occasional one even appearing in a champion.

At the point on the muzzle where bone is replaced by cartilage, there is a desirable and decided droop in the muzzle down to the nose. This is termed roman-nosed. It would seem unnecessary to define nose, but due to some confusion that occasionally comes up it should be pointed out that the nose is only the hairless tip of the muzzle. Possibly this confusion is added to by that term roman-nosed which might possibly be better expressed as roman-muzzled.

The nose itself must be black, fully pigmented. Above the nose the hair is very short and thin. When pink skin shows through this area, some people have questioned this color as lack of pigmentation in the nose. However, not being a part of the actual nose, this pink is of no significance nor application.

When the profile of the head is observed, an important aspect must not be overlooked. After observing the topline of the muzzle, the depth of the muzzle must also be assessed. There must be depth to the muzzle with good depth of lower jaw which denotes strength. In dogs with shallow and

The Borzoi skull is ovoid having an arched back skull due to the prominent occiput. The Whippet lacks a backskull having a more wedge-shaped outline to skull.

Correct Borzoi head with correct length of skull to muzzle. Good depth of muzzle.

The topline of head is correct but there is decided lack of depth of muzzle with weak underjaw.

This incorrect head shows a decided stop at the juncture of skull and muzzle.

A Roman-headed Borzoi with a convex curvature of the skull running into muzzle. Totally incorrect.

weak underjaws, there is often a problem with early tooth loss from the lower jaw particularly when the dog is mature. The teeth must be set in a powerful foundation.

Checking the mouth involves alignment of the teeth, positioning of the jaws and number of teeth. The most desirable bite is a scissor bite in which the upper six incisors fit neatly and closely over the lower six incisors. Also acceptable is the level bite in which the upper and lower incisors meet edge to edge. In both of these acceptable bites, the four canine teeth "mesh" with upper and lower canines side by side in the closed mouth. Sometimes in a level bite, with age, one or two of the incisors may "pop" or move slightly out of alignment. This is not a desirable condition certainly but the bite is still considered level. If all the lower incisors slip forward and "flare out," this is an undershot condition. In a bad malocclusion, the canine teeth are positioned behind one another rather than side by side. A wry mouth is sometimes seen. In this condition the jaws do not meet squarely and it is as if the upper jaw had been pushed slightly to one side. The bite may appear overshot on one side and undershot on the other. Many times a wry mouth is caused by an injury and can occur easily in puppies prone to many types of accidents.

However, unless it is definitely known that the condition was caused by a specific accident, a wry mouth must be considered as a serious fault with the strong possibility that it is of genetic origin.

Missing teeth have plagued the breed for many years. Generally, reference to missing teeth applies to the premolars, but there are now occasional cases of missing molars turning up in young dogs. Genetic faults should be assessed in dogs at their early prime (about two to four years of age in Borzoi) since much can mask the genetic truth during old age. After six years of age or so, teeth can be missing from accident or abscess, toplines can flatten or sag from overweight or multiple pregnancies, hip joints can deteriorate leading to faulty movement due to arthritis, etc. The premolars of most dogs have erupted by six months of age and certainly by a year of age. To count teeth, one must first know the formula and placement of all the normal dog's teeth. It should be remembered that a Borzoi's jaws are quite long as compared with those in other breeds although the actual number of teeth placed in those jaws is the same. There will often appear to be gaps in the line of teeth leading the unknowledgeable person to think he is detecting missing teeth, but a count will determine if any are really missing. The formula for canine dentition is included in the chapter on puppy development.

The reference to missing teeth in the standard was included in the 1972 revision. The wording is perhaps unfortunate in that some read that sentence almost to mean that missing teeth are a disqualification. When

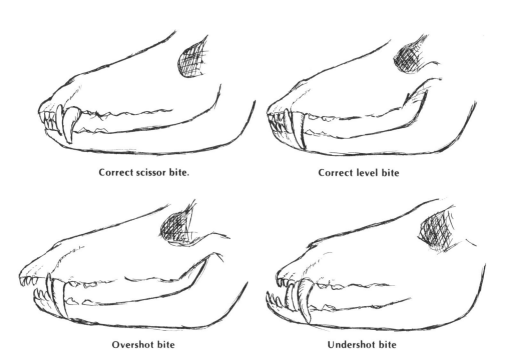

Correct scissor bite.   Correct level bite

Overshot bite   Undershot bite

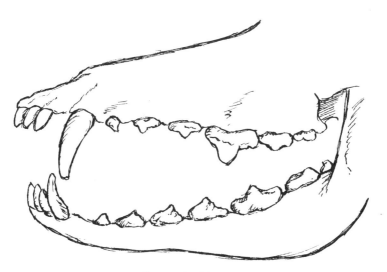

Correct dentition

211

the standard says "missing teeth should be penalized," it means that missing teeth as a fault should be penalized just as any other deviation from the ideal should be penalized. The degree of the fault, and the resulting penalty, rests with the answer to the question of the effect the fault would have on the ability of the dog to fulfill the original purpose of the breed. All faults must be penalized. Since 1972, because of the attention suddenly focused on missing teeth, fewer dogs without full dentition are being bred.

Ears

The ears of the Borzoi are similar to what is called "rose" ears which means that they are laid back in a curled position on the neck. They are "almost touching behind the occiput," the degree of which will depend upon the set of the ears and the width of the backskull.

The ears rise to a semi-pricked position when the dog's attention is attracted by such stimuli as bait, sudden or unusual noises, or the sight of a live or artificial lure. The Borzoi may occasionally bring his ears to a full prick, but this should not be encouraged and the ears must always be brought back to the correct position.

I have seen very few Borzoi with small, fine ears incapable of a momentary pricked position during extreme excitement (notably when sighting game or a lure) so I cannot find myself willing to penalize prick ears severely in a young dog in any situation where he is intensely alert as long as he returns them to a proper position promptly. However, I must admit I abhor the look of a Borzoi standing with prick ears for several minutes looking for all the world like a jackass.

Large ears may tend to hang hound-like as in the Dachshund or even some sighthounds as the Afghan Hound or Saluki. These ears are as incorrect as are ears thrown straight back as in a running jackrabbit. Ear carriage in puppies may vary widely.

Eyes

The proper dark color, shape and set of the eyes give the Borzoi the elegant expression of the true aristocrat. Often, there is a direct relationship between coat color and eye color although the darker the eye, the better in any case. The eye should not be pale yellow, grey or blue. A dark eye gives a softer expression than a light eye. A light brown eye in a dark colored head is less pleasing than the same light brown eye in a light colored head.

The third eyelids, or nictitating membranes, commonly referred to as "haws" should not be prominent. When large or light colored they tend to detract from expression. A dog that is sick or out of condition will often

212

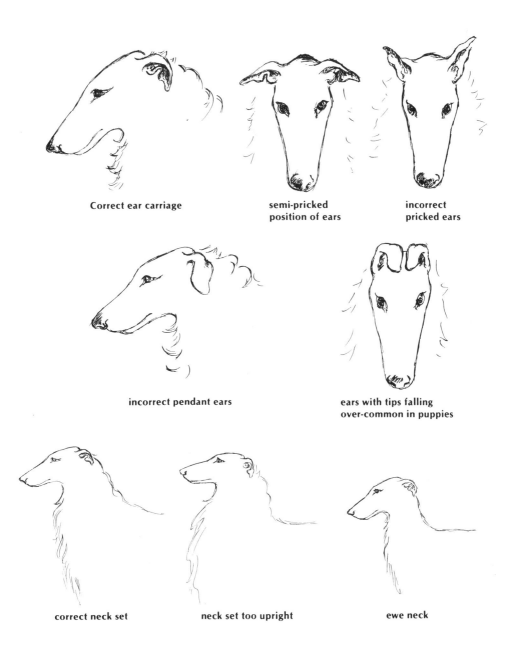

Correct ear carriage

semi-pricked
position of ears

incorrect
pricked ears

incorrect pendant ears

ears with tips falling
over-common in puppies

correct neck set

neck set too upright

ewe neck

213

pull the membranes over the eyes more than would be normal due to lack of pressure within the eye.

The set of the eye is slightly oblique — to the side — giving better peripheral vision. The shape of the eye is slightly almond or oval shaped, never round. A round eye has a staring effect which is incorrect.

The entire eye rim should be pigmented with black just like the nose. Sometimes the eye rims as well as the nose may be slate grey or liver which is definitely incorrect as it does change expression. I remember several years ago seeing a lineup of self-black Borzoi on a bench at a specialty show, all with totally black heads, all from the same litter, all with liver colored eye rims. The heads were lovely in length and shape but the expression was wrong. They looked as if they were all recovering from hangovers! A black eye rim forms the best frame for an expressive eye.

There have been attempts from time to time to equate light eye color either to intelligence or to temperament. In 1934 E.S. Humphrey and L. Warner in the *Journal of Canine Genetics* published the results of a study of inheritance in German Shepherds. One of their conclusions was that there is a strong correlation between light eyes and high intelligence. There have been references in articles from time to time relating light eyes to viciousness. Will someone, some time, try to put these two allegations together to state that intelligent dogs are more often vicious dogs especially if they have light eyes? Nonsense. I cannot accept either relationship of eye color to intelligence or temperament. I cannot accept the theory that the amount of pigment in the eye can affect the amount of intelligence or the amount of stability in the head. In my opinion eye color affects only one thing — expression. And expression is only important in the overall general appearance of the Borzoi.

Neck

There should be no flews or dewlaps and the Borzoi should have a head and neck that is clean, often referred to as "dry." The lips should be tight and firm. The line from the underjaw over the throat and down the neck should be tight and firm with no extra skin or "double chins."

In the standard prior to 1972, the neck was said to be shorter than a greyhound's, but this was removed in the revision of that date as it was felt unwise to refer to another breed in the Borzoi standard. In the Borzoi the neck length is in proportion to the head length. The longer neck in the greyhound contributes towards that breed's ability to produce great initial speed. As endurance is as necessary as speed in the Borzoi, a moderately long neck is required. A too short neck would shorten the length and action of the muscles controlling the shoulder blade and the forward movement of the legs sacrificing speed and endurance.

214

The neck should be set on at an angle of about 50°-60° to the longitudinal axis of the body to use the description in the Russian standard. If the neck is set on too upright or too low, shoulder action and forward movement are inhibited. The importance of the neck set can be seen by the way a dog can change his action when handled on lead in different ways. If the dog is "strung-up" to the point where the neck is forced upright, the forward gait is restricted. Given a loose lead, the neck on the same dog will assume a more natural angle and the dog can better reach out to his full potential.

The arch of the neck required by the standard applies to the area high on the dorsal side of the neck between the second and third vertebrae. A ewe-neck which is a concave curvature of the neck is improper indicating a weakness of the neck ligament.

Shoulders

The shoulder bone or scapula is mobile as it is attached to bone only at its lower extremity (attached to the upper arm or humerus) whereas it is attached at its upper end to muscles and thereby to the spinous processes of the top of the vertebrae in the thoracic region. This muscle, rather than bone, attachment at the upper end allows it to shift position more readily with movement of the forelegs or the neck. The upward spires of the vertebrae running between the scapulae are very slightly above the tips of the scapulae when the dog's neck is in a normal semi-upright position. As the neck moves downward the tips of the scapulae move forward and upward above the spires.

The standard calls for a sloping shoulder. This means that the scapulae should slant at an ideal or most efficient angle of about 50° from the horizontal. Some authorities opt for a 45° angle but this is rarely found and there is question as to whether that angle is even desirable. The lower end of the scapula, the point of shoulder, attaches to the upper arm or humerus. The American standard unfortunately has nothing to say about the humerus or its positioning. The Russian standard, however, calls for an open angle of 110-120°. If the shoulder is laid back at the ideal 50° and using the average of 115° in the Russian standard, this would put the layback of the humerus at 65° from the horizontal. As noted above, the upper end of the scapula is quite mobile due to its attachment to muscles rather than bone so that exact measurements of angles can vary in the same dog due to slight changes in positioning especially of the neck. For this reason the shoulder angulation is best expressed as a range in the open angle as in the Russian standard.

As you run your hands down the chest and then in under the upper arm, you should feel the close, firm attachment of the upper arm to the

215

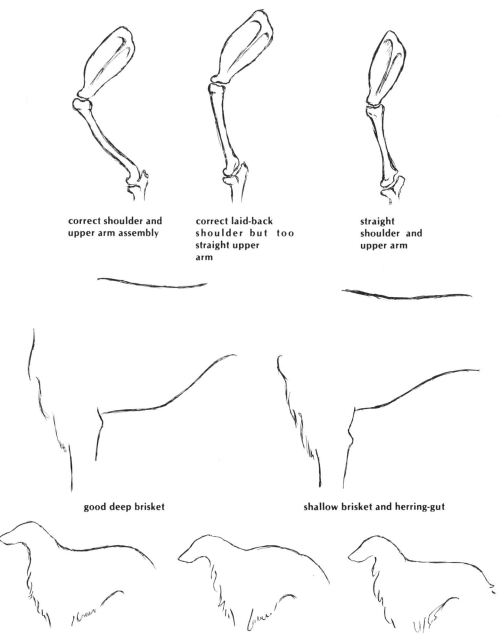

correct shoulder and
upper arm assembly

correct laid-back
shoulder but too
straight upper
arm

straight
shoulder and
upper arm

good deep brisket

shallow brisket and herring-gut

correct topline rising a little at the
loin in a graceful curve

wheel-back arch starts at the
withers

flat topline with no perceptible
rise over loin

body. Application of slight outward pressure to the elbows at the same time should not make the elbows flip outwards easily. The total shoulder-upper arm assembly that is well balanced and properly angled will produce the most efficient forward movement as viewed in profile with full extension of the forelegs. Defects in this assembly will restrict the forward action producing a short, stilted stride.

If there is excessive muscle development or excessive pads of fat under the upper shoulder, it is termed "loaded." Shoulder angulation can be changed slightly due to this. In order to gain strength, the upper end of the scapula is forced outward at the same time bringing the lower end inward usually forcing the elbow out and distorting the desired straight column of bones in the foreleg. The standard calls for fineness at the withers, but this doesn't mean that the opposite extreme of loaded shoulders, which would be a pinching of the blades, is any more desirable.

Chest and Ribs

To carry through with all the other features designed for streamlining and speed, the ribs must not produce a barrel shaped chest but should only be slightly to moderately sprung. It stands to reason that a coursing dog will put great demands on heart and lungs, so adequate room must be allowed for these organs. If the width of their housing is limited by the slightly sprung ribs, compensation has been allowed by calling for great depth of brisket. The spinous processes on the sides of the thoracic vertebrae protrude outwards and then slightly downwards leading into the thirteen pairs of ribs which curve slightly and continuously out, down and under the chest. It should be stressed that the curve is continuous to the sternum. If the processes of the vertebrae are too short or slant too suddenly downward or if the lower portions of the rib curve inwards too abruptly, there is not sufficient spring of rib. Too little spring creates a slab-sided Borzoi humorously referred to by one author as a "canine angelfish."

The brisket line runs parallel to the horizontal back to the base of the eighth or ninth rib. If the line starts to sweep up at the third or fourth rib, the condition is known as herring-gut. Obviously a herring-gut limits heart and lung capacity.

Some standards for sighthounds require great depth of brisket often calling for the brisket to reach to or below the elbows. This requirement is misleading as the depth of brisket is relative to length and angle of the upper arm. The hand and eye are more useful in determining whether there is adequate depth of brisket than measurement of brisket to elbow.

While the general impression of the chest is narrowness, it should never be so narrow that the front appears pinched with the forelegs "coming out of the same hole." The width between the forelegs is relative to the overall size of the dog, but generally it is about the width of your hand. The sighthounds certainly don't have prominent forechests as many scenthounds do. However, they should have sufficient fill rather than a hollow between the forelegs.

Back and Loins

The term "back" is often used interchangeably with the term "topline." Technically, the back is that part of the backline composed of the five vertebrae between the withers and the loin, the 9th to 13th vertebrae. According to the wording of the standard, it would seem that this section really should be entitled "topline." It would then require the topline to rise a little at the loin in a graceful curve. Topline would include the entire line from the withers to the loin and through the croup.

If a caricature of the Borzoi were to be drawn, there would be two features exaggerated immediately to imply "Borzoi:" an exaggerated length of head and an exaggerated curve to the topline. Unfortunately too many novices tend to accept this caricature and thus find this type of Borzoi in the flesh to be most attractive. It is only later when these novices go on to learn about and question function that they realize that the caricature is completely without proper function. This exaggerated curvature of the topline usually starts immediately behind the withers and is termed a "wheel-back" or "camel-back." An extreme case would have about as much flex as an overstretched rubberband.

The topline starts out as level over the actual back with the slightly arched part of the topline starting and peaking over the loins. The graceful arch is carried out through the croup and is extended by the sweep of the tail. It should be kept in mind that the Borzoi is a heavily coated dog and that this covering of the basic structure can often distort the total picture. Just as too thick a neck ruff can make the neck look too short, so also can too much coat over the croup make the croup and the arch over the loin look too flat. Judicious use of thinning scissors can help the eye to see what sometimes only the hand can feel. Of course, excessive coat can also cover faults and can be "sculpted" to create the illusion of angulation or topline, but discussion of that belongs in another chapter.

The graceful curve should be equal at both ends. The beginning of the curve is at the beginning of the loins; the ending of the curve is the croup. Neither should be exaggerated. If the ending is steeper than the beginning, there is an exaggerated fall-away at times referred to as goose-rump usually sloping more than 30° to the horizontal.

The lumbar vertebrae over the loin area are the largest of the vertebrae as they should be to anchor the heavy, powerful muscles of the loins. Because there are no ribs in this area to contribute to a degree of rigidity, the loins remain completely flexible. Where they do not remain flexible, but remain in a state of tension, the Borzoi will not only have too steep a croup, but will often tend to be overangulated in stifle from the naturally induced crouch position. A dog with a rigid arch will usually move in a stilted manner. A proper topline will appear to flatten somewhat as the dog moves into a fast trot. A dog with a rigid topline will appear to maintain the exact same topline no matter what speed the trot.

Because of the great depth of chest, the tuck-up gives the illusion of being exaggerated. The tuck-up or line of the belly somewhat follows the curvature of the topline.

The English standard requires a topline quite a bit different from that called for in the American and Russian standards. The English standard states that the curve in the topline should start as close as possible to the withers. This sort of topline is inconsistent with efficient motion in a coursing hound. With the influx of English imports into this country, there is beginning to be confusion as to the correct toplines among fanciers, but only among those who have not taken the time to study and understand the American standard. Too many people are faulting proper toplines which are indeed "rising at the loins in a graceful curve" as being too flat, when in fact they are totally correct.

Forelegs

The bones of the forelegs are usually referred to as bladed bone. Since this by itself might not give an adequate description, the standard describes it more fully comparing the bone to a knife blade with the narrow or sharp edge forward. Actually, the bones are ovoid as would be consistent with the general pattern of streamlining found in all parts of the dog's anatomy. The bone should be strong but not gross. It must be in proportion to the dog. A very tall dog with lots of body substance would look as out of place with long, thin "toothpick" legs as would a small sized dog with heavy, almost round bone. Round bone occurs from time to time, but is entirely improper on a coursing hound. Dogs dependent upon forward speed should have oval bones as in fast forward movement the greatest stress is on the front and the rear of the bone. Sometimes a Borzoi with a truly bladed bone may have thick hair on his legs giving a false appearance of round bone. Sighthounds have longer, lighter, narrower, straighter bones throughout than do dogs of other breeds. This is most visible in the long bones, and comparison of those bones in radiographs is most convincing.

Seen from the front, the forelegs from the point of the shoulder to the feet present a straight column of bones. Immature dogs often have bumpy

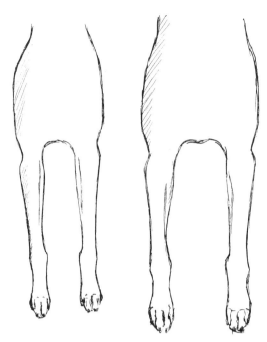

Correct forequarters as seen from the front. The dog on the right is obviously larger and correctly has more relative width between the forelegs.

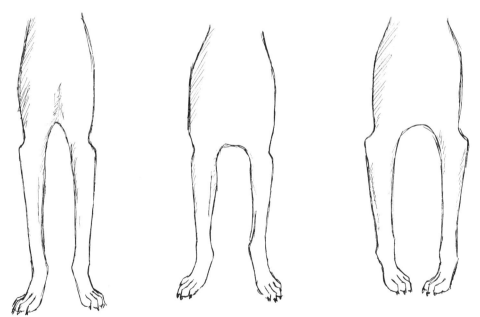

Incorrect forequarters as seen from the front. The first one is too narrow and lacks full. The second one has the correct width but like the first one has pasterns turned out. The third one toes in throwing the elbows out.

correct pastern with
slight incline

pastern too upright

pastern knuckling
over

broken down
pastern

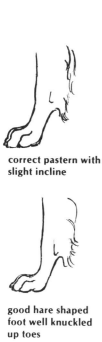
good hare shaped
foot well knuckled
up toes

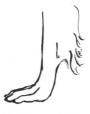
flat foot with thin
pads

splayed foot

incorrect round cat
foot

correct croup and rear
angulation

goose-rump sickle hocks

goose-rump over-angulation

flat croup high in hock

too short in upper and lower
thighs

flat croup, no angulation of
stifle or hock

221

knees or enlargements at the pastern joints. This entirely normal condition will disappear as the bones lengthen and the dog matures. A young dog should not be penalized for this, even though in appearance it detracts from the smooth, straight look desired in the forelegs.

Although the area from the juncture of the foreleg down to the foot is often called the pastern, technically the pastern is only the assembly of small bones at the juncture of the foreleg (radius and ulna) with the metacarpus. It is said that a long metacarpus (with a long metatarsus in the rear assembly) are necessary in the sprinter. A dog which needs to exhibit endurance as well as speed would need only a moderately long metacarpus. A slight incline of the metacarpus is highly desirable for spring and resilience. After all it is the metacarpus that receives the impact from the ground when the dog is running or jumping. While the eye can rarely catch it, the metacarpus practically flattens to the ground immediately after impact and just as immediately straightens. The camera can better stop the action and show this flattening, which until seen on film is pretty hard to believe. An entirely upright metacarpus does not absorb the impact nearly as well as the one bent at about $10°$. Weakness in the metacarpus or pastern can take either of two forms: it can knuckle over or it can go the other direction and break down. Constant stress will accentuate the problem. Unfortunately, both extremes have occurred on top winning sighthounds of all breeds. Viewed from the front, the requirement for a straight column of bones will require that the feet and pasterns as well as the elbows must turn neither in nor out.

Feet and Dewclaws

To obtain more leverage, the feet should be well knuckled up and oval or hare shaped. A round or cat-foot is incorrect. The difference in length between these two shapes comes from the longer third phalanx or digit. Splayed feet, or chicken feet, have space between the toes leading to weakness. They will not serve the dog well for long running on rough ground. Sometimes roadwork or changing the surfacing of the kennel runs will improve a bad foot. However, environmental changes will not change the genetic determination of such bad feet. The pads must be heavy and thick to serve as the shock absorbers for the running dog.

The nails should be kept at a length that just clears the ground. I recall a post-show discussion where the judge was asked for her general impression of the entry. One of her observations was that exhibitors should take better care of their dogs' feet particularly the nails as the nails on the majority of the dogs she had seen that day were entirely too long. One exhibitor took exception to this comment stating that many of the dogs were used for coursing and needed long nails to "dig in" when running.

This notion is unfounded. The nails are not used like the cleats on golf shoes. If the pads are thick and firm on good feet, they will grip the ground and gain purchase as the dog runs.

The removal of dewclaws on the front legs is commonly done in young puppies. This not only improves the neat appearance of the legs but also prevents injury to this extra toe in the field. However, the removal is not mandatory according to the standard and remains the option of the breeder or owner. Occasionally there will be dewclaws on the hindlegs that are smaller and less well attached than those on the front. These should be removed when found.

Hindquarters

Power for drive and speed is generated by the hindquarters. Therefore, the hindquarters must be long, muscular, powerful and wide. The croup, or rump, must be neither flat nor steep but with the pelvis set at about a 30° angle from the horizontal. The measurement of this angle can be deceiving as it changes with the manner in which the hindquarters are set up. With the rear set so that the hock is perpendicular to the ground, there should be an open angle of the femur and the pelvis equalling the open angle of the forequarters.

The stifle joint is the articulation of the upper and lower thighs, the femur to the tibia-fibula. Both upper and lower thighs should be long and muscular with a good bend of stifle. Overangulation, often with a steep croup, will often go along with sickle hocks as the dog attempts to get his feet under the vertical center of gravity. Lack of angulation of the stifle joint usually goes with a lack of definition of hock joint creating a somewhat straight line from femur to foot.

The term "hock" is often loosely used not to pertain to the joint alone but to the entire length of the metatarsus. Because it is used so commonly in this way, it will be used here with that loose definition.

The phrase "hocks well let down" requires a short distance from hock joint to the ground. As with the metacarpus (or pastern as again commonly usage calls it) a long hock is required for speed whereas a shorter hock is more compatible with the combination of speed and endurance. Two faults in hocks showing up more and more often in Borzoi today are sickle hocks and popping hocks. The first is a rigidity of the hock joint while the second is a looseness or double-jointedness. In sickle hocks the hock is set at an angle rather than vertical to the ground. When the dog moves, this angle is not straightened and the dog's gait is stiff, sometimes shuffling, as there is no effective use of the hock joint and no push from the rear. Popping hocks almost always occur when there is lack of definition of hock angle. The hocks in this case are able to straighten in the follow-through

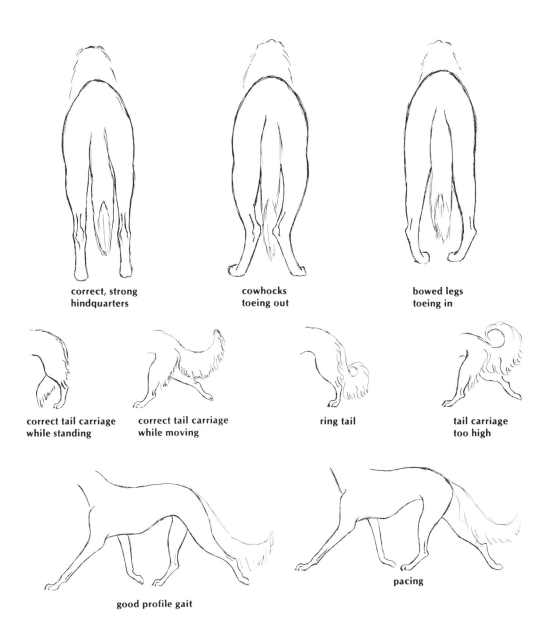

correct, strong
hindquarters

cowhocks
toeing out

bowed legs
toeing in

correct tail carriage
while standing

correct tail carriage
while moving

ring tail

tail carriage
too high

good profile gait

pacing

224

but then go beyond the normal; they collapse forward. If you push forward on these hock joints of a standing dog with your thumbs, they "pop" forward. A quick eye can catch this at any gait speed, but slower eyes can see it at a slow trot or a walk. Since the greatest strength and thrust is provided when the muscles and bones are extended in a straight line, both of these hock defects severely affect the power and effective thrust of the hindquarters.

As in the forequarters viewed from the front, the bones of the hindquarters viewed from the rear must be in a straight column never cowhocked or bowed. When there is insufficient or weak musculature, the hocks are inclined inward to a cowhocked position. Weak or undeveloped musculature will pull the legs inward at the stifle for support. There must be relative width of the pelvis avoiding the weak appearing "A-frame" rear. The strength of the total hindquarter assembly must come from all of the parts working together.

Tail

The tail is long, well feathered, set on low and carried low. If the croup is flat, the tail set will naturally be high and this in turn will lead to a tail carried much too high. When the dog is standing, the tail will be carried straight down or gently curved forward between the hindlegs. (Unlike some other breeds, this type of tail carriage is not a sign of timidity in the Borzoi, unless, of course, it is not only between the legs but pulled up almost to the belly.) As the dog breaks into a trot, the tail will be raised but should never go above the level of the back. If the tail falls to the hock or below, it is the right length. Some measure the length of the tail by pulling it between the legs and up over the loin to the spine. This is really unnecessary as the length in comparison to the hock is sufficient.

Coat

The texture or feel of the coat is more important than the type of coat whether it be wavy or curly or straight. It should be silky, soft and lustrous never woolly or harsh and wiry. (Often, just after a coat drop, the texture of the remaining guard hairs may feel a little coarse but this is temporary.) Extremes in straightness or curliness do not make for an aesthetically pleasing picture of the typical, elegant Borzoi. A Borzoi should not carry too profuse a coat or he may lose elegance or appear to be unsuitable as a coursing dog.

The male Borzoi will carry a heavier coat than the bitch with a heavier neck frill, a longer bib on the forechest and brisket and longer feathering on the legs and tail.

Color

All colors and patterns are permitted.

There have been and probably always will be color prejudices to one extent or another. For many years there was a definite prejudice that was fairly widespread against self-black, black and tan and any other dark self-color. Possibly this was a carryover from the first American Borzoi standard approved in 1905 in which it stated: "Solid black or black marked with tan to be considered a disqualification." This disqualification was removed in 1940. Today, while there is a natural preference in most people for one color or another without actual prejudice against the other colors, Borzoi color can be summed up by: anything goes.

Size

Today I would say that the majority of mature Borzoi males being shown successfully are between 31 inches and 33 inches at the shoulder while the majority of mature bitches range between 28 inches and 30 inches. However, a larger or smaller dog should not be penalized on size alone if the conformation is correct. Extremely large or small dogs should be avoided because they tend to lack type soundness. Maturity and adult coat can often create an impression of greater size than actually exists.

It is interesting to note that while the upper limit is left flexible by a qualifying phrase, the lower limit is quite definite. Dogs and bitches below 28 and 26 inches respectively should be *severely penalized.*

Possibly it is unfortunate that there is no upper limit suggested. In the American standard prior to 1972, as in the Canadian standard today, there was a range of height: dogs 28 to 31 inches, bitches 26 to 29 inches. The English standard now calls for dogs to be over 29 inches, bitches over 27 inches but has nothing to say about the quality of larger dogs. The Russian standard calls for dogs 27¼ to 32½ inches and bitches of 25¼ to 30½ inches. Comparing these heights to those mentioned in the first paragraph of this section as the normal range found in the better dogs of today, it would seem that the Russian standard is the more realistic.

Since the time both the English and the American standards were written — over 75 years ago — there has been criticism of the lower range limits as being unrealistic, uncommon and undesirable. In 1904 the Duchess of Newcastle put the ideal range in height at 29 to 32½ inches. At that time the English standard called for two inches less in range. This was changed in 1906. In 1912 Major S. P. Borman, Secretary of the Borzoi Club in England and a leading Borzoi breeder at that time, wrote the following in regards to size: "Although the Club standard of height has been raised from 27 and 26 inches to 29 and 27 inches for dogs and bitches respectively, it must be borne in mind that the best dogs of to-day far exceed these measurements, and, unless *exceptionally* good in other points, a dog of 29 inches at shoulder would stand little or no chance in the showring under the majority of English judges; indeed, bitches of 29 to 30 inches are by no means uncommon.'' He lists as examples: the dogs Ch. Velsk and Ch. Statesman at 31 ¾ inches, the dog Ch. Kieff at 33 inches, the bitches Ch. Tatiana at 30¼ inches and Ch. Miss Piostri at 31 inches.

At the turn of the century at the time of the great Russian Hunts, many highly regarded dogs were measured at the higher limits. The Tschel-ischtscheff Hunt had many measuring 33 inches.

In almost every book on the Borzoi there are similar comments on the heights found in various standards as being unrealistic. In each case, however, the additional comment is made that extra large sizes (generally 34 inches and over for males) are acceptable only *when the extra size is not acquired at the expense of symmetry, speed and staying quality.*

Weight depends on the individual dog, so I don't feel that any numerical description of weight should appear in the standard. A proper weight is determined by the hands, and to a certain extent by the eye, rather than solely by a scale. If all the obvious bones such as those of the hips and the spine are well fleshed out and can only be barely felt by the hands, the weight is correct. An excessive amount of coat on a dog can give the illusion of too much weight just as a certain amount of extra weight can give the illusion of a bit more coat than actually exists on the body. Excessive weight is not conducive to good health and may have an undesirable effect upon the dog's breeding ability and performance in the field or showring.

Gait

The most important sentence in this section is the last: ''The overall appearance in motion should be that of effortless power, endurance, speed, agility, smoothness and grace.'' This is sure to follow if the dog's structure is correct and well balanced, and he is using that structure to its full potential with all parts in harmony.

The showring gaits by which the Borzoi is judged are the walk and the trot. There are those who say that this is an unfair way to judge the Borzoi as (they claim) the Borzoi's gait in the field is the double suspension gallop. But think about that. Picture one of the old Russian Hunts. The Borzoi wolf teams (leashes of three Borzoi to a mounted huntsman) *walked and trotted* for miles at the sides of the horses. Then when a wolf was flushed from a wooded copse, one team was released to gallop in pursuit of the wolf while the other teams waited for the next wolf to be flushed. In most cases, the Borzoi spent more time at the walk and trot than at the gallop.

double suspension gallop

Also, in the showring, the walk and the trot will demonstrate many of the faults to which the dogs are prone and better allow the judge to make his final evaluation of each individual dog against the specifications of the standard.

As pointed out many times, there must be structural balance of the proper kind. Lack of it leads to incorrect gaiting in one form or another. The dog moving at a trot must be viewed in profile as well as coming and going.

As a dog moves directly away from you and picks up speed when he breaks from a walk to a trot, the legs will move towards the center line for balance, the column of bones remaining in a straight line even though the angle of that line may have changed slightly. This tendency to single tracking is normal and desirable. If the column of bones is no longer straight, if the stifles tend to be out and the hocks are in with the hocks moving parallel yet close, *this* is moving close and it is faulty. If the legs actually brush against one another or if they cross, this is even faultier. If the dog moves at a trot with legs as far apart as when he was standing, he is said to be "traveling." This is movement that is definitely out of balance and obviously so as the dog tends to compensate with a rolling waddle. Some people are wrongly impressed by that incorrect wide moving rear.

If the rear feet are toeing in, the dog is said to be "hocking out." Toeing out, on the other hand, is a sure sign of cowhocks. If the hocks are flexing properly, the pads of each hind foot will show as the leg is at its fullest extension. If you do not see the pads, the dog may be doing a sickle hock shuffle as described earlier. If the hocks are double-jointed and are popping, the dog may appear to have what comedian Ernie Ford would have called "a hitch in his git-along."

When the dog turns and gaits directly back towards you, many of the same principles apply. Again, the straight column of bones in the forelegs must remain straight even though the forelegs, like the hindlegs, tend to move in towards the center line at a fast trot. At no time should they move so close that they weave or cross, however. The elbows should move cleanly with no winging out, thus maintaining that straight column of bones. If the dog has a narrow, pinched front and if the elbows are also pinched, he will tend to move forward with the feet hitting wider apart than they normally stand. This is called "paddling" and is comparable to traveling in the rear and causes the same rocking motion of the body.

The most beautiful sight to behold is a Borzoi moving in profile at any gait be it a trot, a canter or a double suspension gallop, but only when he is moving properly. He should give the impression of power and speed as well as effortless grace.

The most effective functioning of a properly structured Borzoi can best be viewed when the dog is moving at a trot. If the dog is correctly angulated in the forequarters, he will reach well forward with a long stride. All points of articulation should flex smoothly. The ultimate aim in good movement in a coursing hound is covering the maximum amount of ground possible with the minimum number of strides and the minimum amount of effort. A well angulated front assembly will move smoothly and take less number of steps due to the swing and the reach of the forelegs than a straighter front assembly. The straighter front with less reach will produce a choppy or bouncy effect rather than the desired smooth gracefulness.

As a general rule the Borzoi's feet should move forward fairly close to the ground so that he is not tired by action (lifting or bending) which is excessive and at the same time ineffectual as far as forward momentum is concerned. A hackney action, which is a high action of the forelegs, is a good example of excessive action of the front which is very tiring to the dog over the long haul. In a few breeds this stylish action is called for, but never in a coursing hound. Padding or flipping is another action of the forelegs that is energy wasting. This is an extra forward flip of the front feet at the moment when the leg is extended and just before it is brought down to the ground. Both of these faults may be caused by an imbalance between the forequarters and hindquarters in which case the hindquarters are thrusting more from the rear than the forequarters are reaching in the front. These are two means by which the dog compensates for the overreach of the rear feet which might otherwise strike the front legs and feet.

The comparison of proper to improper action of the forequarters might be similar to a description of the Australian crawl as performed by a top Olympic swimmer compared to a little boy just learning to swim. The former will reach forward with long, powerful strokes cutting the water cleanly and moving forward rapidly. The latter chops at the water with short strokes producing lots of splash but little progress. Just so, the Borzoi must move forward with a smooth, purposeful stride covering a lot of ground quickly, effortlessly and gracefully.

It has been mentioned that many of the problems and faults in gaiting viewed in profile are due to an imbalance between forequarters and hindquarters. In many breeds today the imbalance takes the form of more angulation in the rear than the front. The rear legs are capable of reaching farther forward than are the front legs. To prevent interference with the front legs, the dog must compensate by crabbing, padding, hackney action, or some other means to move the front out of the way of the rear or to gain time in the air to keep out of the way of the rear. A dog that is equally straight in front and rear may be balanced but the gait will not be the desirable graceful, ground-covering stride. When a handler moves such a dog at an extremely fast trot, the eye, unfortunately, can be fooled into thinking that the dog is reaching and driving more than he actually is. A slow motion movie camera would show how many more steps he took over a given distance than a dog with more reach and drive from more angulated quarters. While their actual speed might be the same, the energy expended would be quite different.

Other faults mentioned earlier that can also be seen in profile movement are weak pasterns, sickle hocks, rigid croups and toplines, popping hocks, tail carriage too high and improper neck set. Even in the best structured dog, however, condition, attitude and manner of handling can create a wrong picture. A too tight lead will distort the normal gait of the dog even while it might be hiding certain faults. For example, if the lead is so tight that the dog is strung up almost to the point of its front never touching the ground, the pastern faults might be hidden, but at the same time the forward reach is greatly restricted and the gait is choppy. Illness, obesity and age can affect the dog's movement. Attitude — whether the dog is moving with purpose, whether he's happy on that day — can also make the difference between a dog looking like a bum one day and like a million dollars the next day.

The Borzoi's fast gait is the double suspension gallop, a type of gallop typical of sighthounds but few other breeds. In this gait, there are two moments when all four feet are off the ground during a complete sequence. One is when the legs are fully extended and the other when the legs are fully contracted to a jackknife position. The diagram shows the positions of the legs in the full sequence. Notice particularly the importance of the flexible topline and the straight extension of the hock on the follow-through during the full extension.

Faults

Prior to 1972, the American standard under this section had a listing of features and a numerical (based on percent) evaluation of the importance of those features. (This point scale can be found at the end of the present Canadian Standard.) During the Borzoi Club of America Board discussions of the point scale there was hesitancy about discarding the point scale as it was felt it served not so much as a score card but as a guide to the importance of various features. Unfortunately, when several features were lumped together with only one value placed on it, it was difficult to determine how to break down that value to assign sub-values to each feature. The head was assigned 12%, but under head would be included — in addition to the shape — length, width, the bite, dentition, depth of underjaw. How much of the 12% would go to each of those? Would a short head have the equivalent degree of penalty as an undershot jaw with several missing teeth? With the additional insistence of the AKC that the scale be dropped, the Board finally agreed. I submitted a substitute section on faults and it was subsequently approved. As a guide to assessing the quality of an individual dog, I feel this sentence is much more helpful and more easily remembered than any listing of points. This sentence at the conclusion of the standard, coupled with the beginning of the standard, makes the body of the standard much more meaningful.

Random Thoughts on the Standard

In addition to the faults listed in this Borzoi Standard, there are also the universal faults specified by the AKC. The presence of one or more of these faults in the show ring makes disqualification mandatory: deafness, blindness, cryptorchidism.

A few standards for other breeds include ideal temperaments, seriously faulting extreme variations such as excessive aggression or timidity. Since temperament faults or mental instability can be inherited, these should be considered faults just as bad as lack of type or structural soundness. As a breeder and as a judge of the Borzoi, I for one would gladly support any move to include temperament in the standard.

For those seriously interested in learning more about proper structure and function, I recommend the books listed below for reading and study. There is no one good book. In each, the authors' opinions vary on certain points. However, these listed authors have seriously studied their subjects and all are worth consulting. Too many articles on type and soundness have appeared in the last few years in various magazines that have a surface gloss and authority but no actual substance or sufficient basis in fact. The best advice to the serious student is to read several recommended books by noted authorities, study and evaluate both texts and applications to living animals. No matter how long any of us are involved with serious breeding, exhibiting, coursing, or judging we must keep an open mind, must continue to learn. Only the novice thinks he knows it all.

Curtis M. and Thelma R. Brown — *The Art and Science of Judging Dogs,* B&E Publications, Hollywood, California 1976

Rachel Page Elliott — *Dogsteps—Illustrated Gait at a Glance,* Howell Book House, Inc., New York, New York 1973

McDowell Lyon — *The Dog In Action,* Howell Book House, Inc., New York, New York 1950

Eadweard Muybridge — *Animals in Motion,* Dover Publications, Inc., New York, New York 1957

Conni Miller — "The Search for Truth in Gazehounds," *The Gazehound,* Encino, California May/June 1976 through May/June 1979

7

Development of the Borzoi from Puppy to Adult

ONE OF THE FIRST THINGS purchased by many parents of a human baby is a book on baby care and development. Dr. Spock's book, for instance, is often considered as important as diapers in the nursery. Many new owners of a puppy also feel they need some sort of written guidance in order to raise the puppy properly. There are many well-written books on general puppy care and training, but in all of them development of the puppy is handled in a general way. For the new owner of a Borzoi puppy a good many questions on development go unanswered in such all-breed books. Every breed has its own peculiarities especially when pertaining to development.

While the rate of development varies from breed to breed, it also varies from puppy to puppy within each breed. Each puppy is an individual and develops at his own individual rate and in his own individual way. Any dissertation on development of a Borzoi from puppy to adult must stress the fact that there are variations within the norm. Good common sense dictates that if good nutrition, good habits and good training are instituted early and continued, the puppy will develop to the full potential dictated by his genetic limitations. The owner's worry adds nothing and it does detract from the full enjoyment of one of the most interesting and enjoyable times in a dog's life, his early months as a puppy.

Birth weights of puppies are not true indications of adult size. Even when nutrition, environment and condition are equal, some bitches normally produce small puppies and some normally produce large puppies. Borzoi birth weights range anywhere from ten ounces to 24 ounces with the average being about a pound. Puppies with large birth weights do not necessarily grow to large adults. Many a male puppy that is a pound and a half at birth has developed into a 31 inch 80 pound adult while a litter brother weighing only 14 ounces at birth may as an adult outstrip him by two inches in height and 20 pounds in weight. Even between the sexes at birth and for several months, there may be no noticeable difference in size. Size of bone may sometimes be a true indicator and yet even this is not infallible.

Having also bred Whippets and having had a litter of both Whippets and Borzoi occasionally whelped within a few days of one another, I have often remarked how easy it would be to lose a day-old Whippet puppy in a litter of day-old Borzoi puppies. The size, general shape, coat and heads are remarkably similar. Only after a week or so could they be separated.

Elsewhere in this book it is stated that correct weight in a Borzoi adult can best be determined with the hands by the feel of the dog rather than the actual weight. I have often had littermates the same height and weight yet one would be in correct weight by feel and the other one would be overweight. A Borzoi is in correct adult weight if the bones of the spine and hips can still be felt even though well covered with flesh.

When Borzoi people discuss common problems, the most common topic is weight — not the problem of removing excess but the problem of getting a dog to eat and to gain weight. Stories abound concerning favorite methods of encouraging appetites. Actually, puppies should be encouraged to eat well right at weaning time. Competition with littermates helps a great deal. At about eight weeks most puppies are little butterballs. The ribspring looks tremendous. However, within the next few months, there is a great growth spurt. Almost as if they were being squeezed in a vice to create that surge upwards, the ribcage lengthens and narrows. If a puppy's appetite remains good and he gets sufficient exercise during this time, any extra weight he can put on will help keep the ribs sprung properly. The faster a puppy grows in height, the more likely the tendency toward slab-sidedness. Some puppies never lose their good appetites so never present this problem to their owners. Unfortunately, many novice owners think puppies of all breeds eat heartily. As a result, they tend to worry about overfeeding. Rarely will a Borzoi puppy overeat.

If an adult Borzoi will not maintain himself at a good weight, he may still be in excellent health but not in good show weight. Show dogs with this problem may have to be force-fed to maintain a proper weight. At one show, a judge (an Afghan breeder) commented on the excellent weight on the Borzoi champion he had put best of breed. "At least you Borzoi breeders allow your dogs to eat. You don't starve them like these Afghan breeders do trying to create those prominent hipbones the standard calls for." The handler of the Borzoi smiled at the judge but chuckled to himself as he thought of all those stuffing balls pushed down this particular Borzoi's throat daily.

Borzoi generally attain adult height at a year of age although some may add another inch over the next year or two. Of course, as the dog fills out and grows a mature coat, he may appear larger and taller. Human nature being what it is, owners of dogs of the so-called "giant" breeds sometimes play the game of "my dog's bigger than your dog." A St. Bernard owner may add 50 pounds to the actual weight of his dog. A Borzoi owner may add two inches to the actual height of his dog. On rare occasions, this may be due to not knowing the proper way to measure height but more often it just involves ego and a desire to win at that game.

Height is measured at the top of the shoulder as the dog is standing. A level is placed across the highest point of the withers and a measurement taken from that point directly to the ground. Since there is no height disqualification in the standard for Borzoi, the actual height really isn't that important anyway as long as it is within the acceptable range typical of the breed. My idea of ideal heights in mature Borzoi is a range of 31½"-33" in males and 28"-30" in females.

While the mature Borzoi head is quite distinctive, the heads of newborn Borzoi are not. They are not unlike those of Whippets or many other breeds. A puppy with a long narrow muzzle would have great difficulty nursing so nature has provided for this giving all puppies a rather short, pushed-in type of muzzle. In fact, in Borzoi puppies up to eight weeks of age, a blocky or rectangular shaped head giving lots of fill below the eye is desirable. A narrow muzzle at eight weeks usually indicates a weak, snipey muzzle at maturity. When judging a Borzoi puppy head before the ears are curled back in a mature position, you should always cup your hand over the skull pulling the ears back out of the way. There is a slight — but only slight — bony protrusion on the side of the head just behind the eye and over the hinge of the jaw. From this point the skull should never widen but rather should gradually narrow to the pronounced point of the occiput.

The head should be examined from many angles. A profile should exhibit a great depth of muzzle. Since a Borzoi has a tight lip-line without loose flews, the depth of underjaw can be easily seen in puppy and adult alike. Exaggerated dips in the muzzle are not desirable as these may lead to a "dished" appearance later. Don't be confused, however, by the bump of the Roman-nose near the end of the muzzle as this is often quite pronounced in puppies with good heads. When the male puppy is about a year old, the head may appear too large for the body, but soon he will "grow into it."

At birth the ears are hard, little triangular flaps with no mobility at all.

They are sealed at birth so the puppy will not respond to your voice. If you dropped a pan next to him at this age, he might react to the vibration but not to the noise. At about two weeks the ears open as do the eyes, and the puppy's horizons expand. The ears have lengthened and softened by the first few weeks but still hang down hound-like. At about eight weeks the ears start to curl back in the proper way but not as a continual thing. In fact, puppies' ears may be carried in any number of peculiar ways for several weeks. Some breeders, mimicking actions of breeders in some other breeds, will try gluing or taping to force the ears to assume the correct curled position and to prevent them from pricking. This is usually wasted effort for the most part.

Puppy eyes open at 12 to 14 days. At first they are only able to see moving objects although they cannot completely focus on them. The eyes for several days have a blue cast, and it is a bit difficult to determine color. At six weeks, holding the puppy up to a window in bright daylight—but not in direct sunlight—will give an indication of depth of color, whether the color will be light brown or dark brown. If the eyes are grey or blue, a definite fault exists. The eyes may remain blue or they may turn yellow which is also faulty. Sometimes the eyes may be dark but have a wedge of blue. There is a slight possibility that the defect might be due to an accident, but more often it is a genetic fault. Eyes may lighten with age; rarely do they darken. Dark brown is the preferable color. Coat color, at least the color of the head, often determines the effect of the depth of the eye color. A medium brown eye will look darker in a white head than in a black head.

In the newborn puppy, if there is color on the head extending down over the eyes, it is very likely that the eye rim pigment will be dark. In all white heads, there may still be a greyish look around the eyes from pigment in the skin rather than the hair. This also indicates that the rims will be fully pigmented. If the area is totally pink, only time will tell if the pigment will come and if it will be complete.

At birth puppies often have completely pink noses although some have spots of black or a dusting of grey on the pink. A few puppies are born with totally black noses. Every day thereafter the amount of black pigment increases until at six to eight weeks most puppies will have completely pigmented noses. In some lines, especially those with many generations of basically white to white breeding, the pigment of noses and eye rims may tend more to a liver color than the preferred black. Also, if the coat color is a dilute, usually a light grey or a blue, the nose and eye rims may be a slate colored, also less than desirable.

Some lines tend to have fading pigment with the pinkish-brown nose coloring more prevalent in the winter months leading to the terms "snow-nose" and "winter-nose." These faded noses often recover the full black coloring at other times of the year. However, the recovery often takes longer each year as the dog grows older until the faded nose pigment is a permanent condition. This type of nose fading should not be confused with the sudden pasty-grey color of a previously fully black nose occurring when a dog is subjected to extreme stress. The dark color returns in such cases when the stress is removed.

Anyone who has played with a young puppy is fully aware of those little needle-sharp teeth. At about three weeks of age, the puppy's dam also starts to become aware of those same teeth as they start to erupt in the previously toothless gums. The discomfort she experiences when the litter nurses leads her to welcome the weaning process. The temporary incisors have broken through the gums by the fourth or fifth week.

In the adult dog, the normal number of teeth is 42. The formula is: each side of the upper jaw—3 incisors, 1 canine, 4 premolars, 2 molars; each side of the lower jaw—3 incisors, 1 canine, 4 premolars, 3 molars. At about three and a half months the first permanent teeth appear as the temporary incisors are replaced with the full set of incisors all through by about five months. It is at this time that the bite should be checked. If the upper teeth closely cover the upper portion of the lower ones, the bite is a correct scissor bite. If there is a decided space between the upper and lower incisors in this position, the bite is overshot. If the positioning is reversed, the bite is undershot. If the upper and lower incisors meet edge to edge, the bite is level. The permanent canines might appear between four and five months just after the incisors. The upper and lower canines in the closed mouth lie side by side in a meshed position with the lower canine in front of the upper one. In the young puppy there may appear to be a slight overbite, but if the canines are correctly meshed, it will usually move closed to a tight scissor position as the more slowly growing lower jaw lengthens. An undershot bite rarely corrects.

The temporary premolars are lost during the fourth and fifth months as they are replaced by the permanent ones. The upper fourth premolar is particularly large and often mistaken for a molar. A Borzoi's jaw is quite long compared to that in many breed yet the total number of teeth is the same. For this reason, there are often spaces between the premolars. These spaces should never be taken as indications of missing teeth. When in doubt, review the formula and count. The molars erupt between the fourth and eighth months and are not preceded by temporary teeth.

Usually the temporary tooth breaks off just below the gum-line and the root reabsorbs. Occasionally the temporary tooth does not break off or loosen and remains even after the permanent tooth erupts. These should be extracted by the veterinarian to prevent misalignment of the permanent teeth, Sometimes a root will not reabsorb and will, like a splinter, work out through the side of the gum adding to the discomfort or an already sore mouth in the puppy.

The Borzoi puppy grows at a very rapid rate often gaining three to five pounds a week during the third to fifth months. He is also growing rapidly in height making him appear like a leggy little colt. Growth knobs appear on the legs at the pasterns and on the ribs. Unless overly large or painful, these knobs are quite normal and desirable. As the legs and ribs lengthen, the knobs gradually disappear. As long as the knobs are visible you can depend on more height and depth of chest in the maturing puppy as he reaches adulthood. The bone of a Borzoi must be strong but not heavy or bulky. If the Borzoi had been bred originally for pulling sleds or carts, the bone in the legs would be heavy and rounded. Since the Borzoi was bred for speedy pursuit of game, the bone must be bladed as described in the standard. Of course, if the hair on the legs is thick, it may take your hand rather than your eye to determine the actual shape of the bone itself.

At about four to five weeks as the puppy starts stumbling around the whelping box, the feet will appear flat and somewhat splayed. With continued exercise on firm, rough-surfaced flooring, the feet strengthen and assume the tight well-knuckled appearance that is desirable. The rough surface of floors and kennel runs will help to whittle down the nails of active puppies with the properly arched toes while nails on feet that are flat will not wear down as rapidly and will need more attention with clippers or grinders. The nails may be black or white or even both black and white. The pads may be all pink or pink with spots of black. The variation in color has no significance.

Dewclaws on the forelegs may nor may not be removed during the first week after birth. They are attached to the legs by ''gristle'' at this time making removal relatively easy. Removal later requires minor surgery with general or local anaesthesia. Dewclaws on the hindlegs can be easily missed during the first few months as they are quite small and undeveloped and occur on only a few puppies. They are always removed when found.

Puppy play can often be rather rough. Young puppies are also rather uncoordinated as they rush through doorways or flop on hard floors for a nap. Elbows, hips and other bony areas unprotected by much hair or flesh are prone to develop fluid sacs from constant bumps. These can be treated successfully by the veterinarian with sterile tapping and the insertion of steroids. The bursae may refill with fluid, but usually after a year of age this is no longer a problem. Soft bedding may help to prevent the problem but with the tendency of many Borzoi to prefer the cooler, bare floor this is not as easy a solution as it sounds.

Young puppies of two or three months often carry their tails gaily, sometimes ringed. This is not necessarily an indication of an improper adult carriage. A correct tailset with the base of the tail lower than the hipbones and separated from them by the moderately declining croup indicates that the puppy over five months will probably hold the tail down properly especially as the feathering develops.

At three months a Borzoi puppy may appear to have the properly moderate spring of rib, wide fronts with strong straight forelegs and wide rears with strong well-angulated hindquarters. You think to yourself, "Terrific! He's show quality." Maybe yes, maybe no. You can no more be sure of picking real show quality in a three month old Borzoi pup than you could in picking a Miss America in a three year old child. There may appear to be great promise but certainly no guarantees. Too much further growth and development lie ahead before full maturity.

As a very general rule — and there may be many exceptions — the slower the growth between the third and fifth months, the better the puppy will hold together and develop properly. Rapid growth at this time may put too much stress on the bone structure and the muscles are not capable of handling the stress. If there are insufficient or weak muscles, the hindlegs may become cowhocked, the stifles may become pinched or the pasterns may break down. These things may or may not improve with further development.

Toplines in Borzoi can vary greatly during the puppy stages making the interpretation of the development during various stages difficult for the novice. Many young puppies can look deceivingly flat-backed especially when they are going through that early stage in which they may carry their tails high. After three months, the topline can vary, it may seem, from day to day. The front may grow more rapidly than the rear producing a ski-slope topline. Then a week later the rear will catch up and may grow faster than the front producing the opposite effect. Indeed, if the rear is higher than the front even the angulation of the hindquarters will appear changed as it straightens to accommodate the unbalanced height of the hindquarters. After six months when the growth rate decelerates, the balance of front to rear will be regained.

As the puppy trots at a rapid pace the topline will seem to flatten. If it does not and a definite roach is visible, there may be a rigidity of the loin which will create a stiffness of gait as the hindquarters are not allowed to work with full power as it were. If the puppy between six and twelve months appears to cross in front as he trots towards you, it may be due to faulty front structure. On the other hand, it may be due to his exuberance, a sort of happy playful wobble. In the adolescent puppy, the topline may be somewhat exaggerated even though he appears to be moving well. Often this topline will drop to the proper slight rise over the loin with adult weight and maturity.

The length of body in the adult should be equal to the height forming a square. The height is measured as described earlier. The length is the line from tip of sternum to the buttock. In the puppy when his legs have not entered the fast growth stage, it may be impossible to predict whether or not he will be square. More often than not, the very young puppy will appear longer than he is high. If the young puppy appears very short in body, you will likely find that he lacks angulation both front and rear. Well angulated quarters need a certain amount of body length in order to work efficiently and properly.

In male puppies, testicles have often descended at birth or very soon thereafter although they may be too small to be palpated that early. Most have both testicles in the scrotum by at least eight weeks. Occasionally some may take a few weeks longer. The American Kennel Club has ruled that the absence of two normal testicles normally descended into the scrotum is a disqualification in all breeds in the show ring. It used to be thought that hormone injections would encourage the descent, but current veterinary opinion is that this is not so. Because of the AKC ruling, any artificial means used to correct a cryptorchid condition is unethical. If the puppy does retain one or both testicles within the abdomen, it is recommended that the dog be castrated at maturity. Puppies that are incomplete may not be shown and should not be bred. If at a year of age one or both testicles appear to be abnormally located in the scrotum, it would be wise to ask for the opinion of your veterinarian before showing the dog and risking a disqualification.

Bitches of the smaller breeds tend to come in season for the first time at six months, but those of the larger breeds come in much later. In Borzoi bitches, the age of the first heat period may be as early as ten months or as late as 36 months. No Borzoi bitch should be bred before she is at least two years of age regardless of whether it is at her first or second or third season. The intervals between seasons vary from one bitch to another and even from season to season in the same bitch. It is just as normal for the interval to be twelve months as it is to be six months.

Dogs and bitches should not be altered until they have reached maturity as they need the natural hormones for proper development. In Borzoi the minimum age would be eighteen months. Altering has no adverse effect upon either sex either mentally or physically. As Dr. Stephen Roberts, formerly on the staff of Cornell Veterinary College, has stated: "Reproduction is a luxury function of the body not physiologically necessary for the life of the individual." No one should ever decide against neutering of either a dog or bitch because of transference of his own emotional feelings about sterilization.

Borzoi puppies are born with short-haired coats. Some develop a short, fluffy coat during the first few weeks; others do not. At first the coat is fuzzy or downy and is then replaced by the silky puppy coat at eight to ten weeks. There is often a streak of the new silky hair at this time down the back first

240

(almost appearing like the saddle in an Afghan Hound) before it spreads down the sides replacing the puppy fuzz. Around four months, the feathering of the legs and tail starts to develop with the entire coat becoming quite profuse by the age of twelve months. Just when your puppy's coat looks its best, he will start losing it. Daily brushing and a warm bath to help loosen the dead coat will hasten the complete loss of and stimulate new growth.

The amount of curl or wave often varies from the puppy to the adult coat. However, a puppy coat that is in very tight ringlets with a somewhat coarse texture will often turn out to be "woolly" and appear rather kinky. A coat of that type will never have the desirable sheen and length.

The growth of new coat is never as fast as you might like and this is especially true of the first adult coat. It takes almost a year in some cases for the first full adult coat to grow. Since the young dog is still immature at that point and needs more weight and fill in addition to the coat, he will very likely not be in condition for showing in the breed ring. I have often advised owners that this is a good time for serious obedience training or lure-coursing. Both activities are excellent for mental and physical development and this is the age at which the god is both mentally and physically ready for such activities.

The Borzoi standard sets limits within which the breeder must work in his breeding programs allowing little leeway for personal preference. In all things that is except color. All colors, all combinations of colors and all patterns are permissible. A few breeders may breed for a single specific color, but most breed for the basic structural soundness and type, then let the color chips fall as they may.

Colors may change more drastically in the developing Borzoi puppy than any other feature. A puppy that is a true black, with black right down to the blue skin, will usually remain black. A very dark brindle or very dark sable may at first be mistaken for a black in a newborn puppy but within a day or two the hint of the ground color will become evident. The terms sable and brindle are not colors by themselves. Sable means black tipping of varying degrees so it should be coupled with the color underneath — silver-sable, gold-sable, red-sable. Brindle means black striping on a colored ground and should be coupled with the ground color — silver-brindle, gold-brindle, red-brindle. A dark reddish-brown color at birth will always change but not always to the same adult color. It may become a brilliant, almost setter, red or a light red, orange, fawn or dark gold. Grey markings at birth will usually become some shade of cream or gold. White puppies may stay all white or may develop ticking later. Ticking may also develop later in the white areas on any parti-colored dog. When the term "self" is coupled with a color, it means that the dog is almost totally that color with white trim only on muzzle, tail tip, feet and forechest. Colors may lighten or deepen as coat grows or blows. Exotic terms to describe colors as well as overly-involved descriptions should be avoided on registrations and pedigrees.

The development of personality and temperament may be affected and controlled to some extrent by training and environment although the basic temperament is hereditary. The Borzoi is a very sensitive breed and responds to extremes in attention and discipline. Firm discipline is essential for all training, but it must be accompanied by love and praise. A shy dog can be brought out of his shell by extra love and attention and early exposure to variations in environment. Harsh discipline untempered by love can make a shy dog even more timid. A puppy that is very shy is quite apt to turn into an evil tempered dog as he grows older, not from innate viciousness but from fear. A shy dog is a scared dog. Most of his fears are imaginary ones to be sure, but they are very real ones to the dog, and as his main weapon of defense is his teeth, he tries to protect himself in the only way he knows. An aggressive puppy will often respond to harsh discipline with even more aggression. If the temperament is such that the dog creates daily problems for those with whom he lives, the dog should be put down. Before purchasing another dog, however, the owner should honestly try to evaluate the situation to see if he himself was at all responsible for the bad situation by lack of training or improper training. Not everyone is suited to a Borzoi. Some people buy Borzoi for the wrong reasons and end up finding themselves completely incompatible.

The many facets of the Borzoi's character have been summed up all too frequently by the overworked adjectives elegant, dignified, beautiful and aristocratric. They are all applicable, but the real beauty of this breed goes much further than, shall we say, coat deep.

The Borzoi possesses an innate sense of the fitness of things. Outdoors he will romp and play as roughly as the occasion may warrant, but in the house one forgets how large a dog he really is because he displays the manners of a very proper guest. He wends his way quietly and gracefully through the house leaving no rugs scattered about nor household articles displaced in his wake. The long, sweeping tail is carried very low when indoors so precious china and bric-a-brac need not be put away for safe keeping just because there is a Borzoi in the house. This, of course, is the adult dog. A puppy of any breed is all puppy and behaves irresponsibly until he is old enough to have learned good manners.

The Borzoi is no fawning type of dog. He meets you as an equal. He is affectionate but displays this emotion with restraint. A gentle nudge with his head will inform you he would appreciate a caress, and after being granted this wish he will retire to his favorite corner and relax with maybe a glance in your direction occasionally out of very expressive brown eyes to let you know he is perfectly contented with the status quo.

242

The Borzoi rarely barks. He is not a nervous dog, raising an alarm over every little strange noise but gives the impression of knowing that his size, speed and strength equip him to meet any emergencies, no need for any show of braggadocio. However, this should not cause his value as a watch dog to be underestimated. His size alone is often a deterrent to those whose intentions are not legitimate. The Borzoi seldom provokes attack, even among other dogs, but will not shrink from fighting in defense if it becomes necessary. His quiet demeanor is not a deceptive pose assumed by an otherwise ferocious animal. Rather, it is the indication of a gentle spirit that displays brute force only when the aggression of others demands it.

I believe the most important trait of all is the Borzoi's capacity for companionship. He will walk miles with you, happy to be taken out for the exercise, or he will lie quietly by your side if you prefer less strenuous pastimes. If you are ill, he seems to sense it and makes no demands, but patiently awaits the time you will resume the usual round of activities with him. If you are sorrowing, you will be apt to find a head laid gently in your lap and expressive eyes looking into yours. No words are necessary between close friends to convey deep sympathy. No matter to what use the Borzoi is put, his most valued role in life is and will remain — companion.

Six week old puppies at Alpine — with friend. *Ludwig.*

243

8

Basic Training
and Grooming

WHETHER YOUR BORZOI is destined to be a kennel dog or a house dog, a pet dog or a show dog, an obedience trial dog or a coursing dog, his basic training should be the same. Rarely is a dog put into one narrow niche for his whole life nor should he be. The Borzoi is a versatile dog to be enjoyed in a variety of ways.

Training a dog for any purpose can begin at almost any age although in many cases, the older he is the more set his pattern of behavior and therefore the more difficult is the training. One thing that cannot be deferred, however, is his socialization, his adaptation to humans and to other dogs. Properly socialized at an early age, a Borzoi can face any type of training at a later age. There are cases, of course, in which the basic temperament may be covered over, molded or modified by extra training, socialization and environment. You should never ignore the fact in such cases that the poor temperament is there ready to be passed on to future generations if the animal is bred.

Many studies have been conducted on socialization of young puppies. From these studies the optimal ages for working with puppies has been determined on the following schedule. The first three weeks of a puppy's life are devoted simply to survival, and as long as the dam is caring for him properly, no human association has much effect. Between three and seven weeks the puppy's eyes and ears open and he becomes aware of things around him besides his dam. He discovers his littermates, he becomes aware of human contact, he hears the noises outside his immediate area.

During these weeks there is much interaction all of which benefits his social development. After eight weeks he starts developing individual traits that form his own personality. Training of various types is best started at this age. If adequate socialization has taken place between eight weeks and three months, the puppy is well prepared to start the next phase in which he starts to declare his independence. Adolescence is between nine months and fourteen months in the Borzoi. At times a dog that has been under-socialized prior to this will suddenly react adversely to strangers or strange situations even though up to this point he has been a very outgoing puppy.

Training of a Borzoi is best done with voice control rather than physical control. An exception to this general rule is in cases of biting or snapping when he must be punished sharply and immediately. All corrections must be immediate to have any effect. Where possible, correction should seem to the puppy to be coming from his improper action itself rather than from you and your hand. Treat gently but firmly. Always follow a reprimand with a word of reassurance, "good boy!" or whatever. This is not taken as contradiction by the dog but rather as a reminder that in spite of his lapse in good manners or training you still love him. He will follow your commands only if he feels he is part of your world and that you are his leader. Borzoi are typical hounds in that they react in an independent manner often interpreted as blind stubbornnesss.

Most Borzoi spend at least part of their lives, if not all, in the home as a member of the household. Even dogs that are kenneled benefit greatly from time spent in the house occasionally. Show dogs need the confidence generated by exposure to various situations. Brood bitches need the comfort of familiar places. By the same token, house dogs need some sort of what might be called kennel training. All dogs benefit from crate training and often consider their crates as their private dens, going into them voluntarily to sleep or to get away from everything for some quiet moments.

Puppies need attention for mental development as well as physical development. Going for several long walks a day accomplishes a lot in both departments. Not only is walking good exercise for physical development, but the changes in the environment and exposure to various distractions encourage an interest in that environment. Puppies must be exposed to people, noises and activity. Otherwise, a puppy easily becomes kennel-bound or house-bound. Then later as an adult he has difficulty adapting to new situations as they arise. This leads to problems in traveling and showing.

Obedience training is always helpful. Organized classes are very good when the Borzoi puppy is mentally ready. However, a few basic obedience commands should be taught early to help the puppy become an acceptable member of the family. Learning the meaning of the word "no" is essential. The word for this command or any other is actually less important than the tone of voice accompanying it as well as your follow-through. Borzoi are sensitive animals and quickly learn to recognize a tone of disapproval or approval. You could call your puppy a "big dummy" but if your tone was one of loving approval, he would wag his tail and wiggle all over in his delight over what he takes as your approval. When you say "no" you must sound as if you really mean it. This is one command the puppy must learn early as almost every activity the puppy gets himself involved in will be hedged with "no-no's."

Two other commands he must learn early are "come" and "stay." Borzoi love to run. If they are allowed to roam freely, owners are surprised to learn the great amount of territory covered by the sighthounds. Their intentions are rarely directed towards running away. Rather, they enjoy the· thrill of the chase and the coursing of anything that moves. In addition, their natural curiosity will take them in ever-widening circles until they are miles from home. They almost always will return home, if possible. The key here is the "if possible." In today's mechanized society crossing any road is a definite hazard for man or dog. Most communities have leash laws prohibiting the free-roaming of dogs with stiff penalties and enforcement. There are many obstacles between a dog's intentions of returning home and the actual return.

Never call the Borzoi to you to be reprimanded or punished. If he has had an accident in the house, never call him to the spot for scolding and punishment. If he runs away, never punish or scold when you catch him no matter how furious you may be. If the dog does not know instantly why he is being punished, the punishment does no good at all. It just lets you vent your anger and yet accomplishes nothing towards the dog's training.

The key to all training is firmness coupled with consistency and persistence. If you ever find yourself losing your patience during a training session, discontinue immediately. Tomorrow comes soon enough. With a Borzoi, anger and a lack of patience accomplish little.

Generally, the exercise that a Borzoi gets running in his own fenced yard and on his long walks with you is enough to keep him in good condition. However, for Borzoi that are being shown and those being raced or coursed, additional exercise in the form of roadwork is necessary. Used properly, this activity can develop and harden muscles, smooth out a gait, relax muscle tensions and have some effect on creating better show attitudes related to endurance. All of this produces a more natural presentation of a Borzoi. Forced exercise or roadwork, however, should never be undertaken with a young, undeveloped puppy in a breed as large and slow-growing as a Borzoi.

Roadwork can be done in several ways. If you yourself are in good physical condition, you might jog several miles a day with your Borzoi.

Starting show training early. Vilovia's
Adeen Suka at five weeks.

Suka at ten weeks after five weeks of
daily practice strikes a show pose.

Roadworking Ch. Loral's Apha Sverkai by car.

247

Otherwise, you could use a bicycle, horse or car with the dog trotting along beside you. Notice the use of the word "trotting." It is the sustained trot rather than the slow gallop that develops the hard condition you are striving for. Just be sure that the road or path you are traveling on is safe for both you and the dog and that the surface is such that it offers good purchase for the dog — rough, not smooth, yet firm and without potholes and obstacles.

Training for the show ring can start well before you are even sure you have a puppy of show quality. Basically, much of the training for companionship and obedience is invaluable as part of show training.

A puppy can be accustomed to standing or stacking at a very early age. Indeed, you tend to do this stacking at an early age, not as a means of show training so much as a means of evaluating the quality of the puppy. However, by no means should this take the place of simple playing with the puppies. Too often I have seen breeders spend time with their puppies only in poking and posing. What the puppies really need is loving and playing whether they be pet or show quality. Some breeders, having determined that a particular puppy is pet quality only, will then pay no more attention to it, will give it no further training. This puppy becomes so kennel-bound if not sold early that a sale at a later date will go sour because the puppy has not been socialized enough to adapt to any other than the basic kennel situation.

It is beneficial to each puppy to alternate play periods with work periods of the time alloted for your socialization with them. The work period consists of setting the puppy up in a show stance, examining the entire body structure. Then it's on to play time. If show training, or obedience training, becomes boring or overbearing, it is wasted effort. It may even send training three steps backward for every two steps forward.

Grooming, no matter how unnecessary at the time, is another way to show train a puppy. Show dogs must be groomed frequently and it works best if the dog enjoys it. Later, when time is limited, it helps to have a cooperative dog when grooming is necessary. Even though you know his bite is a perfect scissor bite and he has both testicles in the scrotum, check these things every now and then while grooming. The puppy needs the handling experience and to learn that it's all part of the routine.

Local handling classes are available for both puppy and handler. Better that the puppy learns to adjust to noise and strangers and other dogs at a handling class than at a point show. The puppy has already learned to walk with you on a lead, but when in a room with several other dogs he is easily distracted and may act as if he's never been on a lead before in his life. If you have worked often with your puppy at home, he will have learned to trust you and to pay attention to you and to your voice. The class instructor will teach you the general things expected of you and your dog in the show ring. However, there are steps you need to know about showing a Borzoi.

Exercising the Borzoi at Aatis Lillstrom's Windhound Farm.

249

To set up or stack a Borzoi in the proper way, place his forelegs in a natural stance so that viewed from the front, the legs are a straight column of bones from the point of shoulder to the feet. This will permit the width between the legs to be the width natural to your individual Borzoi. When you view him from the side, the forelegs must be perpendicular to the ground. If he tends to lean back so that the legs are at an angle, he is "posting." This seems to be very common at first but should be corrected. If he continues to do this, concentrate on getting, and keeping, his attention as you stand slightly ahead of him. Your voice or even a favorite tidbit as bait should get his attention and make him straighten up. The hindlegs are positioned so that the hocks are also perpendicular to the ground both as viewed from the side and the rear. To check for the correct distance between the two rear feet, stand at the dog's head and look straight at him. You should just barely see the two rear feet at the sides. To improve the topline you may give him a slight nudge in the belly. In this case, experience and daily practise in stacking may relax him into a more normal topline.

After the puppy has learned to remain in this standing position, have people, preferably strangers, go over him with their hands. Dream up all sorts of different situations with which to confront him. Have your "judge" wear a floppy hat, glasses, or a loose coat. Have him use a somewhat heavy hand occasionally, have him use slow hand movements as well as fast, have him approach the dog from all angles.

Practise gaiting the dog in a straight line. Common problems that must be corrected by confidence-building practise are: head-hanging, lunging, forging, dragging and over-responding to noises outside the ring. Have others stack and gait your dog for you so you can see his problems for yourself.

Eventually, your Borzoi will stand patiently in the proper show stance for several minutes; he will take all of the judge's actions in stride; he will gait in a straight line by your side on a loose lead. Then, and only then, is he ready to be entered in a point show.

He may be ready for entry at a show but he is still not ready to go into a show ring. Grooming is essential for a show dog. A dirty, unkempt dog in the ring is an insult to the judge and to the breed, an embarrassment to you his owner. You too should be well groomed. You and your dog should be a team in appearance, behavior and attitude.

Grooming is not only for show dogs, of course. A dog with a clean coat and skin, trimmed nails, clean teeth and a brushed coat is more comfortable. A regular routine for basic grooming should be established and adhered to during the entire life of the dog.

Bathing is not the chore you might expect as most Borzoi soon learn to like the routine. Indeed, in the heat of summer your dog will love it, especial-

A Borzoi bitch, bathed and brushed, but untrimmed.

The same bitch after hocks have been cleaned, tuck-up trimmed, withers and croup thinned out.

ly if done outside with a garden hose. There are innumerable shampoos on the market. Use a good brand of shampoo that has been especially formulated for dogs. Human shampoos are rarely recommended due to the difference in pH. The normal pH range of human skin is 4.5 to 5.5 or slightly acidic. The normal pH range of the average dog skin, on the other hand, is 6.2 to 8.6 or slightly alkaline. Complete rinsing is absolutely essential. Special creme rinses and conditioners are often used especially in show dogs whose coats are subjected to constant shampooing. Powder or chalk as cleaning agents should only be used for spot cleaning and then usually for emergency cleanup. Routine use of such powders in the coat dries the coat and changes the texture. Every Borzoi should be completely bathed before a show or a weekend of shows. On a longer circuit, if another full bath is impossible half-way through the circuit, at least the legs and feathering should be bathed. After toweling dry, most prefer to blow-dry to fluff up the coat and have it lie in the proper way.

It should be stressed that the kind of shampoo, conditioners and oils used on the coat are of little importance if the health of the dog is poor. The outer condition of the coat reflects the inner health of the dog. Nutrition and freedom from internal and external parasites are essential to a good, basic coat.

Routine grooming of nails, teeth and ears is simple and can be learned by anyone. The key here is thoroughness. The appearance of an otherwise well-groomed dog can be spoiled by long nails, teeth caked with tartar and filthy, smelly ears. The nails can be clipped down close to the quick with ordinary canine nail clippers or ground down with a special grinder or file. The tartar is scraped from the teeth, sometimes with great effort if you've let it go, with a universal scaler you can obtain from your dentist. If tartar buildup is too great, your veterinarian may have to remove it with his ultrasonic Cavitron. The ear wax can be softened up with a sebum dissolving solution and then swabbed out with cotton tipped applicators.

Scissoring various areas on the Borzoi is not necessary for the house or kennel dog but is used for show dogs to give them that finished look. It can also emphasize good points and minimize bad points. Starting with the head, snip off all whiskers on muzzle, cheeks and over the eyes. The ears are often the most difficult area for both the novice and the oldtimer. Basically what you are trying to do is to make the outline of the head longer and sleeker. The hair grows in clumps at the base of the ear to the side of the head giving the head a broader and fuzzier appearance than it truly has. Thin out these tufts gradually with thinning scissors but by no means try for a shaved look. The neck curls on some dogs lie forward up and over the occiput. These also can be trimmed back or thinned out with a thinning scissors or a stripping knife. It's just about impossible to describe this sort of trimming of the head and ears. Look at several dogs at the shows. Ask the owners of those dogs whose heads appear well groomed to you to show how it's done. Never try this type of grooming, except for whiskers, just before a show. It's always best to try it well ahead of time in case you take too much hair off and it must grow back.

The feet should be trimmed so that they are neat and tidy. The nails, of course, have already been trimmed so that they just clear the floor. Trimming the hair on hocks and pasterns is optional. Severe trimming of pasterns below well-feathered upper legs gives a very unnatural look.

Often there is less coat over the center of the back with heavier coat over the withers and from the his over the croup. Left in the natural state, a dog with this uneven distribution of coat can appear neckless and flat-backed even though he is actually neither one. Judicious thinning of the thicker areas following the natural topline improves the general outline of your Borzoi.

The belly coat is often so profuse it hides all appearance of tuckup. Trimming here is advisable but it should never appear that trimming has been done. To accomplish this, I like to hold up the hair on the outside of the belly area and trim only the hair along the center belly to about an inch in length following the natural line of the tuckup. Then when the "side-curtains" are lowered, light comes through this thinned area showing tuckup in a more natural way.

Brushing is a simple procedure but one that is so often done improperly. Brush out the dog before a bath and again after drying. Brushing once a week is usually sufficient. During the coat drop season, daily brushing will be necessary though to keep up with all the loose hair. Using a pin brush, you can feel and even hear when you hit a mat or tangle. Never try to rake it out with the brush. Rather, use your fingers first and work it apart before resuming the brush work. On areas of profuse, long hair, hold it up with your left hand and starting at the bottom, brush it down in layers in order to do a thorough job. Never be so lazy that you settle for top brushing only. Mats and tangles don't go away by themselves; top brushing only covers them over. If your brush has bent pins, remove them as they tend to break hair. You want to remove all tangles while leaving as much coat as possible.

Proper grooming on a regular routine basis will make your dog happier and healthier. Well trained, well groomed, well loved. Could you settle with less for your Borzoi companion?

9

Borzoi in Obedience

SINCE THE 15th AND 16th CENTURIES attempts have been made to classify or group the known breeds of dogs according to their original purposes. Dame Juiliana Berners and Dr. John Caius made the first such attempts in England during those centuries. Not that many years ago in America the sporting group at dog shows was comprised of both the sporting dogs and the hounds as we know them today. The split was made based on the hunting instincts of the individual breeds. Those breeds that hunted with some amount of dependence upon the master for direction were classified as sporting dogs. Those breeds that hunt independently from the master were classified as hounds be they scent hounds or sighthounds. Using the Borzoi as an example, remember how he is used in the hunt. Once he is slipped after the quarry is sighted, he is off on his own doing his own thing in his own way until the quarry is caught or lost.

Training a Borzoi for obedience trials, for coursing, or for just ordinary companionship with his family and their friends is basically similar to the training of any breed. However, there are differences in training methods all based on adaptation to the basic character of the individual breed and to individual dogs within that breed. There are many books, good books, on obedience training written by experts in the field. Anyone wishing to obedience train his Borzoi should read and study several of them. Several are better than one for better understanding in the long run. Each author, each trainer, has his own pet theories and methods. Finding what appear to be contradictions may at first lead to confusion in the mind of the reader. To

The "Long-Sit" exercise being done by Ch. Sunbarr's Bengal Lancer C.D.X., Ch. Buk's Susan O'Grady C.D., and Ch. Ben Nilance C.D., all trained and owned by Chester and Irene Bukwaz in Michigan.

Ch. Trezor Trasanya C.D.X., T.D., the first Borzoi to earn a tracking degree in addition to her other titles. *Ritter*

255

resolve these doubts and confusions, more reading and studying are necessary. Studies have been done on dog behavior: common problems and their origins, common behavioral patterns, normal behavioral development. To understand the "why" of various patterns of behavior is the key to learning how to cope with, control or change that behavior. And this is just what obedience training is all about: coping with, controlling and changing behavior.

It is true that certain temperament characteristics are genetically produced. They can be modified to some extent by environment and training. The very shy, introverted dog must be trained by extra love and persistence so that he can cope with life and all that this involves. An excessively timid dog that is mollycoddled and protected will never learn to cope with problems on his own except, at times, by fear-biting. This type of dog benefits greatly from sound, basic obedience training by an understanding trainer as he learns to depend on his trainer for support while developing a degree of boldness. An overly aggressive dog, on the other hand, must have the benefit of training subject to the authority of his master or trainer so that he does not develop into a dog that is a hazard to himself and to all others around him. Most important of all, however, is the realization by anyone who would breed a litter, that while some undesirable temperament traits can be covered over by training, they should be fully recognized as serious faults disqualifying dogs with such traits from any and all breeding programs. Today we have all sorts of gadgets and devices to make our lives easier than was possible during our grandparents' times. Why then should we not apply all the knowledge and experience produced by scientific studies on canine breeding and behavior to breed dogs with suitable and stable temperaments also to make our lives, as well as the dogs' lives, easier?

The ideal temperament traits in a Borzoi (indeed, in all breeds) are a combination of confidence, boldness, endurance or persistence, willingness to please and intelligence. Each puppy will develop these traits to varying degrees and at varying stages. A puppy that establishes his role as boss of the litter certainly develops confidence and boldness early in life. His littermate that always gets left out, is always picked on by the others in the litter, will naturally lack confidence early in life. Now if that same puppy goes to a home where he is the center of attention and is given exposure to all sorts of stimuli early in life, he may then develop the same degree of confidence and boldness as his littermate "boss." If the potential is there, love and training can bring it out.

Novice breeders too often tend to overprotect their puppies. If a puppy is trapped behind his dam in the whelping box, he will at first lie there and scream. the tendency for most people is to rush to the box and rescue the puppy. Unless he is in serious trouble, it is often best to let him struggle a bit to work out his own solution to his problem. With a little effort, he finds that he can work his way up and over his dam's body. The next time will be that much easier if he has overcome the obstacle successfully by himself. The same applies to all life's problems for the developing puppy.

The dog must learn early that his owner is his master, his "leader of the pack." This is taught through the use of firm authority, not force. Reward for good behavior stimulates a willingness to please, and it is this willingness to please that makes all training so much easier on all concerned. It also leads to a happy worker in the obedience ring, such a joy to see. A dog responding to your commands because he wants to please you is a happier dog than one who responds out of fear of punishment. This would seem to be just plain, common sense although I've seen dogs trained by fear and force too often to believe that common sense is a common trait of all dog owners. One of my favorite pastimes at shows is people-watching as well as dog-watching. Around the obedience ring I find it fascinating to observe the owners of the dogs outside the ring as well as inside the ring. There is often a strong correlation between the attitude of the owner-trainer and the performance of his dog in the ring. By performance here, I'm not referring to the precision of the performance but rather to the attitude of the dog during the performance: whether he is a happy worker or a mechanical worker.

No matter how many books one reads, however, there comes a time in a dog's training when an owner can benefit most from a training class conducted by a knowledgeable, understanding trainer. Very rare is the owner who can completely train his dog all on his own. There is no problem so unique that someone, somewhere has not experienced the same problem. Sharing problems and solutions benefits all.

General dog books written in the twenties and thirties often expressed the same opinion of Borzoi intelligence and trainability. They all seemed to state that the long, narrow head of the Borzoi allowed no room for brains; the breed was beautiful but stupid. That myth persists even today to some extent. Often a judge or trainer will express surprise at seeing a Borzoi in the obedience ring. And should the dog turn in a creditable performance, as he often does, these same people are almost stunned by disbelief. Statistics prove the Borzoi can do very well in obedience. Hardly a month goes by but what at least one Borzoi earns an obedience degree; usually several do. Success breeds success. Once a Borzoi owner has learned the satisfaction and pleasure of training his dog through one degree, he soon goes on with further advanced training of that dog or starts training with another.

In 1935 the American Kennel Club granted its approval of obedience training as a vital part of dog activity. Rules were formulated and obedience trials were sanctioned as part of dog shows. Today almost every point show offers classes for obedience. Obedience clubs hold sanctioned shows for obedience only, sort of independent obedience specialty shows.

258

The first Borzoi to earn a U.D. in both Canada and the United States—Ch. Lady Tasha of Kamaroff U.D.—owned and trained by Gladys Dykstra.

Ch. Denton's Matvey C.D.X., owned and trai by John and Mary Gamber in Pennsylvania.

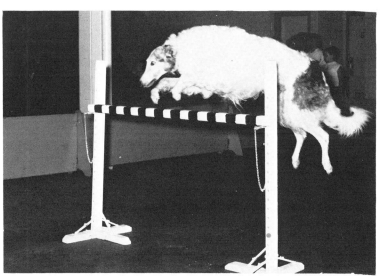

Ch. Buk's Shadow U.D., the first male Borzoi to earn a U.D. owned and trained by Chester and Irene Bukwaz. *Frank*

257

Ch. Buk's Omar of Nayra C.D.X., owned and trained by Chester and Irene Bukwaz, doing the retrieve over the solid jump. Omar also won several hound groups and was highest scoring obedience Borzoi in 1976.

Ch. Loral's Matvey C.D.X. taking the solid jump, owned and trained by Jane Maddox in West Virginia.

Ch. Rugay Aspor of Pheasant Hill C.D.X. retrieving over the solid jump, owned and trained by Ed and Ann Filetti. Rugay also has earned his field championship, a very versatile hound. *Turner*

The year 1939 saw the first Borzoi earning a companion dog (C.D.) degree: Madge Cluxton's Ch. Czar III of Glenwild C.D.. It is most interesting that this first obedience Borzoi had already attained his breed championship. This was not the only time a Borzoi sported titles at both ends of his registered name either. The reader must have noticed in the two chapters on history in America, the great numbers of Borzoi since 1939 boasting the same achievement.

Gordon and Sylvia Sohr of the Twin Elms Kennels in Wisconsin owned and trained the first Borzoi to earn a utility degree (U.D.) in 1950. This dispelled another rumor about the breed, that because Borzoi are sight hounds they have no sense of smell. (The utility degree requires one exercise in which the dog must show scent discrimination.) The gold and white bitch Bourtai of Malora U.D. continued to display her versatility and her obedience trained prowess by her public performances. She was a favorite at many Independence Day celebrations where she would carry a ten foot pole bedecked with red, white and blue streamers and small flags over a six foot high jump and a seven foot broad jump.

Gladys Dykstra had three Borzoi, all with U.D. titles. The first was Ch. Lady Tasha of Tamaroff U.D. (by Ch. Rachmaninoff ex Ch. Mazar-Zorka of Pavlov Crest). Tasha was the second U.D. Borzoi in the United States and the first to earn a U.D. in Canada as well. Her American U.D. title was earned in 1963, her breed championship was earned in 1965. Gladys was well known in the Springfield, Massachusetts area as an excellent obedience trainer. Training handicapped people in obedience work was one of her specialties. In addition to Tasha, Gladys also owned and trained Meyer's Beautiful Tanya U.D. and Wilolea's Lucky Triska U.D.

In the East, many well-known breeders have combined breed and obedience quite successfully. Joan and Michael Carusone owned and trained Ch. Wilolea's Sweet Diana U.D. Gwen and John Pinette's Ch. Czarina of Gwejon C.D.X. (companion dog excellent) earned her American and Canadian C.D.X. titles at nine years of age proving you *can* teach an old dog new tricks. Other kennels combining breed and obedience are Karen Staudt's Majenkir Kennels, Alfred Edlin's Ridgeside Kennels, Debra and Lorraine Groshans' Loral Kennels, among others.

In the Midwest, the kennels of Chester and Irene Bukwaz stand out in the history of Borzoi obedience. To date they have bred, owned and trained more U.D. Borzoi than any other owners: Ch. Buk's Shadow U.D. (first male U.D. Borzoi), Ch. Buk's Arrow U.D., Ch. Buk's Calliope U.D. and Ch. Buk's and Fox Run El Toro U.D. Referring back to the history chapter for additional obedience achievements will prove that the record of this small kennel is indeed a remarkable one.

Ernestine and Janet Shelton trained and own the only Borzoi to date to

Marbob's Toniscott of Malora C.D., owned and trained by Betty and Jim Forry in California, doing the broad jump.

Borzoi and handlers of the Borzoi Brigada in one of their costumed demonstrations.

Bogardia's Guenevere U.D., the first Canadian U.D. Borzoi owned by Marg Coleman in Ontario.

earn a tracking degree (T.D.), and this in addition to a breed championship and a C.D.X. on their Trezor Trasanya (by Ch. Trezor Lubyanka C.D. ex Ch. Trezor Meta).

On the West Coast, the first champion Borzoi to earn an obedience degree was Ch. Zonazo Perchinoff C.D. owned and trained by June Forry. June was only twelve years old at the time. Phyl and Lyle Gillette of Ranch Gabriel Kennels put many obedience degrees on their Borzoi as has been seen in the history chapter. Lyle conducted an obedience training class for several years. Phyl and Lyle were instrumental in initiating the Borzoi Brigada, an obedience drill team. Gail McRae owned the outstanding brother-sisteer brace of Ch. Shahzana Kochab of Hethivar C.D. and Ch. Sascha Kochab of Hethivar C.D.X. bred by Gail's parents Marge and Sid Cox. This brace won many best brace in show awards. In the Pacific Northwest, the outstanding breeder combining obedience and breed is Lois Cooper of Chulista Kennels.

In Canada, the first and only U.D. Borzoi to date is Marg Coleman's Bogardia's Gwenevere U.D.. Marg is a gifted obedience trainer who shares her thoughts, theories, and training suggestions with others through articles in various breed magazines.

To close this chapter on Borzoi Obedience, I'd like to quote from one of Marg's articles:

"Whether in the hunt, the coursing field, the show ring, or the intricate challenges of advanced obedience, the dog who runs only to please himself can be unpredictable — even in the chase — often a perpetual harassment — even embarrassment to his owner, while the dog who is in tune with the wishes of his master is a joy to experience."

10

Coursing and Racing with Borzoi

VOLUMES COULD BE WRITTEN about wolf hunting with Borzoi in Russia particularly during the late years of the 19th century. Indeed, volumes have been written. One of the most interesting, the most vivid and the most widely read accounts of such hunts is "The Perchino Hunt" written in 1912 by His Excellency Dmitri Walzoff, a translation of which is included in Winifred Chadwick's book *The Borzoi*. Mr. Walzoff at one time owned his own hunt but later was put in charge of the Perchino Hunt of the Grand Duke Nikolai Nikolaivitch. Every Borzoi fancier interested in the history of the breed should read his account.

Short descriptive accounts of wolf hunting with Borzoi appear in several Russian novels: Leo Tolstoy's *War and Peace* and Ivan Nazhivin's *The Dogs,* to name but two. The Russian-produced movie of Tolstoy's novel included several sequences of hunts which were interesting but failed to capture the pomp and pageantry of the actual hunts which were by all accounts true extravaganzas. The money spent on maintaining the extensive kennels, staging the hunts and wagering on the outcome of hunts must have been phenomenal.

Many of the larger hunts staged events that involved the marshalling of small armies of men, horses, hounds and equipment necessary for the establishment of field kitchens serving up sumptuous feasts of food and drink following the day's hunt and camping sites for occasional overnight comfort and convenience.

Leashes of three Borzoi comprising a wolf-team were matched not only

Two Borzoi, Riva and Borloff, look over a trophy from their day's coursing.

Ch. Natalie of Chulista C.D.X. returning with her quarry to owner Lois Cooper.

Princess Natacha taking a hurdle in her record-setting-style at Tiajuana, Mexico.

for compatible abilities but often for color. Each hunt or kennel bred according to its own interpretation of the necessary qualities for successful wolfhounds. In the early days there was no single standard of excellence to which all breeding programs were geared. Each hunt more or less developed its own standard which accounts for the various distinctive types bred by each hunt. Color differences in the hounds of various hunts were often based not so much on an historical basis as on personal preferences.

According to all the old Russian accounts of wolf hunting, the Borzoi were generally trained not to kill the wolf but to catch and hold the quarry. The huntsman would ride up and deliver the fatal blow. A few Borzoi in Russia did earn reputations as solo wolf killers and they were prized for their strength and courage. Trials were held in Moscow at which wolf and hound met on a one-to-one basis in closed arenas. However, the majority of the Russian Borzoi were hunted in the open by the organized Hunts.

Today such extensive hunts would be impossible to stage, but the desire to view the working of superbly conditioned Borzoi in the field and to experience the thrill and excitement of watching hounds flying over the fields in pursuit of game is still strong.

Early in the 20th century, the first few Americans visited some of the larger Russian estates and participated in wolf hunts staged for their benefit. It isn't difficult to imagine the enthusiasm that was engendered and the tales that were related upon the travelers' return home. Joseph Thomas was one of those in whose breast the fire burned brightly. He imported many fine Borzoi from the better Russian Hunts. His Valley Farm Kennel was located in Connecticut, an area not well suited for this type of hunting either by terrain or available quarry. Several of his Borzoi, however, were sold to men in the western plains states where the hounds could be trained for hunting wolves and coyotes. The training facilities and methods could hardly equal those in Russia so hunting proceeded on somewhat different lines. Greyhounds and deerhounds were used with the Borzoi plus crosses of the three breeds by the hunters. The dogs usually killed the coyotes they caught, but often needed help from the hunters after catching a full-grown wolf.

Mr. C. E. Miller of Wisdom, Montana trained the OVF wolf team of Ivor, Gillick and Appraxin O'Valley Farm on coyotes and wolves. In one season this team caught and killed 47 coyotes and nine wolves.

Theodore Roosevelt at the beginning of the 20th century wrote in his book *Ranch Life and the Hunting Trail,* "Coursing is the sport of all sports for ranchmen, now that big animals are growing scarce; and certainly there can be no healthier or more exciting pastime than that of following game with horse and hound over the great Western plains." While non-ranchers such as Roosevelt may have considered this type of hunting as sport, the ranchers themselves found coursing a very necessary function to deplete

Princess Natacha, owned by Marietta Gregory and Edith Green, in a quiet moment between races.

Ch. Joseph Alexander Austerlitz and Ch. Berbeg Odette Odile chasing the lure at a trial in Missouri. Borzoi owned by Jeff and Lyn Rissman.

Many Borzoi can course small game in the field and still live in harmony with small animals in the home.

the numbers of coyotes, wolves and rabbits that made daily forays on their livestock and crops.

In South Africa and Rhodesia during the 1950's Borzoi and other sighthounds were used to hunt jackals and cape hunting dogs. Jackals cause great financial losses to sheep ranchers every year with their raids on the flocks. The cape hunting dogs live and hunt in packs killing off many animals including the springbok and other swift antelopes. They are killed on sight by rangers in the national parks and wildlife refuges. Borzoi and other sighthounds are used on a regular basis to help in the hunting and killing of both jackal and cape hunting dog. Maxwell Riddle, one of our fine all-breed dog judges of today, actually attended such hunts when visiting in South Africa and Southern Rhodesia in 1955. He wrote of these exploits in his weekly column in a Cleveland newspaper.

There are still ranchers today who know the value of using sighthounds for keeping down the population of unwelcome predators. From time to time there are stories appearing of modern day coursing exploits. Some follow the same coursing methods used at the turn of the century with only the substitution of trucks for horses. Unfortunately there are some who have added other modern embellishments and refinements such as planes acting as spotters or beaters to spot or concentrate the coyotes which rather takes such mechanized coursing out of the category of sport and puts it in what many would consider wholesale slaughter.

From Russia come accounts of Borzoi being used by the fur industry. Because a Borzoi kills its small quarry instantly by a snap of the neck, he is invaluable in hunting fur-bearing animals. A pelt from a Borzoi-killed animal is usually in much better condition because of the way in which the animal is killed than one from an animal killed by a gun or caught in a trap.

There are also accounts of coursing sighthounds for other useful and necessary purposes. At Reese Air Force Base in Texas, for example, sighthounds have been used for controlling the jackrabbit population on the base. With many square miles fenced off, the jackrabbits had taken over, safe from their usual enemies. However, rabbits on the runways presented potentially fatal hazards as they ignored the traffic of planes landing and taking off. The situation was ideal for sighthound coursing, providing sport as well as a vital service on the base.

In 1959 one of the first organized coursing clubs originated in California known as the Pacheco Hunt sponsored by the Borzoi Club of Northern California. California was a natural location for such sport as it had favorable weather, proper terrain, non-restrictive laws and suitable game. Interest and enthusiasm ran high in this group as the open field meets were held more and more often on winter and spring weekends. Soon after starting with Borzoi, other sighthound breed clubs supported the activity. The

Ch. Apollo's Malachi Del Viento C.D. shown winning the BCOA Western Specialty in 1975 under judge Del 'Glodowski, handled for owners D. and L. Larsen by Barbara Binder, trophy presenters Helen Colstad and Harald Sundt. Malachi was the second Borzoi to earn a lure coursing field championship and was highest scoring Borzoi in lure coursing in 1973. *Rubin*

coursing took on a more organized aspect as rules and procedures were formulated, tried and revised. Since 1970, organized open field coursing has been governed by the National Open Field Coursing Association. An Annual Grand Course is held at which only that season's course winners and past coursing champions are entered. The top winning Borzoi in open field coursing in 1975 was Manon of Rancho Gabriel owned by Lou and Fern Lockrem. In 1977 the honor went to Tzoyuz Tzar of Virshina owned by C. Wells and C. Bradley.

Areas for open field coursing are chosen with care to assure safety for the dogs. Natural obstructions — trees, gopher holes, rocky ground, loose shale and manmade obstructions, open pipes, poison bait, domestic animals, irrigation pipes, barbed wire — are avoided whenever possible. Fields are checked before coursing meets for the presence of game. Pasture, range land, fallow cropland all make ideal areas for open field coursing. The Huntmaster at the meet controls the timing and areas when the dogs are slipped, turning the line of advance to avoid close obstructions should a rabbit be raised near them.

The hounds and handlers are assembled at dawn on the day of a coursing meet. By luck of the draw, hounds are grouped in threes for slipping in assigned order upon the "Tally-Ho" signal from the Huntmaster when a jackrabbit is raised by the advancing gallery. The Huntmaster occupies a position of extreme importance on the day of a meet as he controls the direction, the time of slipping, the end of each course when the hounds must be recalled.

With organized coursing meets there are breed stakes as well as open stakes with each meet hosted by a breed club. Judges come from the ranks of coursing enthusiasts, serving an apprenticeship before becoming licensed by the Association. Success in open field coursing is not determined by the number of rabbits actually caught. Indeed, it has been estimated that only 5% of the rabbits raised are actually caught and killed. Hounds are judged on a point system based on their speed, endurance, agility, contact with the quarry, enthusiasm and searching, compatibility and the recall.

As you may have gathered by now, the quarry involved in organized open field coursing is the jackrabbit. Unlike the Eastern cottontail, the jackrabbit is a hare with larger and longer ears and extreme angulation front and rear. Also unlike the cottontail, the jackrabbit rarely "holes up" having confidence in his speed for his escape from the pursuing dogs. The eyes are positioned to the sides of the head for excellent peripheral vision which allows the jackrabbit to determine the exact moment to turn ahead of the dogs. In California where the sport of open field coursing is the most popular, the most common rabbit is the Blacktail Jackrabbit whose running stride has been measured at 12 feet and speed clocked at up to 40 mph. With

Modern day open field coursing with "hunters" armed with cameras rather than guns and knives. This hunting trio is moving in line with the rest of the gallery waiting for the Huntmaster's Tally-Ho.

A Borzoi and Saluki chasing the lure. The Borzoi here is Mulberry Street's Blyunca, a field champion owned by Robert Schulze going Best in Field at his first coursing meet. He was coursed seven times, going best of breed five times.

this speed and his natural agility and his knowledge of the immediate area, it is no wonder that Mr. Jack so often lives to see another day.

Open field coursing enthusiasts are often lyrical in their descriptions of the joy and excitement of this form of field work with their hounds. About ten years ago when I was in California to judge, I was fortunate to participate in some open field coursing myself. It was not an organized meet as holding it was a spur of the moment decision. Someone threw out the question, "Who'd like to go coursing tomorrow?" Immediately there were responses from several people even though the next day was Monday, a work day for many. Arrangements were quickly made, times and places agreed upon. The next morning before dawn we started off for the fields thought best for the day's sport. The early morning hours were cold but as the sun climbed the sky, it became quite hot. Unfortunately it was a bad time of year as the fields were dry and dusty providing sparse cover for any game present in the fields and allowing the rabbits we did raise too much of a headstart before dogs could be slipped. We only raised maybe four or five all day, and the dogs made up of a group of Salukis and Borzoi, never even got close enough for an attempt at a take. But in spite of all this, the ground-in dust, the weary muscles, the feeling of excitement for the sport and the beauty of the dogs coursing the fields made me an ardent supporter of the sport wishing for all the world that I lived in California instead of Pennsylvania.

From written and personal accounts of the sport of open field coursing, many sighthound owners in parts of the country other than California dreamed of holding similar events. In fact, in 1962 Eli Fleischer was appointed by the Borzoi Club of America to investigate the feasibility of an organized coursing event on his farm in Pennsylvania using imported jackrabbits. All the plans were progressing well and enthusiasm was running high when it was learned that State Game Laws prohibited the killing of all wild game by any means except gun and bow. Coursing of live game is illegal in almost all states of the country. As a watered-down alternative, interest then turned to racing.

In the 1920's there was a great deal of interest in racing Greyhounds and Whippets. In California the Pacific Coast Russian Wolfhound Association was formed with Miles S. Gregory as president. The major interest of the club was racing with Harold F. Wilson as chairman of the racing committee. The TiaJuana Kennel Club in TiaJuana, Mexico, just over the California border, had opened its beautiful new Aqua Caliente track. Most races involved greyhounds but the nightcap each evening was the hurdle racing of Russian Wolfhounds. The appearance of these stately hounds in the paddock and on parade was greeted with exclamations of admiration. Originally introduced as a novel means of publicity, races for Russian Wolfhounds met with such keen interest that they soon became a regular feature. Many of the participating Borzoi were AKC champions of record proving the breed worthy of its place as both a show and sporting dog. The members of the PCRWA sent the best hounds in their kennels to the training camp at Lankershim to be schooled and conditioned by trainer Charles Snell.

The great favorites at the Caliente track were Diablo (by Astor ex Ch. Olga XIII) owned by A.V. Wilson and Princess Natacha (by Rolf of Anoakia ex Princess Ski). On a 5/16 mile, four foot hurdle track, Natacha established a record of 37 seconds, the record holding for many years. Natacha was bred by J. Miller in 1924 and was co-owned by Marietta Gregory and Edith Green with most of her training done by Miss Gregory.

In the 1960's an attempt was made to feature Borzoi races at one of the Florida Greyhound tracks but it was shortlived as the Borzoi were unschooled. Besides, the Borzoi is really not the sprinter the Greyhound is and tends to excel in long distance running requiring endurance rather than initial speed.

Racing for fun became popular in the 1960's at informal tracks set up by various sighthound clubs and is still a feature attraction at some dog shows. It was thought for a while that racing would have to satisfy the thwarted desires of many Borzoi owners to course their hounds.

In 1970 a lure coursing system was developed as an answer to many of the problems with open field coursing both in California and other states. Actually, this system combines the best features of both open field coursing and racing. So enthusiastic was the response to lure coursing on a local basis in California where it originated, that Lyle Gillette in 1971 toured the country to all areas where there was a concentration of Borzoi owners interested in coursing.

In September of that year, the Borzoi Club of America scheduled a match show and picnic with a demonstration of the new lure coursing system as an added attraction. This was held at the Kostroma Kennels in Bucks County, Pennsylvania which had several acres of more or less open hillside which was freshly mowed. A zig-zag course was set up with pulleys mounted on plywood set into the ground at all the turns. The lure itself was a bundle of white plastic strips attached to a line run through the pulleys. At the end of the line was a manually operated unit with a gear assembly giving about a 1:13 ratio allowing for speeds up to 55 mph. As the lure was whipped around the course, it bounced and hopped over every bump in the terrain appearing for all the world as a wildly scampering cottontail. Many of the Borzoi there that day had participated in racing so they were not completely green. They took to this new form of racing, this lure chasing, with great enthusiasm matched only by that of their owners.

Much progress has taken place since then in the training and conditioning of the hounds, the sophistication of the lure system and the formulation of rules and procedures to make it a competitive sport. In 1972 an organization of the National Provisional Committee was formed by fanciers of Salukis, Whippets, Afghans and Borzoi with the purpose of initiating and promoting lure-coursing trials on a national basis. This committee became the American Sighthound Field Association (ASFA) with delegates from many sighthound bred clubs and coursing associations and Lyle Gillette as its first president. Annual meetings are held at which the delegates discuss and vote on rule changes and clarifications. The ultimate goal of AFSA is to obtain the sanction of the AKC in holding lure-coursing trials leading to the officially recognized title of Field Champion. (Many dogs today are listed in ads and catalogs with a F.Ch. designation but to date that is a title recognized only by AFSA.) AFSA publishes the *Field Advisory News,* a magazine which keeps fanciers up to date on new rules, procedures, and decisions as well as including results of all trials held with AFSA sanction under AFSA rules. As in open field coursing, wins in lure coursing are based on speed, agility, endurance and enthusiasm as determined by three judges on the field.

In Europe, open field coursing is prohibited, so for many years organized racing was enjoyed by sighthound fanciers. Now the lure coursing fever has caught on there also.

Since 1972 the annual top winning Borzoi in lure coursing based on points earned at sanctioned trials are as follows:

1972	Tasia's Contiga del Viento, owned by C. de Frietas and B. Binder.
1973	Ch. Apollo's Malachi del Viento C.D., owned by Dale and Louis Larsen (It should be noted that Malachi was best of breed at two specialties in 1975 — a very versatile hound indeed.)
1974	Lira of BeeGee, owned by W. and S. Clawson
1975	Manon of Rancho Gabriel, owned by Lou and Fern Lockrem (This dog also excelled in open field coursing.)
1976	Anastasia of Marzoi J-Khan C.D., owned by P. Anuta and D. Darling

In 1976 AFSA approved a new Bowen system of computing placings, so there was a second top winning dog that year.

1976	Mytarkha's Lalejana Shadowfax, owned by Marian McNeil
1977	Caspian Prince Pyerun Duncan, owned by R Manteiga
1978	Birchwood Caspian Princess Zorya Am. F.Ch., LCM owned by G.A. Manteiga

| 1979 | Fairyfort's Flute, LCM—owned by Jean and Steve Kurdziolek |
| 1980 | Birchwood Seryosha v Songmaker L.C.M., owned by Jan McKenney |

As of March 31, 1979 there have been 119 Borzoi field champions with eight of them earning the more advanced title of Lure Courser of Merit. The first Borzoi field champion was El Jaco of Rancho Gabriel owned by Kay Maccagno in 1973. The second one was also a bench champion with an obedience degree, and a two time specialty winner, Ch. Apollo's Malachi del Viento C.D. owned by Dale and Louis Larsen. The first bitch to earn a field championship was Pat Hillyard's Timber Ridge's Tara del Viento in 1974. The first Lure Courser of Merit was Caspian Prince Pyerun Duncan owned by R. Manteiga in 1977 in Pennsylvania.

Even though there is no question now that lure coursing is and will be for a long time the most available coursing-type sport open for sighthounds on an organized level, there is still controversy about the advantages and disadvantages of lure coursing versus open field coursing. Open field coursing does offer a continual variety of coursing patterns as determined by the quarry whereas lure coursing patterns are predetermined by field committees and must be manually changed regularly to outfox the lure-smart hounds. Experienced hounds can key in on physical indications of a rabbit's decision to make a turn since a rabbit will slightly raise his ears as he slows for a turn as opposed to well laid back ears on a straight course at top speed. An artificial lure gives no indication of an impending turn and a very fast dog, especially when he is in the lead, will almost always overrun at the turn and can easily become unsighted. A dog in open field coursing is in a constant state of warm-up as he trots along with his handler in the gallery waiting his turn to be slipped. At a lure coursing trial a dog may be run in only three heats all day while between heats he spends most of his time sitting or lying down. All forms of coursing involve some risk although usually there are fewer risks on the grounds of a lure course as the course is laid out over a known territory. However, a discussion of the advantages and disadvantages of the two types of coursing is only academic outside a very few states which allow both.

Some people say that they will not course their Borzoi for fear of injury. Of course there is always the possibility of injury, but there is also a chance of injury running around his own back yard. I had the horrifying experience of watching one of my own Borzoi, a champion of only a few weeks, die of a broken neck as he made an abrupt turn running in the exercise paddock. Recently, a friend's Afghan broke her leg while in her usual crate for the night. Accidents can happen anywhere, any time. It has been said that less than 5% of coursing injuries result in permanent disability. Many of the more common injuries have been due to improper or insufficient conditioning. This might be comparable to a person spending five days a week at a soft non-physical job, watching TV every night, smoking too much, and then taking five or six dogs to two shows on the weekend and running around the ring with them. It can be done, but it will usually not be a top performance and the dogs are not shown to their best advantage. Injuries or problems in coursing range from simple muscle cramps and serious fractures of various bones to ruptures of tendons, cut or bruised pads and torn nails. Young dogs that are forced beyond their capabilities at various growth stages may more easily develop the temporarily debilitating effects of osteochondritis dessicans or panosteitis.

Another controversial aspect concerns the effect of coursing on temperament. Many fanciers have refused to course their Borzoi for fear of adverse effects upon temperament. Lure coursing by its very nature does stimulate a competitive spirit, although often more so in the human than in the canine participants. Those dogs that do exhibit undesirable characteristics, such as interference with other dogs in the course by bumping or attacking them, are either basically unstable or have been improperly trained for clean coursing. Most clubs offering coursing trials also hold practice or training sessions, and it behooves any fancier interested in the sport to take advantage of them for his novice dogs. Occasionally, a dog fails to correct behavioral faults in spite of all attempts at proper training. Such a hound should not be coursed as he is a hazard to himself and to other hounds on the field. Aggressive behavior directed towards catching the lure is desirable but when directed towards the other hounds is an unreliability that cannot be tolerated.

In open field coursing, coursing live game may present additional problems. It has been felt by many experts from experiences in the field that catching and killing jackrabbits, the usual quarry in open field coursing trials, will not affect temperament as the rabbits put up little resistance. Other types of quarry that tend to fight when caught, such as coyotes and other large game, may present a different picture. As one expert, Steve Copold, has stated in various articles on coursing, "I do feel that any time a hound takes game that fights back, it will most certainly act to degrade the dog's temperament." A basically stable temperament coupled with proper discipline and training minimizes the effects of this. The majority of our Borzoi are family dogs. Coursing the neighbors cats and other small pets is certainly undesirable, embarrassing and degrading to the reputation of the breed. Hounds coursed on large game might be compared to attack-trained dogs of the working breeds used by law-enforcement agencies and the military. All such dogs must be worked under reliable control.

Controversy also exists over the humane aspects of coursing live game. Of course, the same controversy exists in connection with the killing of game by hunters with gun, bow and arrow, and traps. The few jackrabbits that are caught in open field coursing are dispatched with a quick toss by the dog, the rabbit dying instantly from a broken neck. On rare occasions, a bad take may be a bit gory as the rabbit is not killed instantly, but this is comparable to a poorly placed shot from the hunter's gun. Neither is intended by dog or hunter, and either situation is immediately corrected by dog or hunter.

Wolf hunting in old Russia was quite different from the present day types of coursing in spite of basic similarities. Reading various accounts of actual hunts, such as those by Walzoff and Thomas, evokes the same passions today that must have been felt in the hearts and minds of those old-time participants. I would urge everyone seriously interested in the Borzoi to read at least the three books described below to understand the coursing heritage of the breed.

Joseph B. Thomas just after the turn of this century visited Russia on behalf of the Valley Farm syndicate searching for superior specimens of Borzoi. In 1912 his *Observations on Borzoi* was published by Houghton Mifflin Co. This book is very difficult to find now in the original edition as most existing ones are highly treasured by those lucky enough to own them. However, the book was recently reprinted by The Dehack Effort in Campbell, California.

In 1904 Mr. Thomas was invited to hunt with the hunt of the Grand Duke Nicholas at Perchina. In his book he describes the Perchina kennels and estate in detail and gives an account of the manner of hunting with Borzoi. He also quotes from an article by James Primrose in *World-Wide Magazine* describing a wolf-hunt near Nijni-Novgorod in which he participated. The photographs and paintings included in the Thomas book add much to the flavor of the text. In other chapters, Mr. Thomas describes the hunting of game with Borzoi in the western states of this country. It is an interesting comparison of cultures of the two countries at that time in history.

In 1952 Winifred Chadwick's book *The Borzoi Handbook* was published by Nicholson and Watson in London. A revised edition retitled simply *Borzois* was published in 1971 in London by Kemp's Printing and Publishing Co. Ltd. In both editions, the second half of the book is a translation from the German of Dmitri Walzoff's *The Perchino Hunt*. Walzoff was the manager of the Grand Duke Nikolai's Perchino estate and a noted Borzoi breeder and sportsman in his own right. It was Walzoff who hosted Joseph Thomas' visits in 1903 and 1904 and arranged a hunt for Mr. Thomas' pleasure and instruction. *The Perchino Hunt* is probably the most detailed accounting of kenneling, breeding practises and hunting on the vast Perchino estate.

There is a third book that I feel is valuable reading for all Borzoi enthusiasts. This is Ivan Nazhivin's book *The Dogs* published in 1931 by J. B. Lippincott Co. While the book has been out of print for some time, copies may still be obtained through rare-book dealers. Mr. Nazhivin, the son of rich peasants, was born in 1874 in Russia living there until the Revolution forced him to take refuge in Belgium. The novel mentions Borzoi and wolf-coursing with Borzoi only incidentally although graphically. The author, quite obviously, was not a Borzoi fancier of his day. Because he was not, there is no attempt to sugarcoat or excuse the weaknesses or mistakes or shortcomings of either man or dog in his description of what could well have been a typical wolf hunt in Russia about the turn of the century. In the chapters devoted to a wolf hunt on the Prince's estate, you tend to wonder if the author patterned his fictitious character The Grand Duke Nikita Vsevolodovitch after The Grand Duke Nikolai Nicolaiovitch of Perchino. I would hope that this was not the case since if it were it would seem to topple the Grand Duke of Perchino from the pedestal on which Borzoi fanciers of this century have placed him. Reading the entire novel *The Dogs* gives the reader an understanding of and a feeling for the times during which the breeding and coursing of Borzoi reached a peak of quality and success before the sudden disastrous cessation brought on by the Revolution with its destruction of the great estates and the obliteration of the Czarist culture.

11
Borzoi Clubs

THE ORIGINATOR of the most famous affix in American Borzoi history, Joseph B. Thomas, who registered his Valley Farm Kennels in 1901, also inspired a small group of Borzoi owners to organize the national breed club. Although his Valley Farm hounds had won many honors in the show ring, Mr. Thomas was convinced that the judging of the breed was inclined to be erratic due to the ignorance of most people regarding the qualities that constitute a good Borzoi. He recognized that there was a great need of a recorded Standard of Perfection to guide judges, show committees, and breeders in their efforts to improve the breed and maintain the points of excellence already achieved. With this goal in mind, a meeting was held at the Brooklyn Bench Show on November 12, 1903 at which an executive committee, consisting of Mr. Thomas, Dr. John DeMund and James Mortimer, was appointed to draft a Constitution and Standard, to be voted upon by the Club at a meeting scheduled for February 10, 1904 at Madison Square Garden.

There had been considerable controversy about the correct name of these hounds ever since their introduction in America. The Russian name for the breed was *Psovoi Barzoi* meaning swift dog. The controversy in this country divided fanciers into two camps: those preferring the name for the breed of Psovoi and those preferring Borzoi. James Watson, a well known judge and author of the day, suggested as a compromise using the name Russian Wolfhound, a suggestion quickly adopted by the fanciers. Joseph Thomas held out for his preference for the name Borzoi as evidenced by his use of this name for the breed in his book published in 1912. In 1936 The Russian Wolfhound Club of America officially changed the breed name to Borzoi mainly to avoid confusion since Borzoi is the name by which these hounds are recognized all over the world. Naturally, the name of the club also was changed at that time to Borzoi Club of America. Etymologists suggest that since the word in Russian is used as an adjective and in its application to the breed is now used as a noun, the word Borzoi should be capitalized in written use and that the plural is the same as the singular.

Despite the argument over a suitable name, the primary purpose of the club was realized when the breed standard was formally adopted September 1, 1905. It remains basically the same today save for some few changes and clarifications in 1940 and 1972. From time to time there have been and there will continue to be attempts to make additional changes to the Standard. Some changes may be justified, of course, but others are often attempts by small groups to justify certain features that they have in their own lines or to justify and accept changes that have crept into the breed line due to fads or careless breeding. Any changes that are proposed by groups of fanciers or by the Board of Governors of the Club must be first voted on by the members of the Club and approved by a two-thirds majority providing that at least fifty percent of the membership has voted. Final approval must be given then by the American Kennel Club.

Originally, the Russian Wolfhound Club of America was strictly an Eastern oriented club with all of its meetings in New York City. In 1927 the Pacific Coast Russian Wolfhound Association was formed in southern California with Miles Gregory as its first president. While this group was composed of fanciers interested in promoting the interest in and the welfare of the Borzoi through breeding and exhibiting at point shows, the interest in organized racing ran high. Most of the members participated in racing their Borzoi at the track in Tiajuana, Mexico. Many of the top racers were also champions of record attesting to the well rounded interests of the club members. This first local club was in existence for less than ten years.

In the early 1950's, recognizing the need for better communication between the members and between the members and the Board of Governors, the BCOA initiated the club's quarterly publication *The Aristocrat*. Prior to this time there had been only yearbooks published on an erratic basis. These yearbooks, however, generally amounted to no more than statistics of champion titles and registrations for the previous year. There had been little attempt at education of the Borzoi fancy or at dissemination of news of various sorts. Columns and articles were written for various magazines for these purposes, but the national, or parent, club itself lacked communication with the growing numbers of Borzoi owners.

In 1961 the decision was made to hold a second specialty during that year. The area chosen was the Pittsburgh area as it was more or less midway between the East and Midwest. The success of this venture was overwhelming, proof that the age of provincialism was drawing to a close. During the years since then many BCOA specialties and meetings have been held in all parts of the country — Illinois, California, Washington, Minnesota and Georgia.

During the war years 1942 to 1945, registrations of Borzoi were cut about in half as breeding and showing were curtailed due to so many war-imposed restrictions. After the lifting of the restrictions, interest in all Borzoi activities and in the breed itself grew and prospered. However, after a few years it became a time of paradox. There were a growing number of Borzoi owners and breeders, great understanding of the requirements of the standard, more and better means of communication, and better means of transporting Borzoi and their owners. Yet on the other hand, there were mushrooming numbers of pet shops appearing which sold increasing numbers of pure-bred dogs including Borzoi, increasing numbers of poorly bred and planned litters of Borzoi, and increasing amounts of restrictive legislation on local as well as national levels. Charles Dickens described the situation in his opening words of *A Tale of Two Cities:*

"It was the best of times, it was the worst of times, it was the age of wisdom, it was the age of foolishness, it was the season of Light, it was the season of Darkness, it was the spring of hope, it was the winter of despair, we had everything before us, we had nothing before us, we were all going direct to Heaven, we were all going direct the other way . . ."

The world of pure-bred dogs faces problems today that are not only local but national and international as well. Solutions do not come overnight and have proven often to be best undertaken at a local level first. It is at this level that there is more personal contact and concern.

Over the years since the late postwar years more and more local clubs devoted to the interests of the Borzoi were organized in all parts of the country. At first, these clubs represented areas large enough to make them more regional than local. Now, due to the encouragement of the AKC, all new clubs represent truly local areas.

The first local Borzoi club of those still in existence today was the Borzoi Club of California including the entire state of California in 1948 with Harald Sundt Jr. serving as the first president. The first specialty show was held at the Golden Gate Kennel Club show in San Francisco in January, 1954. The membership of the club was concentrated in two areas, greater Los Angeles and greater San Francisco. Show sites and meeting locations were alternated between the north and the south for several years until it proved to be unworkable and the club was split into two, one in each area. The club in the south retained the original club name.

280

Right on the heels of the California club, a club in the midwest was formed named the Midwest Borzoi Club. This club, formed in 1949, included five states: Ohio, Indiana, Illinois, Michigan and Wisconsin. The first president of the çlub was Major Chester J. Clark. Following the first specialty show in 1950 at Grand Rapids, Michigan, the location of the annual specialty has been in various places throughout the midwest area although since 1966 it has been held in conjunction with the Detroit Kennel Club show. Entries at the MBC specialties have ranged from eight to over 200. During the last ten years it has not been at all uncommon for the MBC specialty entry to surpass that of the national specialty in the same year.

The Borzoi Club of Northern California was formed in 1957 when the original Borzoi Club of California was split into the northern and southern California clubs. The area of greatest club influence is generally thought to be the Bay Area of San Francisco. The first president of BCNC was Phydelma Gillette. The club has held annual specialty shows for over twenty years with the usual site that of the Golden Gate Kennel Club show where the first BCOC specialty was held. The BCNC was the first breed club to sponsor coursing with its Pacheco Hunt, and it held coursing events between 1960 and 1966.

With interest waning in open field coursing within the BCNC in 1967, a new club was formed in the same general area although centralized just south of the San Francisco Bay Area. This club, the Mission Trail Borzoi Club, elected Hal Stanger as its first president. The club sponsored many open field coursing trials and was the first to actively promote lure coursing. With many members actively training their Borzoi in obedience, it was a natural thing for someone to originate the idea of an obedience drill team. This drill team, known as the Borzoi Brigada, presented many demonstrations before various groups thereby gaining much favorable publicity for the breed.

The following year the Gold Coast Borzoi Club of South Florida was founded in the Miami area with Paul Einstein serving as its first president. Their first specialty was held in 1975 and has been held every year but one since then.

The year 1968 also saw the formation of the Puget Sound Borzoi Club in the greater Seattle area. Elected as the first president was Larry Clements. The national club held a specialty, hosted by the PSBC, in the area in 1976. The following year the PSBC held its first specialty as well as hosting another BCOA specialty the next day.

In January, 1969 the Borzoi Club of Greater New York was organized with Lena Tamboer as its first president. As its name implies, the club's area of influence extends to a fifty mile radius of New York City. The first BCGNY specialty was sanctioned in September of 1972 in conjunction with the New Brunswick Kennel Club show. Several of the more colorful recent specialties have been on the grounds of the Tolstoi Foundation.

Founded in January of 1972, with Terry Fulmer as the first president, the Borzoi Club of Delaware Valley set its boundaries to cover an area within a fifty mile radius of Philadelphia, Pennsylvania. This covers portions of New Jersey, Pennsylvania, Delaware and Maryland. The first specialty was held in 1978 in conjunction with the Penn Treaty Kennel Club show. The BCDV has been quite active in promoting lure coursing on the East Coast being the only eastern Borzoi club holding AFSA-sanctioned coursing trials on a regular basis.

Sharon Roske was elected president when the Greater Twin Cities Borzoi Club was formed in March, 1974. The area of the club generally covers the Minneapolis-St. Paul area of Minnesota. In 1977, the club hosted a national specialty as a step towards the sanction of its own specialty which followed in 1979.

Other clubs have been in the process of organization in the Phoenix area of Arizona and the Maryland-Virginia area. As the popularity of the breed increases, there will be more and more local clubs organized.

The value of these local clubs is in the service they can render members and thereby the breed. Members of local clubs can more easily attend meetings for educational programs, group discussions and demonstrations involving members in a learning process that can only benefit the breed. The American Kennel Club encourages the formation of truly local breed clubs for this very purpose.

On a national level, almost every AKC recognized breed has its own parent club. The Borzoi Club of America, like the majority of such parent clubs, is a member of the AKC and as such has an AKC delegate to represent Borzoi interests at the AKC quarterly meetings. The differentiation between parent and local breed clubs was very well summed up by William Stifel, currently president of the AKC but then executive secretary, in a letter to the BCOA delegate in February, 1972:

"The purpose of local clubs is very different from that of a parent club. Local clubs hold regular meetings and activities. They sponsor matches and training classes as well as specialty shows. Their principal aim is to bring in newcomers to the breed and to serve the breed on a largely local basis. A parent club, on the other hand, is the group which under our by-laws writes the Standard for its breed. It selects a delegate to the AKC who attends the quarterly meetings, giving the club a voice in the making of rules, and in electing new member clubs and delegates, and in electing the AKC Board of Directors. A parent club membership is generally made up of persons who have along range interst in the breed. Membership in a parent club is usually not of interest to the newcomer, and we think that is just as it should be.''

As I recently wrote in a Club Yearbook, we are at a point in history where the choices made, or the lack of choices made, will determine the course of Borzoi history for some years to come. Communications must be improved and maybe even changed in means so as to conform to the growing demands of the Borzoi fancy. Education of the general public must assume prime importance through the clubs and individual breeders. Potential sales must be restricted so that Borzoi puppies are placed only in the proper homes, and promiscuous breeding is curtailed. The welfare of the breed must be paramount; the protection of the breed can only be through wisdom and common sense and honesty. Within the Borzoi Club of America and within the regional and local clubs and within the ranks of individual Borzoi owners, the potential exists. That potential must be developed.

Borzoi Registrations with the American Kennel Club

Year	Reg.	Year	Reg.	Year	Reg.	Year	Reg.
1891	2	1913	172	1935	85	1957	162
1892	3	1914	140	1936	100	1958	115
1893	11	1915	184	1937	120	1959	178
1894	1	1916	166	1938	1'1	1960	143
1895	8	1917	174	1939	110	1961	329
1896	17	1918	147	1940	147	1962	275
1897	23	1919	246	1941	98	1963	230
1898	4	1920	272	1942	86	1964	330
1899	13	1921	302	1943	80	1965	429
1900	3	1922	317	1944	52	1966	508
1901	30	1923	378	1945	114	1967	617
1902	34	1924	468	1946	201	1968	760
1903	53	1925	530	1947	159	1969	980
1904	83	1926	482	1948	109	1970	1138
1905	87	1927	406	1949	153	1971	1445
1906	115	1928	272	1950	170	1972	1447
1907	101	1929	323	1951	126	1973	1703
1908	120	1930	197	1952	215	1974	1656
1909	103	1931	147	1953	163	1975	1515
1910	127	1932	81	1954	142	1976	1519
1911	155	1933	85	1955	153	1977	1392 +
1912	205	1934	102	1956	151	1978	1545
						1979	1050 +
						1980	1309

PRESIDENTS AND SECRETARIES OF THE
BORZOI CLUB OF AMERICA

(formerly the Russian Wolfhound Club of America)

	President	Secretary
1903-1908	John E. DeMund	Joseph B. Thomas
1909	Joseph B. Thomas	J. Peter Hoguet
1910-1915	J. Peter Hoguet	J. Bailey Wilson
1916-1919	Henry W. Shoemaker	J. Bailey Wilson
1920	R.W.K. Anderson	J. Bailey Wilson
1921-1929	Ralph C. Stewart	J. Bailey Wilson
1930-1933	John E. DeMund	Louis J. Murr
1934-1938	George J. O'Reilly	Louis J. Murr
1939	Louis J. Murr	Mrs. Robert Gundlach
1940	Carroll G. Stewart, Jr.	Mrs. Robert Gundlach
1941	Carroll G. Stewart, Jr.	Fairfield Pope Day
1942-1943	Louis J. Murr	Mrs. Rosanelle W. Peabody
1944-1945	Louis J. Murr	E. H. Berendsohn
1946-1948	Louis J. Murr	R. A. E. Herbhold
1949-1950	Louis J. Murr	William Schmidt
1951-1952	R. A. E. Herbhold	Mrs. Erma Denton
1953	Chester J. Clark	Mrs. Erma Denton
1954	Virginia Mauer	Mrs. Erma Denton
1955-1956	Arnold Brock	Mrs. Erma Denton
1957-1958	Weldon J. McCluskey	Mrs. Erma Denton
1959	Clarence R. DeCraene	Mrs. Erma Denton
1960	Mrs. Grace Dusenbury	Mrs. Erma Denton
1961	Mrs. Grace Dusenbury	Weldon J. McCluskey
1962-1963	John H. Gamber	Mrs. Lorraine M. Groshans
1964	Leonard Tamboer	Mrs. Lorraine M. Groshans
1965	Byron Avery	Mrs. Lorraine M. Groshans
1966-1967	John H. Gamber	Mrs. Lorraine M. Groshans
1968-1969	Russell Everhart	Mrs. Lorraine M. Groshans
1970	Mrs. Grace Conally	Mrs. Lorraine M. Groshans
1971	Mrs. Grace Conally	Jeff Campbell
1972	William Reddick	Jeff Campbell
1973	Miss Lena Tamboer	Mrs. Lorraine M. Groshans
1974	Miss Lena Tamboer	Mrs. Marcia Melamed
1975-1977	Mrs. Lorraine Groshans	Mrs. Patricia Murphy
1978	Mrs. Marcia Melamed	Miss Lena Tamboer
1979-1980	Dennis Jones	Miss Lena Tamboer

Original painting by Russell Hoover owned by Lorraine Groshans.

287

BIBLIOGRAPHY

ALL OWNERS of pure-bred dogs will benefit themselves and their dogs by enriching their knowledge of breeds and of canine care, training, breeding, psychology and other important aspects of dog management. The following list of books covers further reading recommended by judges, veterinarians, breeders, trainers and other authorities. Books may be obtained at the finer book stores and pet shops, or through Howell Book House Inc., publishers, New York.

BREED BOOKS

AFGHAN HOUND, Complete	Miller & Gilbert
AIREDALE, New Complete	Edwards
AKITA, Complete	Linderman & Funk
ALASKAN MALAMUTE, Complete	Riddle & Seeley
BASSET HOUND, New Complete	Braun
BLOODHOUND, Complete	Brey & Reed
BOXER, Complete	Denlinger
BRITTANY SPANIEL, Complete	Riddle
BULLDOG, New Complete	Hanes
BULL TERRIER, New Complete	Eberhard
CAIRN TERRIER, New Complete	Marvin
CHESAPEAKE BAY RETRIEVER, Complete	Cherry
CHIHUAHUA, Complete	Noted Authorities
COCKER SPANIEL, New	Kraeuchi
COLLIE, New	Official Publication of the Collie Club of America
DACHSHUND, The New	Meistrell
DALMATIAN, The	Treen
DOBERMAN PINSCHER, New	Walker
ENGLISH SETTER, New Complete	Tuck, Howell & Graef
ENGLISH SPRINGER SPANIEL, New	Goodall & Gasow
FOX TERRIER, New	Nedell
GERMAN SHEPHERD DOG, New Complete	Bennett
GERMAN SHORTHAIRED POINTER, New	Maxwell
GOLDEN RETRIEVER, New Complete	Fischer
GORDON SETTER, Complete	Look
GREAT DANE, New Complete	Noted Authorities
GREAT DANE, The—Dogdom's Apollo	Draper
GREAT PYRENEES, Complete	Strang & Giffin
IRISH SETTER, New Complete	Eldredge & Vanacore
IRISH WOLFHOUND, Complete	Starbuck
JACK RUSSELL TERRIER, Complete	Plummer
KEESHOND, New Complete	Cash
LABRADOR RETRIEVER, New Complete	Warwick
LHASA APSO, Complete	Herbel
MALTESE, Complete	Cutillo
MASTIFF, History and Management of the	Baxter & Hoffman
MINIATURE SCHNAUZER, New	Kiedrowski
NEWFOUNDLAND, New Complete	Chern
NORWEGIAN ELKHOUND, New Complete	Wallo
OLD ENGLISH SHEEPDOG, Complete	Mandeville
PEKINGESE, Quigley Book of	Quigley
PEMBROKE WELSH CORGI, Complete	Sargent & Harper
POODLE, New	Irick
POODLE CLIPPING AND GROOMING BOOK, Complete	Kalstone
PORTUGUESE WATER DOG, Complete	Braund & Miller
ROTTWEILER, Complete	Freeman
SAMOYED, New Complete	Ward
SCOTTISH TERRIER, New Complete	Marvin
SHETLAND SHEEPDOG, The New	Riddle
SHIH TZU, Joy of Owning	Seranne
SHIH TZU, The (English)	Dadds
SIBERIAN HUSKY, Complete	Demidoff
TERRIERS, The Book of All	Marvin
WEIMARANER, Guide to the	Burgoin
WEST HIGHLAND WHITE TERRIER, Complete	Marvin
WHIPPET, Complete	Pegram
YORKSHIRE TERRIER, Complete	Gordon & Bennett

BREEDING

ART OF BREEDING BETTER DOGS, New	Onstott
BREEDING YOUR OWN SHOW DOG	Seranne
HOW TO BREED DOGS	Whitney
HOW PUPPIES ARE BORN	Prine
INHERITANCE OF COAT COLOR IN DOGS	Little

CARE AND TRAINING

BEYOND BASIC DOG TRAINING	Bauman
COUNSELING DOG OWNERS, Evans Guide for	Evans
DOG OBEDIENCE, Complete Book of	Saunders
NOVICE, OPEN AND UTILITY COURSES	Saunders
DOG CARE AND TRAINING FOR BOYS AND GIRLS	Saunders
DOG NUTRITION, Collins Guide to	Collins
DOG TRAINING FOR KIDS	Benjamin
DOG TRAINING, Koehler Method of	Koehler
DOG TRAINING Made Easy	Tucker
GO FIND! Training Your Dog to Track	Davis
GROOMING DOGS FOR PROFIT	Gold
GUARD DOG TRAINING, Koehler Method of	Koehler
MOTHER KNOWS BEST—The Natural Way to Train Your Dog	Benjamin
OPEN OBEDIENCE FOR RING, HOME AND FIELD, Koehler Method of	Koehler
STONE GUIDE TO DOG GROOMING FOR ALL BREEDS	Stone
SUCCESSFUL DOG TRAINING, The Pearsall Guide to	Pearsall
TEACHING DOG OBEDIENCE CLASSES—Manual for Instructors	Volhard & Fisher
TOY DOGS, Kalstone Guide to Grooming All	Kalstone
TRAINING THE RETRIEVER	Kersley
TRAINING TRACKING DOGS, Koehler Method of	Koehler
TRAINING YOUR DOG—Step by Step Manual	Volhard & Fisher
TRAINING YOUR DOG TO WIN OBEDIENCE TITLES	Morsell
TRAIN YOUR OWN GUN DOG, How to	Goodall
UTILITY DOG TRAINING, Koehler Method of	Koehler
VETERINARY HANDBOOK, Dog Owner's Home	Carlson & Giffin

GENERAL

A DOG'S LIFE	Burton & Allaby
AMERICAN KENNEL CLUB 1884-1984—A Source Book	American Kennel Club
CANINE TERMINOLOGY	Spira
COMPLETE DOG BOOK, The	Official Publication of American Kennel Club
DOG IN ACTION, The	Lyon
DOG BEHAVIOR, New Knowledge of	Pfaffenberger
DOG JUDGE'S HANDBOOK	Tietjen
DOG PSYCHOLOGY	Whitney
DOGSTEPS, The New	Elliott
DOG TRICKS	Haggerty & Benjamin
EYES THAT LEAD—Story of Guide Dogs for the Blind	Tucker
FRIEND TO FRIEND—Dogs That Help Mankind	Schwartz
FROM RICHES TO BITCHES	Shattuck
HAPPY DOG/HAPPY OWNER	Siegal
IN STITCHES OVER BITCHES	Shattuck
JUNIOR SHOWMANSHIP HANDBOOK	Brown & Mason
OUR PUPPY'S BABY BOOK (blue or pink)	
SUCCESSFUL DOG SHOWING, Forsyth Guide to	Forsyth
WHY DOES YOUR DOG DO THAT?	Bergman
WILD DOGS in Life and Legend	Riddle
WORLD OF SLED DOGS, From Siberia to Sport Racing	Coppinger